Our Tour of Doors Open Niagara-on-the-Lake October 22, 2022

Photography by Barbara Raué ©2022

Series Name: Doors Open

Cover photo: Willowbank

The Ontario Heritage Trust works with communities across the province to open the doors, gates and courtyards of their unique and most fascinating cultural sites so you can explore the stories inside. Every April to October, many of Ontario's heritage treasures are opened to the public with free events across the province. From historical houses to modern marvels of construction, Doors Open Ontario showcases the buildings, natural spaces, infrastructure and cultural landscapes that shape and define our communities. The program was launched in 2002 to allow people to learn about heritage conservation and local history.

From historical houses to modern marvels of construction, Doors Open Ontario showcases the buildings, natural spaces, infrastructure and cultural landscapes that shape and define our communities.

The first Doors Open Day (La Journée Portes Ouvertes) took place in France in 1984. The idea soon spread to neighboring countries, including the Netherlands, Sweden, the Republic of Ireland, Belgium and Scotland. In 1991, these events were united as European Heritage Days at the initiative of the Council of Europe. In 2003, all 50 signatory states of the European Cultural Convention participated in European Heritage Days.

In 2000, the City of Toronto launched the first Doors Open event in North America. In 2002, the Ontario Heritage Trust launched Doors Open Ontario, the first provincewide event of its kind in Canada, attracting visitors to unique heritage sites and cultural tourism experiences. The Doors Open concept continues to spread across North America with events being held in Newfoundland, Alberta, Massachusetts, Western New York State, New York City and Denver.

In 2020 with the COVID-19 pandemic with the aim of continuing to engage visitors across Ontario, and beyond, the way the program was delivered was changed. With **Digital Doors Open** – a year-round program – there is unique access to hundreds of sites, creating digital experiences that offer everything from virtual tours and videos about the sites to online games, activities, searchable collections and additional resources. This way, you can still have that Doors Open experience, but with a digital twist, as you experience sites from anywhere in the province from the comfort of home, and even explore sites that are impossible to visit in-person.

After two years of a pandemic, doors are open to places that are not usually available for public tours. They are fun, free, and family-friendly for everyone involved.

Doors Open Niagara-on-the-Lake features architecture, culture and heritage. We were able to tour historical buildings that are being reimagined as new adaptive reuse spaces. Venues that were once derelict are being transformed. My sister, Shirley, and her husband, Edward enjoyed our visit to the sites presented in this book.

Table of Contents

Niagara-on-the-Lake

Generations of Indigenous people lived in this area centuries before the first permanent settlers arrived during the American Revolution. They gave the river a name which early French explorers recorded as 'Niagara.' The earliest inhabitants were nomadic hunters and gatherers. Native settlements became more permanent with the cultivation of crops becoming an important food source.

Joseph Brant (1742-1807) (Thayendanegea meaning 'two sticks bound together,' or 'symbol of united strength') dedicated his life to uniting the various native groups under one confederacy. Brant entered military service at age 13; he fought with the British army under Sir William Johnson.

Molly Brant (1736-1796) was the older sister of Joseph was "married" (not recognized under English law) to Sir William Johnson, Superintendent of Indian Affairs and they had eight surviving children. She was a British loyalist and her allegiance to the Crown remained even after the death of her husband. As a clan mother, Molly held much power among the Mohawk people. She lived at Fort Niagara for a few months in 1779 after coming there at the request of Colonel John Butler who recognized her usefulness as an intermediary between the British and the Iroquois. While at the fort, Molly was involved in six Native Conferences held at Niagara.

In the winter of 1778-1779, Butler's Rangers, a Loyalist Regiment came from the overcrowded Fort Niagara to settle the west bank of the Niagara River, to build barracks, and later, farms with their families. There was a lot of growth in the area after the Revolutionary War ended. Hundreds of disbanded Rangers and Loyalist refugees settled here.

A town was laid out in a grid pattern of four-acre blocks and grew quickly, gaining prominence as the first capital of Upper Canada from 1792 to 1796.

A few crude log cabins greeted Lieutenant-Governor Simcoe and his family in 1792. A few years later, almost one hundred homes were built in the capital. Most were 1½-storey clapboard homes with brick chimneys and shingled roofs on a half-acre or more of land. The backyards had fruit and vegetable gardens. Then came the war between the British and Americans. The town was captured by American forces on May 27, 1813; upon their withdrawal on December 13, 1813, the American forces burned the town. During the three years, Niagara suffered three invasions and occupation of the enemy. Civilian casualties and hardships were severe.

Following Niagara's destruction, the citizens rebuilt. The town's colonial buildings became one of its greatest resources. Beginning in the 1950s, residents rehabilitated and restored old structures, demonstrating an exceptional commitment to the preservation of local heritage.

The Upper Canada Gazette or the American Oracle was the first newspaper in what is now Ontario. It was published in the town of Niagara. The first issue, edited by Louis Roy, appeared April 18, 1797. The Gleaner was published here from 1817 to 1837 under the editorship of Andrew and Samuel Heron. It was one of the most prominent newspapers in Upper Canada.

The Second Welland Canal opened in the mid-1840s, by-passed Niagara, and killed the trans-shipping business. In the 1870s, summer visitors and citizen-soldiers training at Niagara Camp swelled the local populations.

Niagara-On-The-Lake, National Historic Site of Canada, is an early-19th century Loyalist town located on the southern shore of Lake Ontario, near the United States border. The historic district covers 25 city blocks and includes more than ninety residential, commercial, ecclesiastical and institutional buildings constructed between 1815 and 1859. Most of the buildings are constructed in the British Classical Tradition, producing similarities in design, materials and scale. The wide, tree-lined streets within the district follow a late-18th century grid plan. The district includes a city park and two early-nineteenth-century cemeteries. The landscape is gently rolling in places, with a creek running through part of the district. The official recognition refers to the approximately forty-one hectares of related buildings and landscapes within the district boundaries.

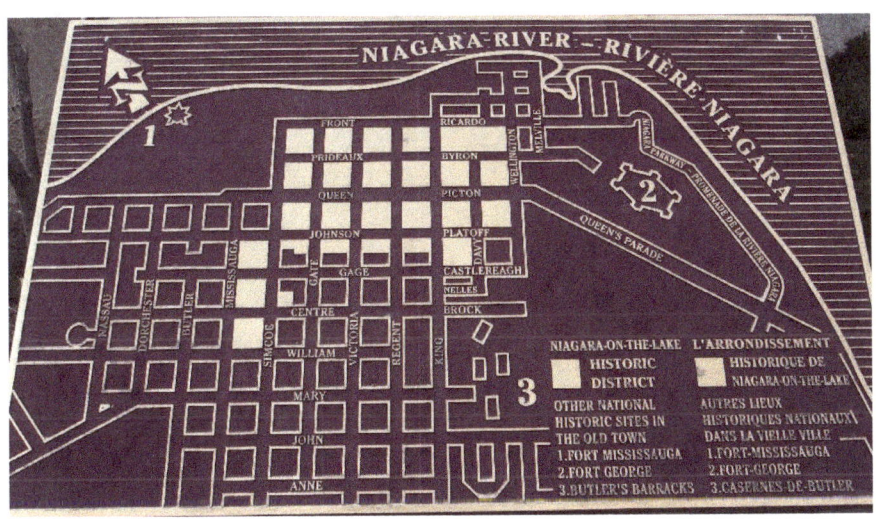

The Prince of Wales Hotel is a historic Victorian hotel.

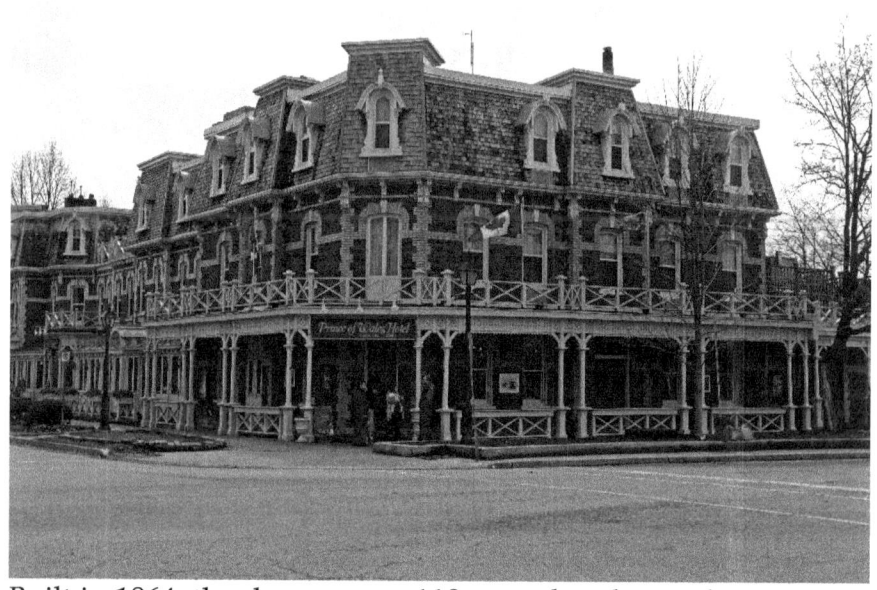

Built in 1864, the three storey 110 room hotel went by several names before being given its current name, The Prince of Wales Hotel, in 1901 after royal guests The Duke and Duchess of Cornwall and York (afterwards known as The Prince and Princess of Wales until 1910) stayed. Queen Elizabeth II stayed at the hotel during her visit to the area in 1973. It is located at 6 Picton Street and King Street along the historic main street. It is in the Second Empire style with a mansard roof, dormers, window hoods, dichromatic brickwork, cornice brackets, second floor balcony.

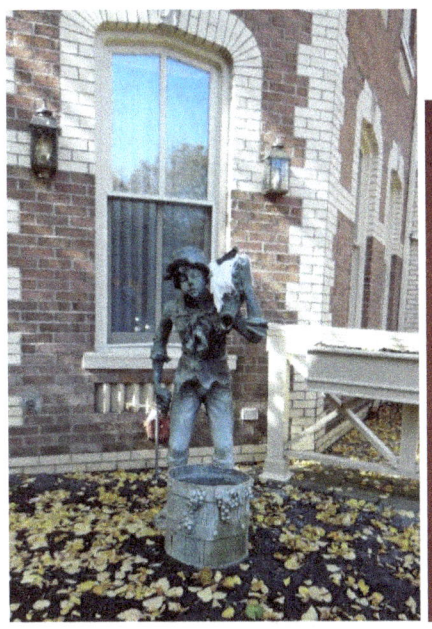

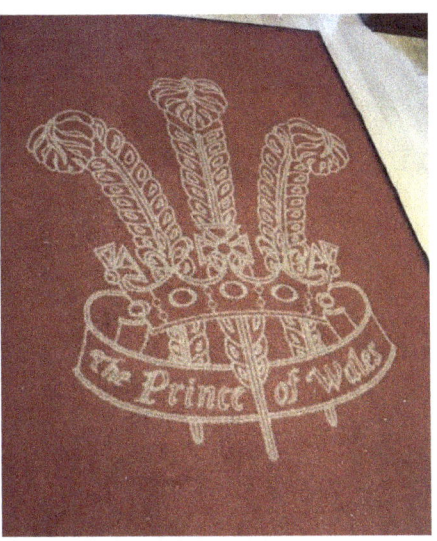

Welcome mat

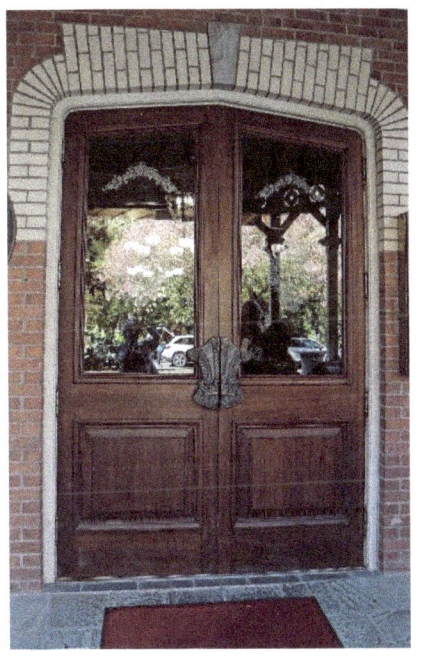

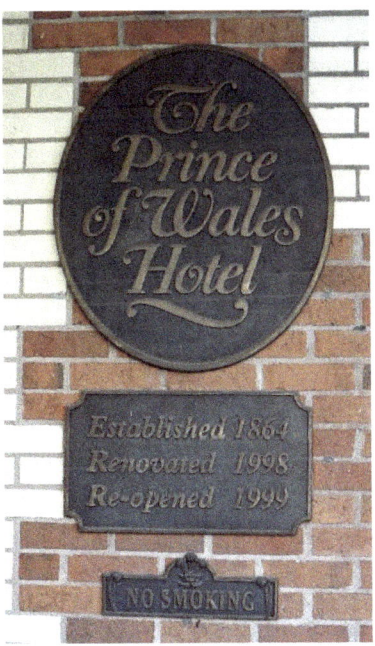

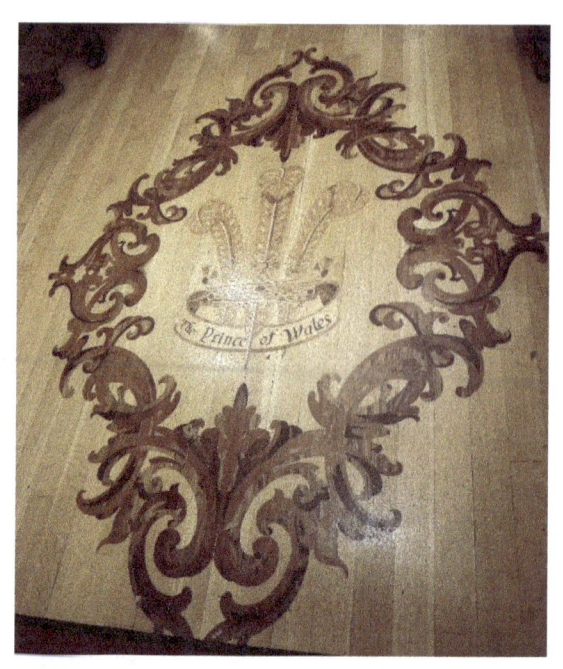

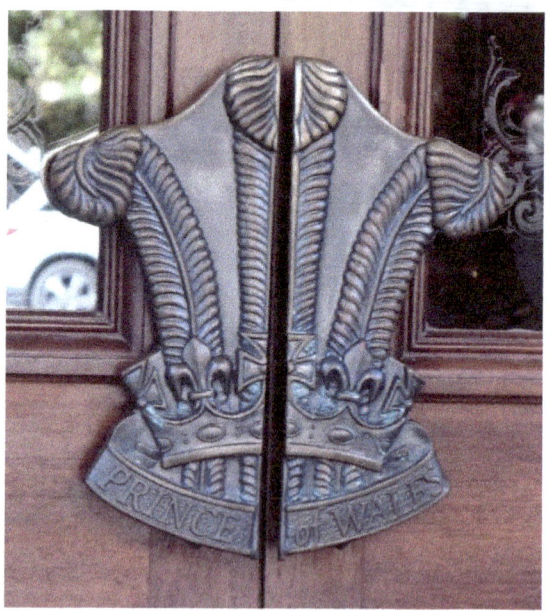

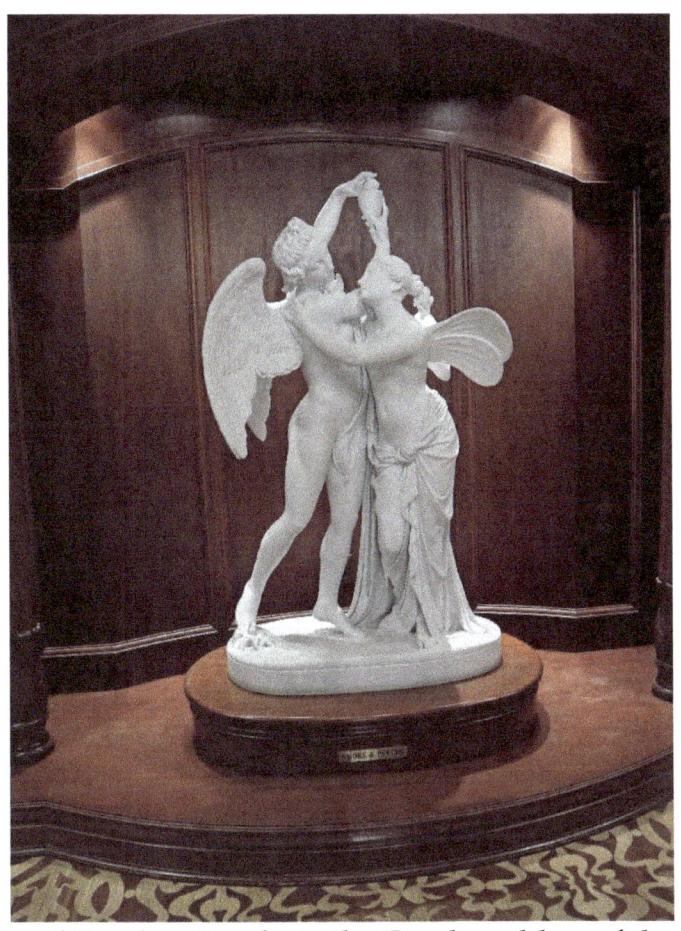

Amoré and Psyche - Psyche is the Greek goddess of the soul and often represented with butterfly wings. She was born a mortal woman, with beauty that rivaled the goddess, Aphrodite. Cupid and Psyche is a story originally from *The Golden Ass* written in the second century A.D. by Lucius Apuleius Madaurensis (or Platonicus). The tale is about the overcoming of obstacles to the love between Psyche (soul or breath of life) and Cupid (or Amor – meaning desire or love), and their sacred marriage.

On December 10, 2013, two hundred years after the burning of the town during the War of 1812 to 1814, the Town of Niagara unveiled its first Town flag. The flag is a symbol of new beginnings and a legacy of peace between the British Crown and United States. It features the Royal Union Flag of 1707 and the shield from the Town's Official Coat of Arms granted by the Canadian Heraldic Authority. The mace within the shield is a gilt wood object dating from 1792 and indicates that Niagara-on-the-Lake, known then as Newark, was the first capital of the province of Upper Canada.

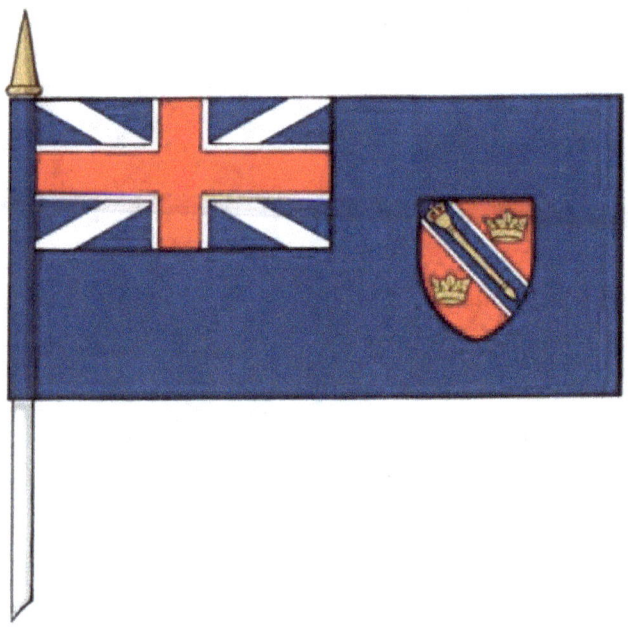

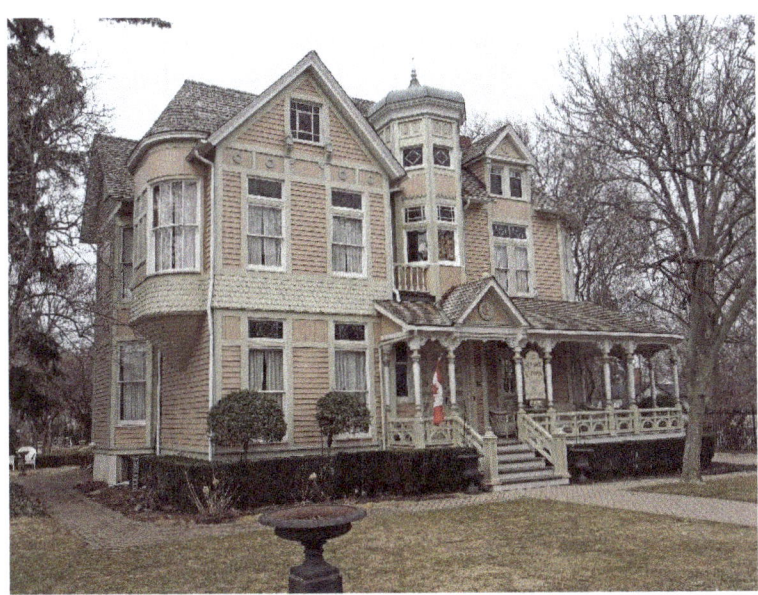

177 King Street - the former Romance Collection Gallery featuring the exclusive works of Trisha Romance and Tanya Jean Peterson – Queen Anne style home 1886

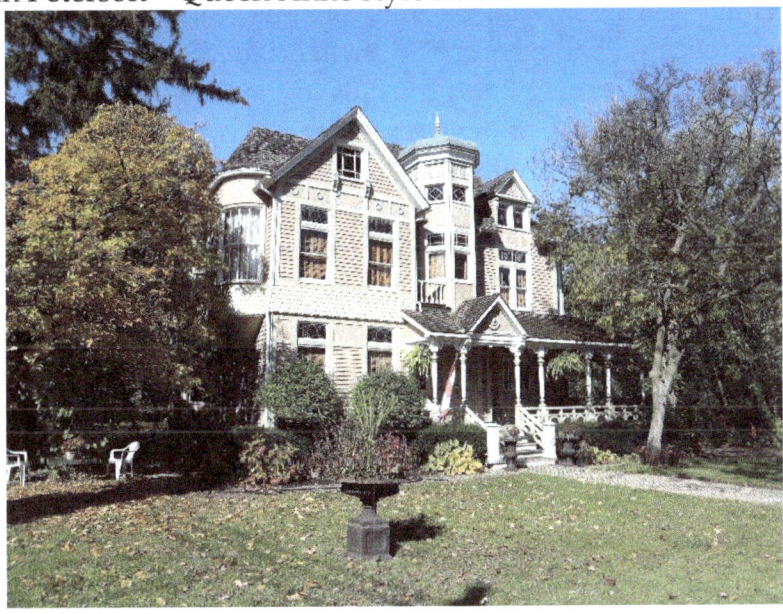

On June 8, 1800, the Niagara Library, the first circulating library in Upper Canada, was established to "diffuse knowledge" among its area subscribers. Library services began with about eighty works for circulation, many on religion and history. Under the management of Andrew Heron, a merchant, the collection was steadily enlarged. The library operated successfully until the occupation of Newark (Niagara-on-the-Lake) by American forces in 1813, when many volumes were lost. In 1820, the holdings were incorporated into a new subscription library begun by Heron, then a publisher and book-seller.

The St. Lawrence and Great Lakes system was the most efficient route to the interior of the continent of North America. Large waterways allowed for substantial sailing vessels to trade and maintain contact with Native allies from Montreal to the Mississippi with minimal portages and transshipment in smaller boats. The one great obstacle along the chain of waterways was Niagara Falls whose dramatic height required some control of the land to allow for a portage around the escarpment and the falls to the lakes beyond. The strategic importance of this area led to the construction of several forts at the mouth of the river to control this critical water route.

Fort Niagara is a fortification originally built to protect the interests of New France in North America. It is located near Youngstown, New York, on the eastern bank of the Niagara River at its mouth, on Lake Ontario. The fort played a significant part in the French and Indian War, and suffered the only European-style siege in North America in 1759. It fell to the British in a nineteen day siege in July 1759, called the Battle of Fort Niagara.

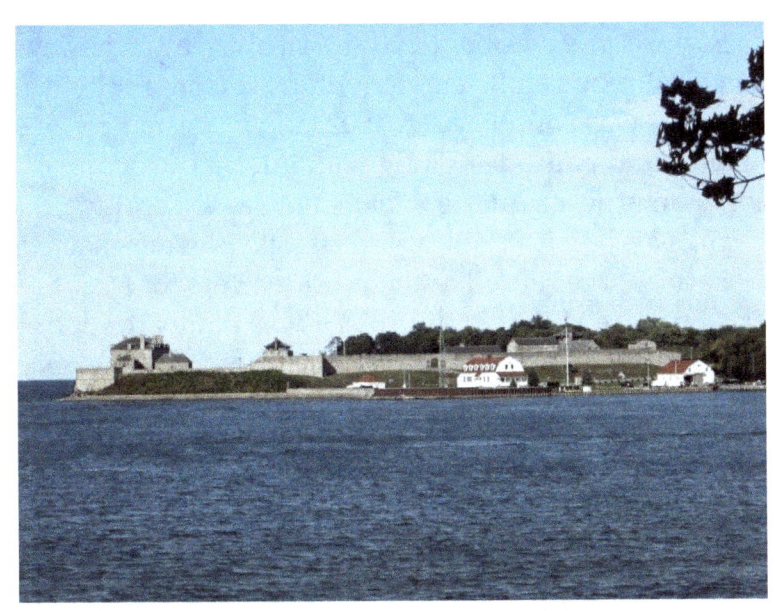

American Fort Niagara

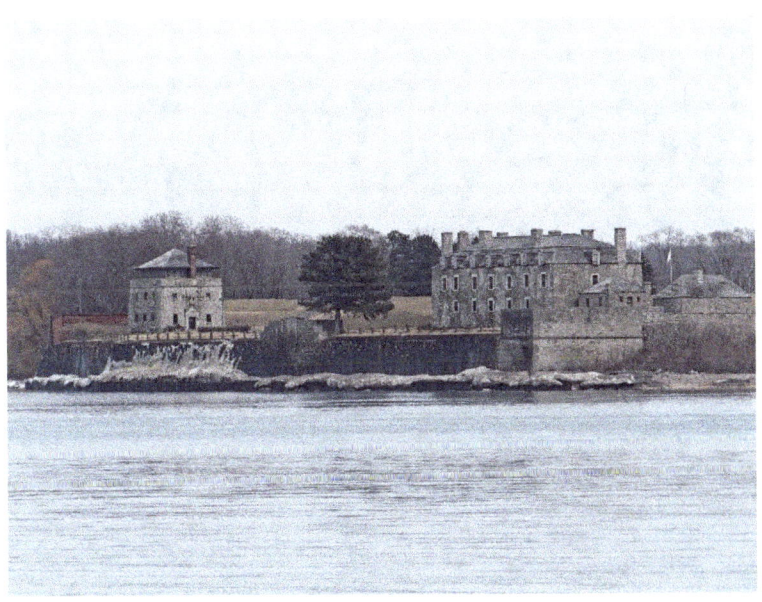

Fort George was built by the British Army after Jay's Treaty (1796) required Britain to withdraw from Fort Niagara. The new fort was completed in 1802, and consisted of earthworks and palisades, along with internal structures, including an officer's quarters, blockhouses to accommodate other ranks and their families, and a stone powder magazine.

Fort George served as the headquarters for Major-General Brock in 1812. In May 1813 it was bombarded for two days by the American fleet and the batteries at Fort Niagara across the river. The British and Canadians, together with Aboriginal peoples allied with them, fought to oppose an American landing on Lake Ontario.

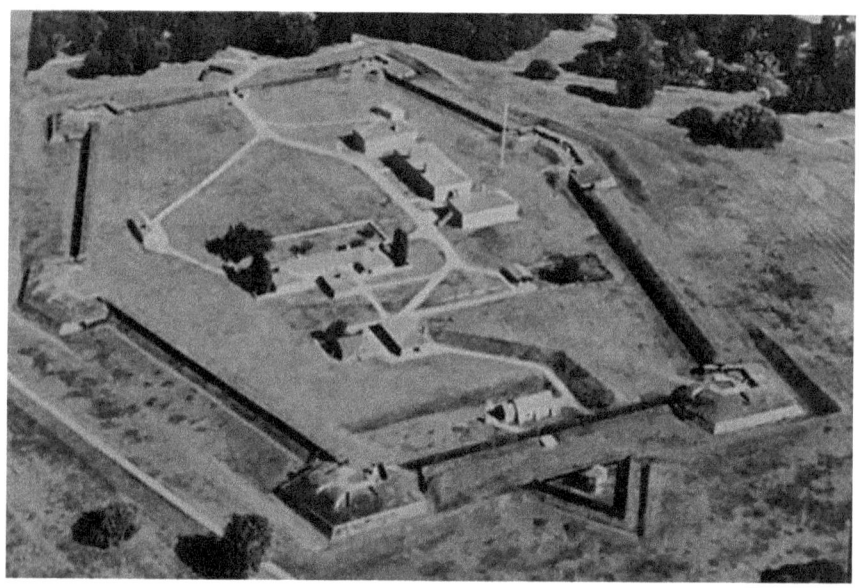

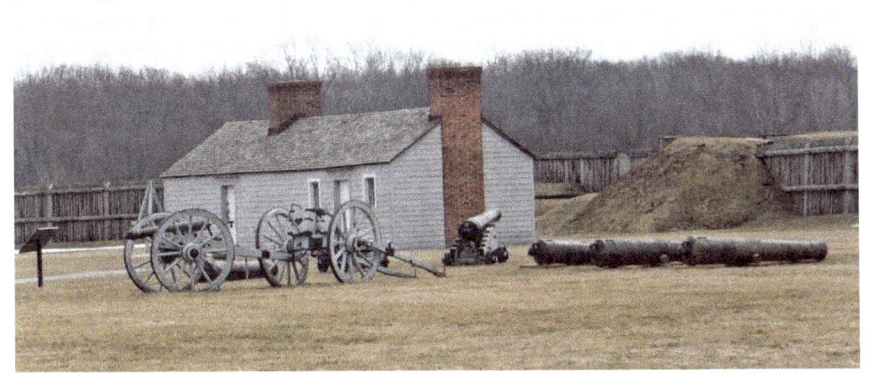

A large American force was landed near Two Mile Creek and after a brief engagement at Fort George in which the Canadian garrison was outnumbered and sustained heavy casualties, Brigadier-General John Vincent made an orderly withdrawal towards Burlington Heights.

The Americans constructed fortifications of their own on the site. The American Army used the fort as a base to invade Upper Canada. The capture of Fort George left the Americans in control of the Niagara frontier, but Vincent's troops a week later repelled the Americans at the Battles of Stoney Creek and Beaver Dams, preventing the Americans from gaining the whole peninsula.

Mississauga Point is located where the Niagara River flows into Lake Ontario. Lakes and rivers were military supply and transportation routes and forts were built to protect them.

After the British captured Fort Niagara on December 19, 1813, a new fort was constructed on the Canadian shore, called Fort Mississauga. Materials for it were obtained from the ruins of the nearby town of Newark (now Niagara-on-the-Lake). With the American navy now controlling Lake Ontario, this work was crucial to the security of British forces in the Niagara Peninsula.

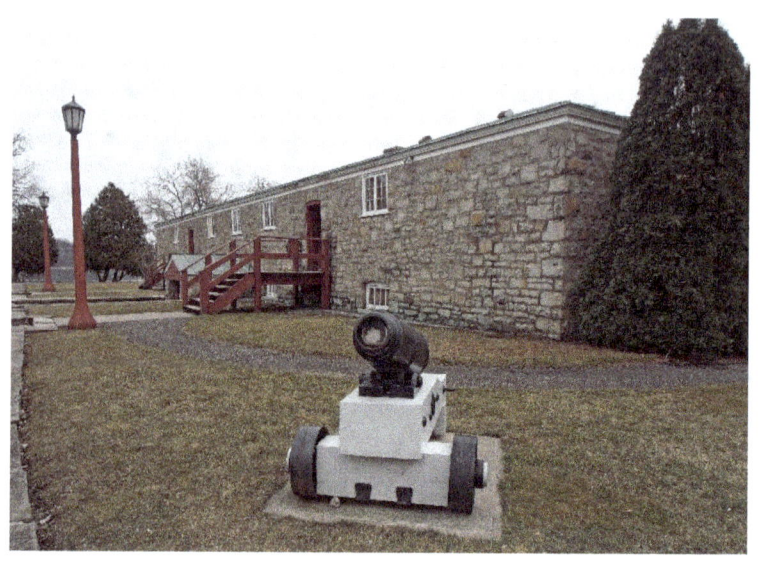

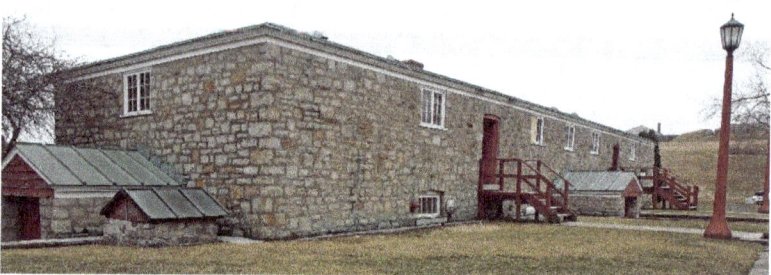

Navy Hall originally consisted of a small shipyard, storehouses, residences and docks which served as a depot for supplies; it also served as a transshipment point for the posts on the Upper Great Lakes. From 1792 to 1796, Lieutenant-Governor John Graves Simcoe had offices and his residence in the complex. These buildings were later converted to military use until destroyed by American artillery fire during the War of 1812.

Immediately after the War of 1812, a new wooden military storehouse was built on this site. It was converted into barracks for British troops during the border troubles of 1838. The building remained in use into the twentieth century, serving as a medical dispensary for Canadian troops during World War I. During the 1930s the building was moved to its present location and encased in stone.

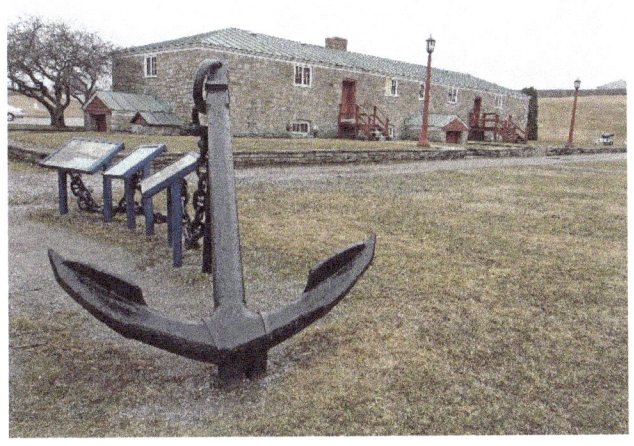

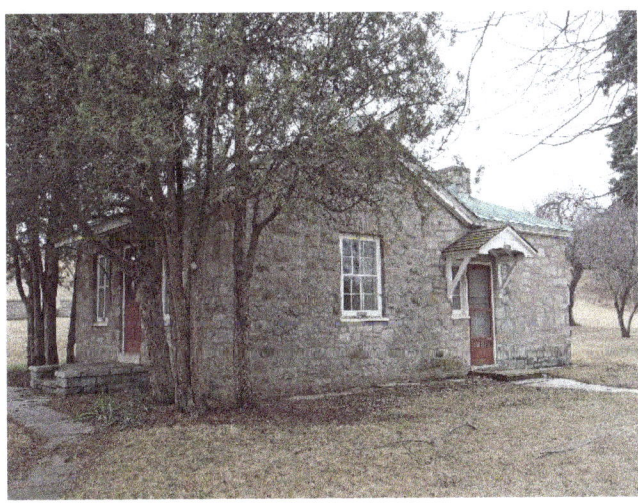

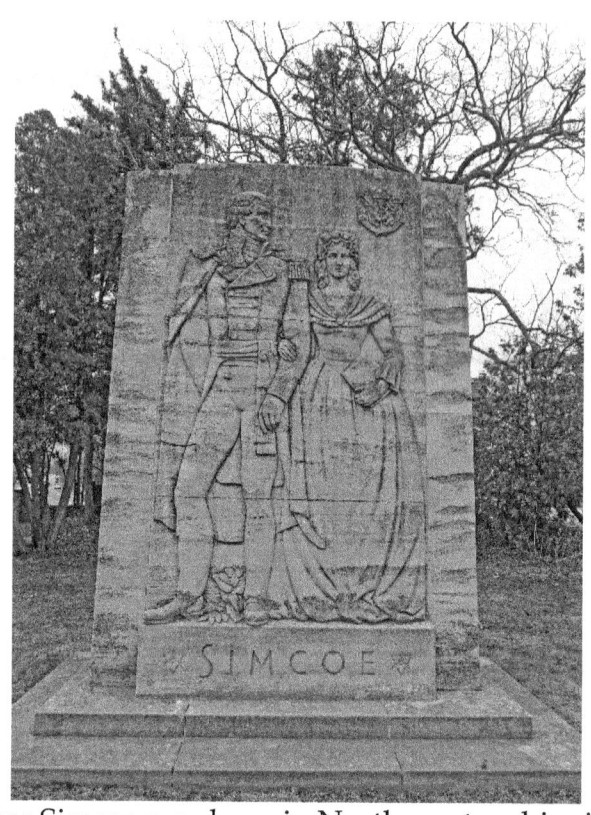

John Graves Simcoe was born in Northamptonshire in 1752
and educated at Oxford. He joined the British army in 1771
and from 1777-1781, he commanded the Queen's Rangers, a
Loyalist corps in America. After the Loyalist influx had led to
the creation of a separate province of Upper Canada in 1791,
Simcoe was named its first Lieutenant-Governor. During his
five years of office, the province's basically British and
monarchical character and institutions took shape. After he
left Canada in 1796, he held a succession of military and
colonial offices, and died in Exeter in 1806 shortly after being
appointed Commander-in-chief for India.

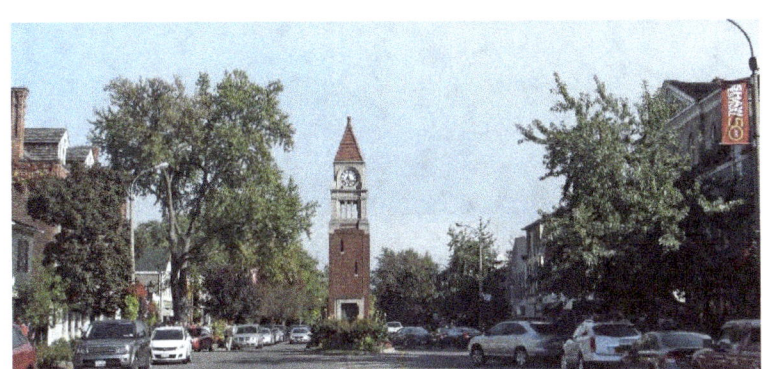

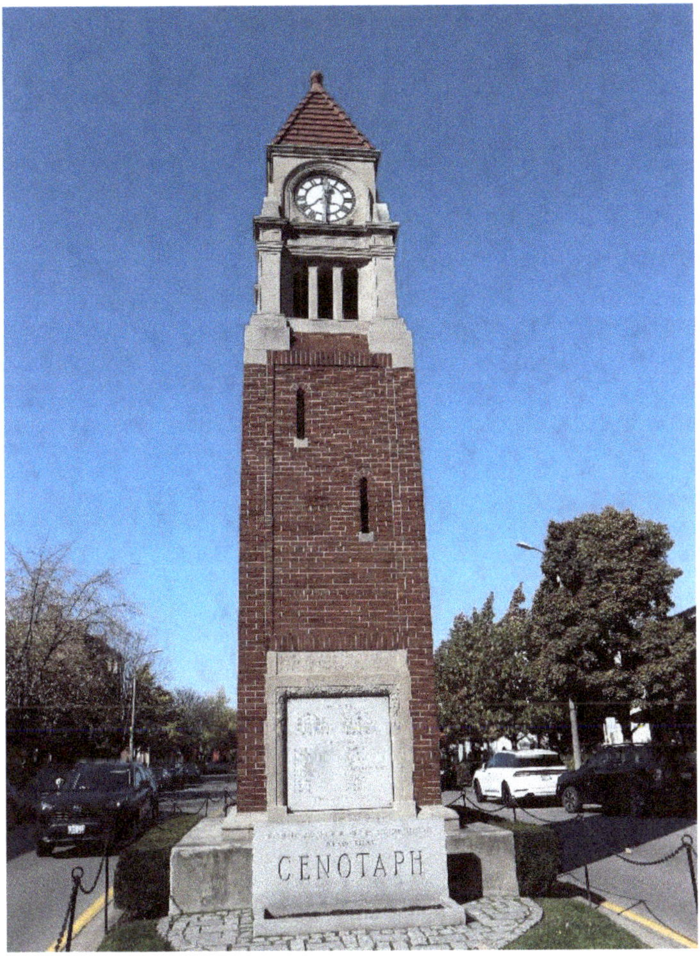

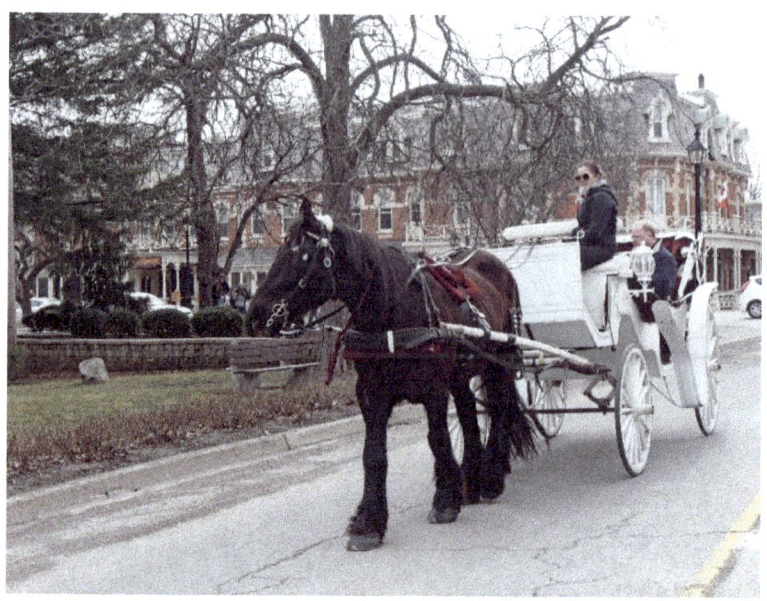

Horses are well-cared for; they are work horses and want to work at pulling the carriages.

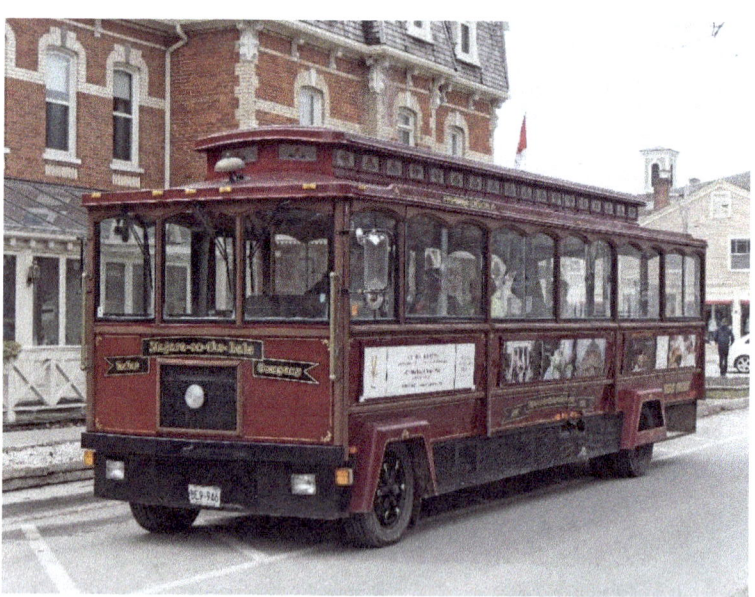

Clare's Harley-Davidson of Niagara
590 York Road

The store was built in 2008; it is a commercial and historical landmark; it is in a Contemporary style of architecture. Throughout this store are architectural touches with reclaimed and re-purposed materials. Outside, a large water tower was relocated from Fort Erie to form the sign. Inside, reclaimed brick creates the industrial feel, along with wooden doors and reclaimed woodwork. There is a vintage window in the sales office and a countertop in the ladies' washroom from a local hotel.

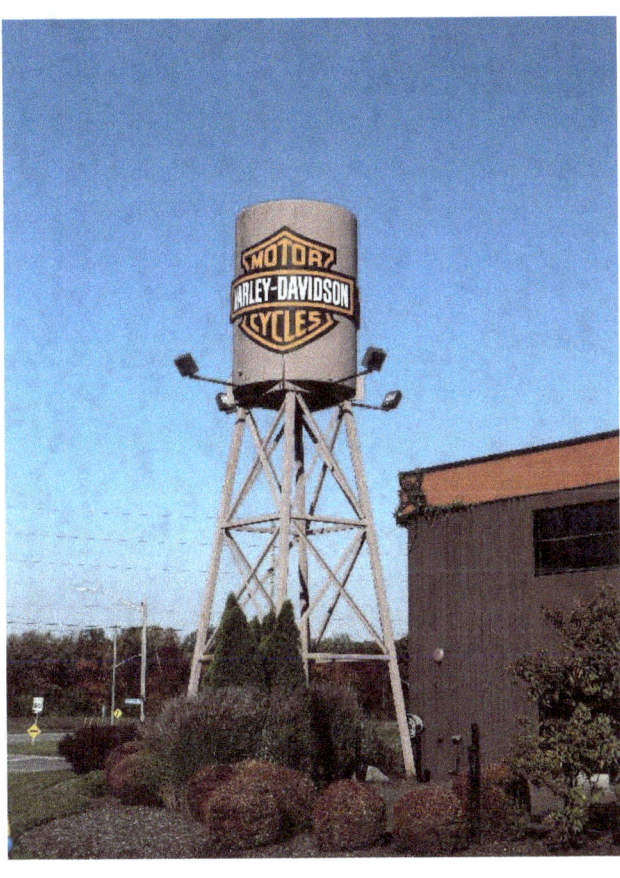

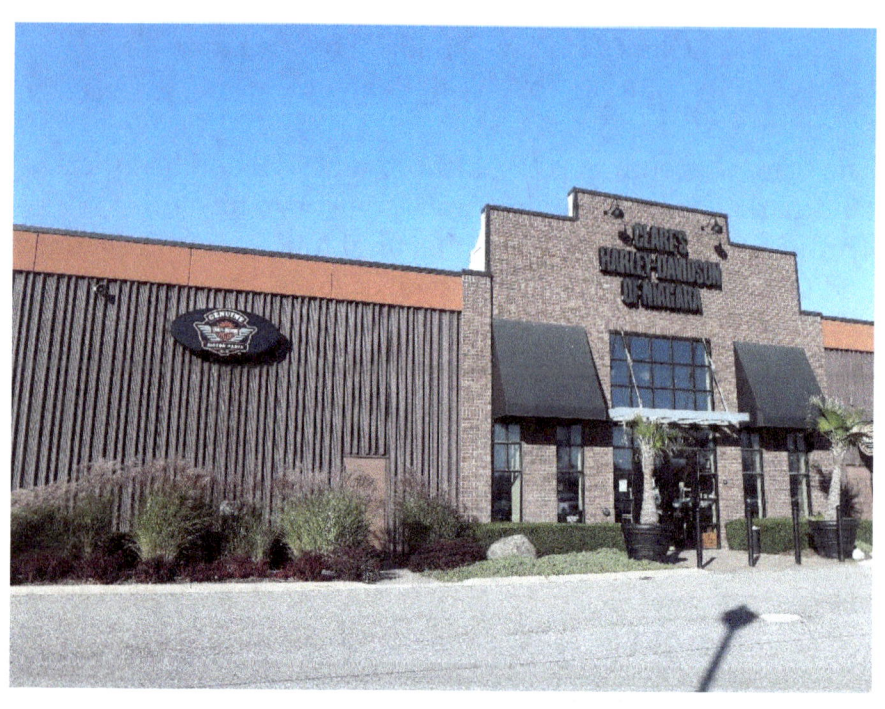

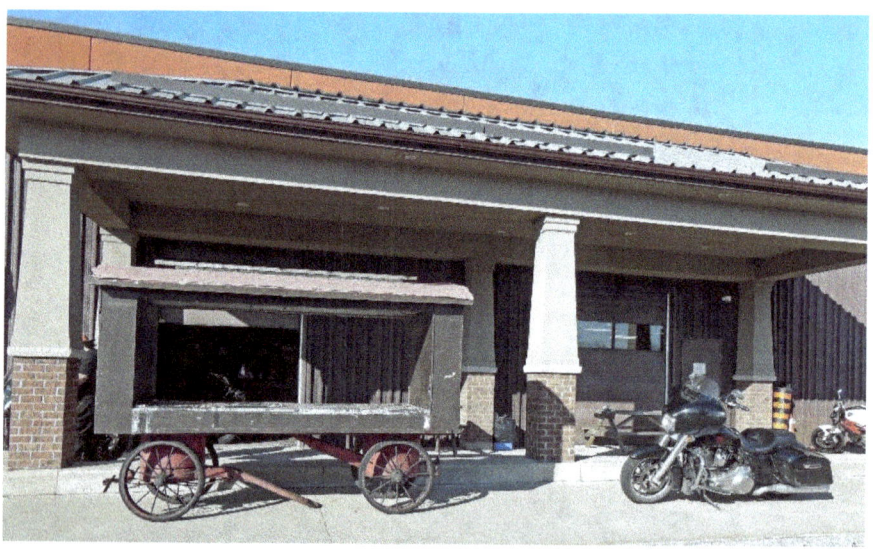

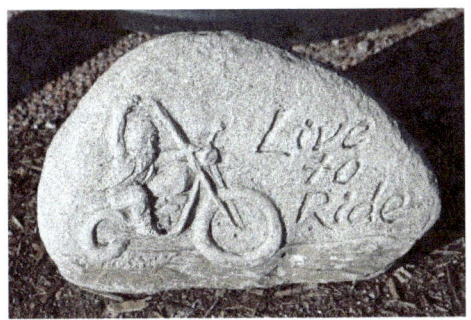

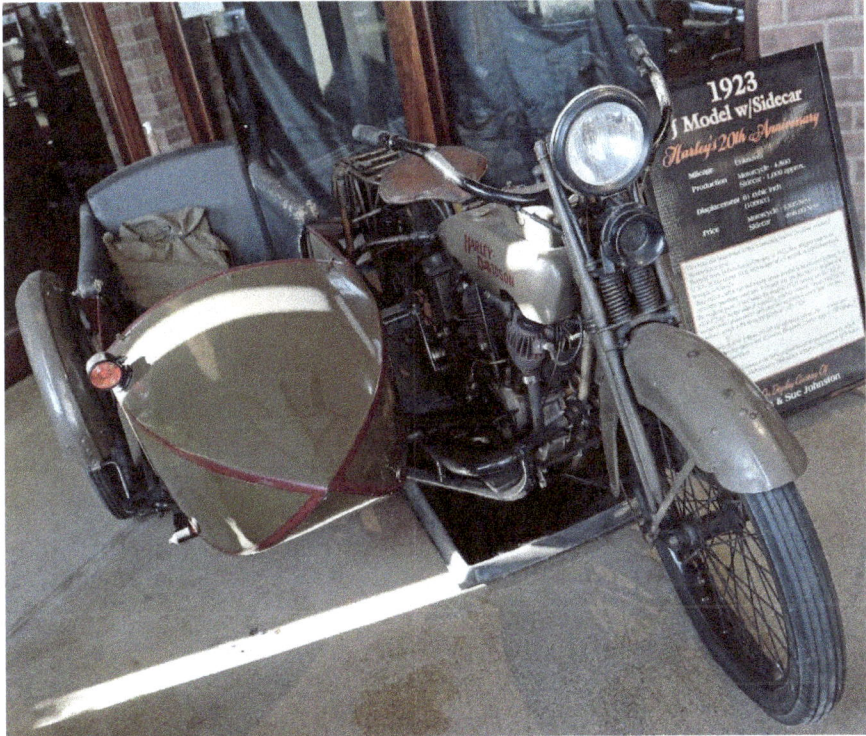

1923 J Model with Sidecar – 61 cubic foot displacement; the engine is an F-head, oil fed via automatic pump; creates about 7 HP using a 3-speed transmission

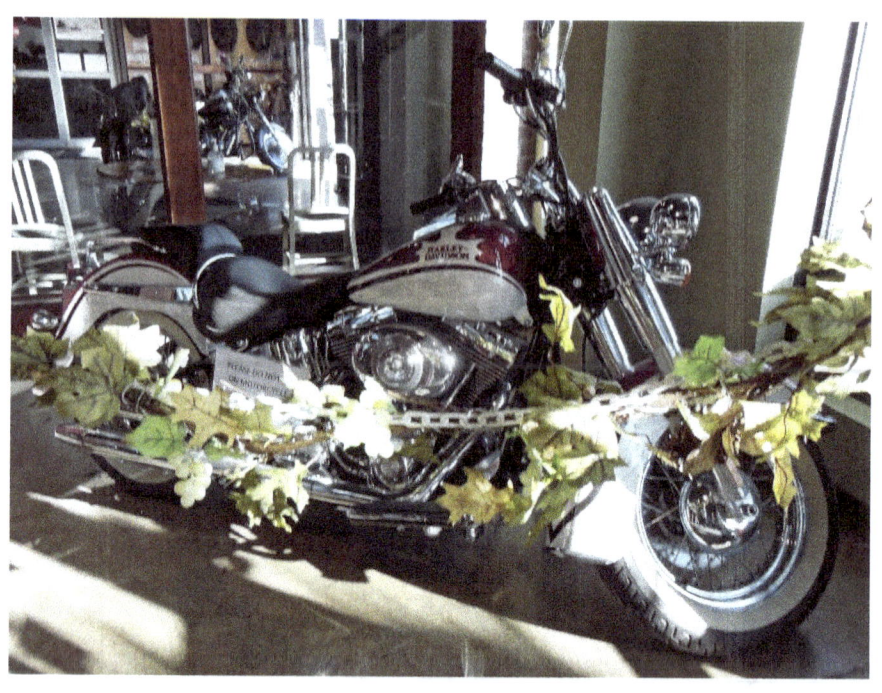

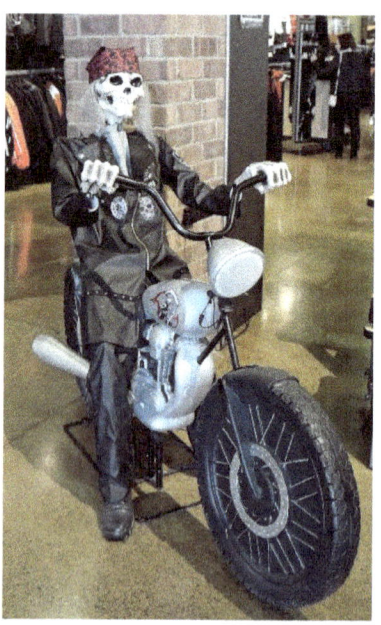

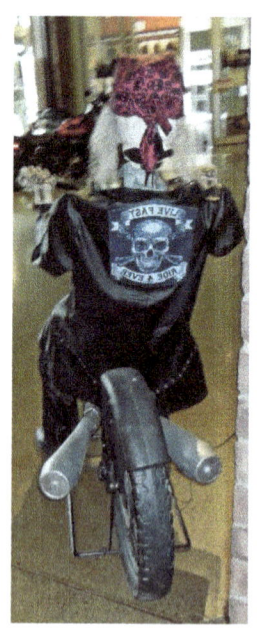

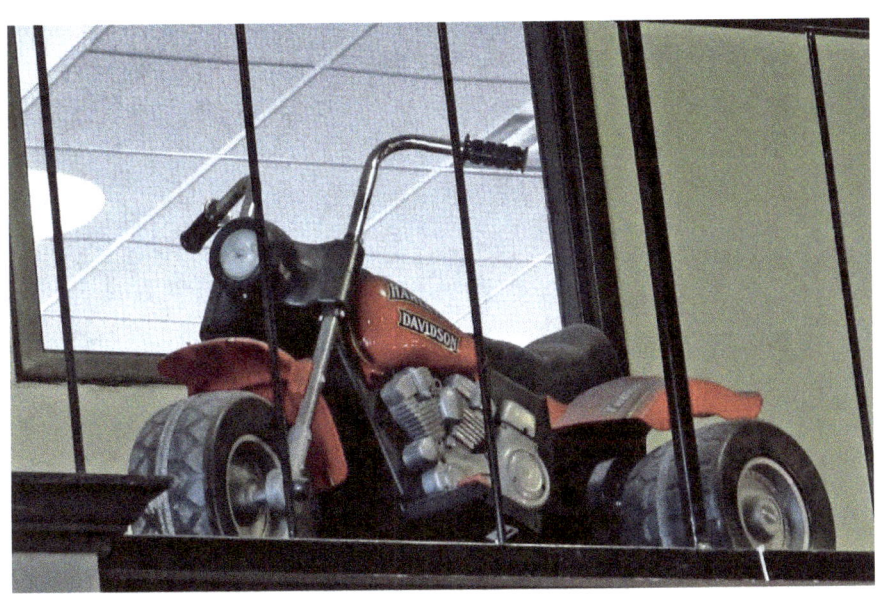

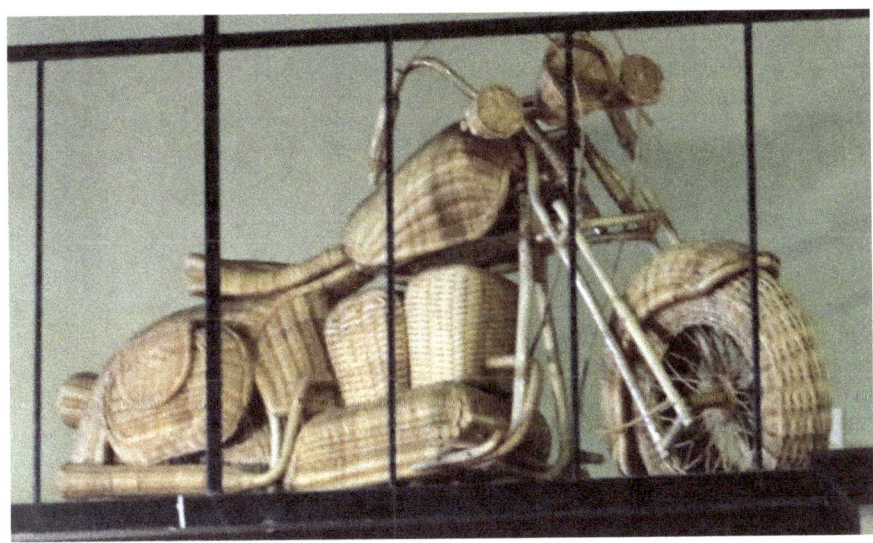

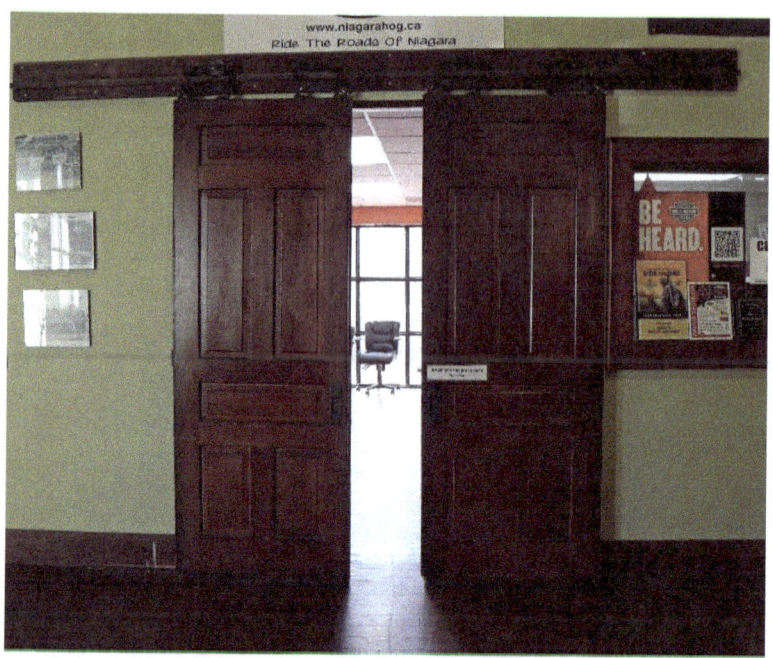

Vintage doors

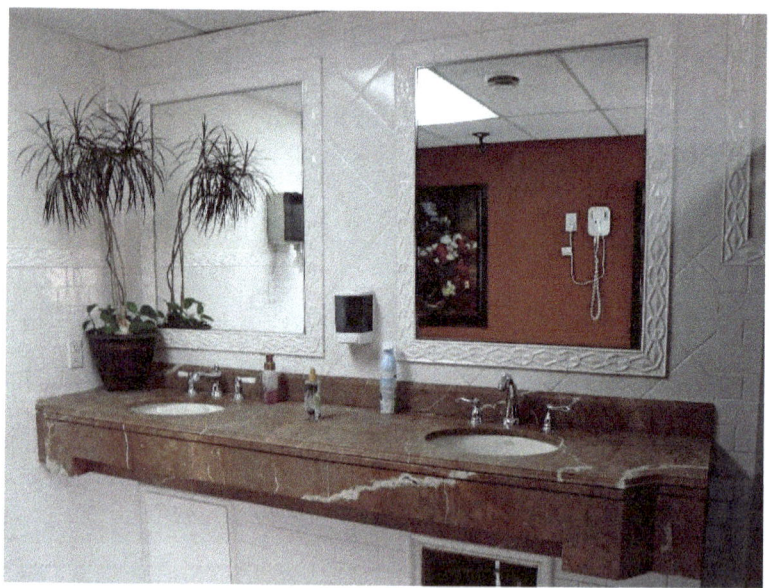

Marble countertop in ladies' washroom from a local hotel

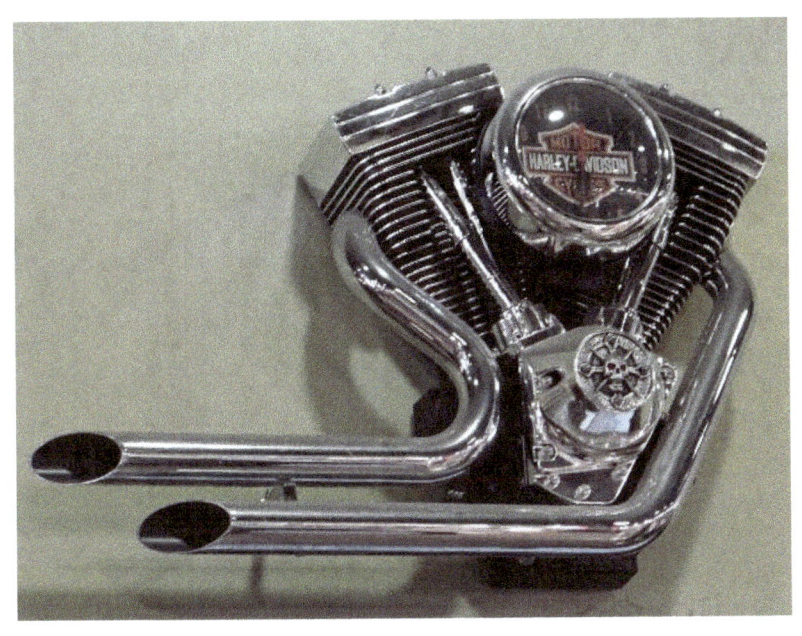

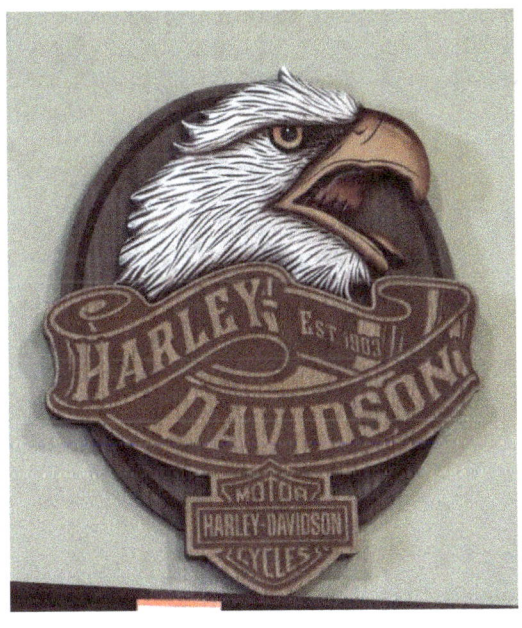

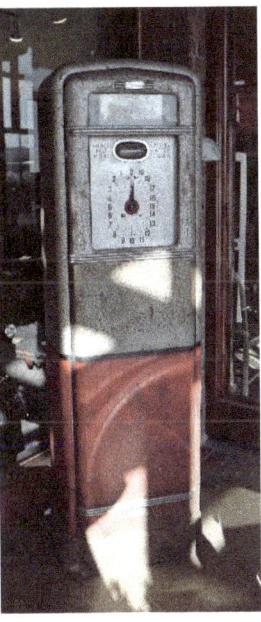

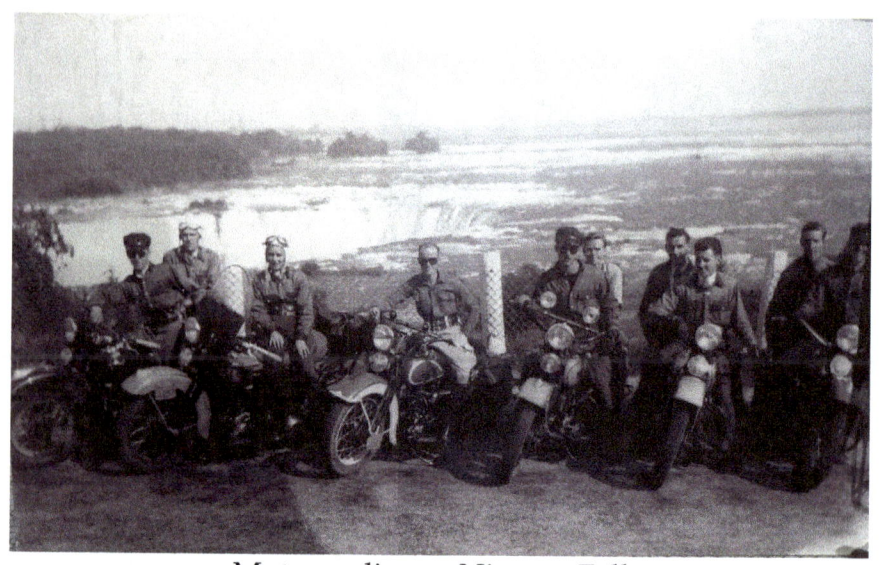
Motorcycling at Niagara Falls

Diana Sweets Shoppe was a candy store/ice cream parlor.
There was a shoppe in St. Catharines, another in Toronto.
They served sundaes, sodas, lunches, and dinners. A Diana
Sweets Shoppe has been replicated in the Clare's Harley
Davidson building.

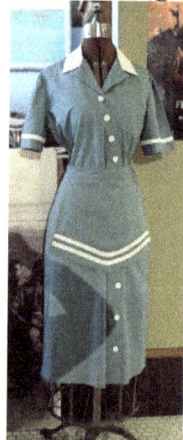
Waitress uniform

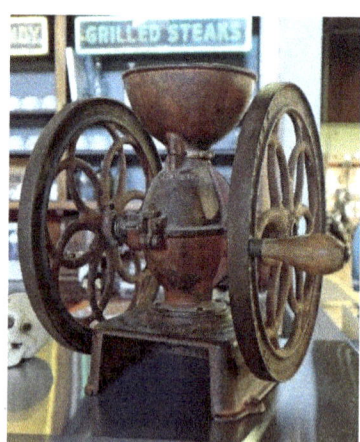
Coffee grinder

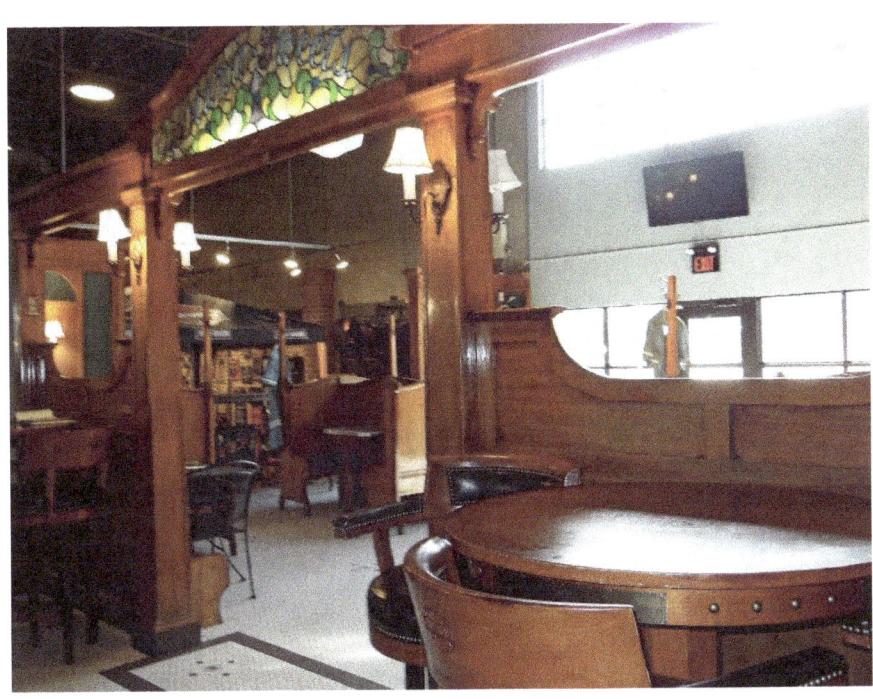

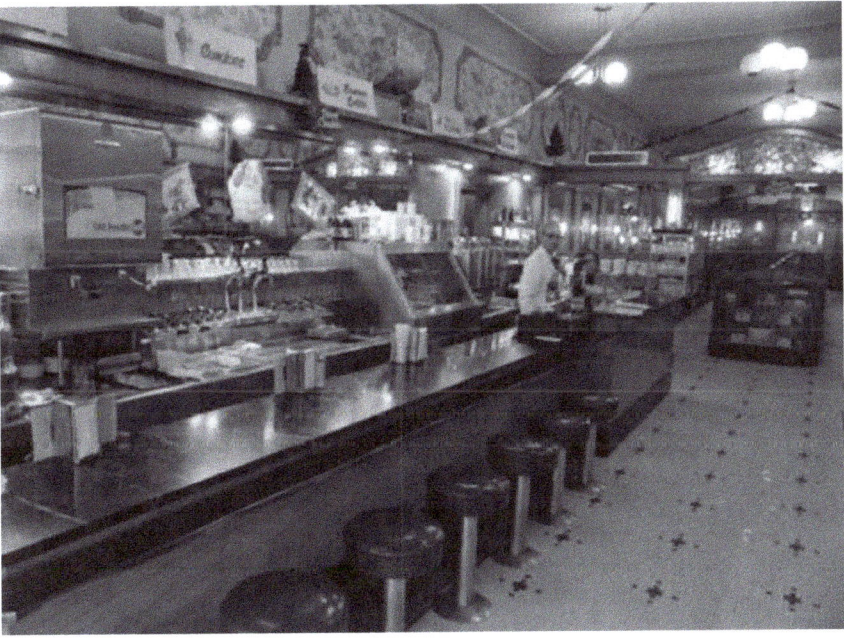

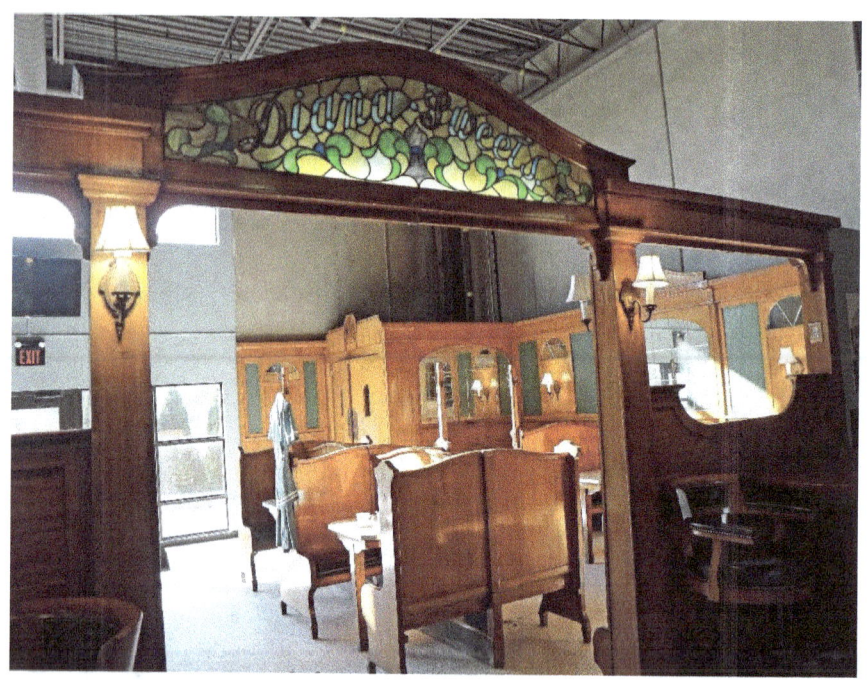

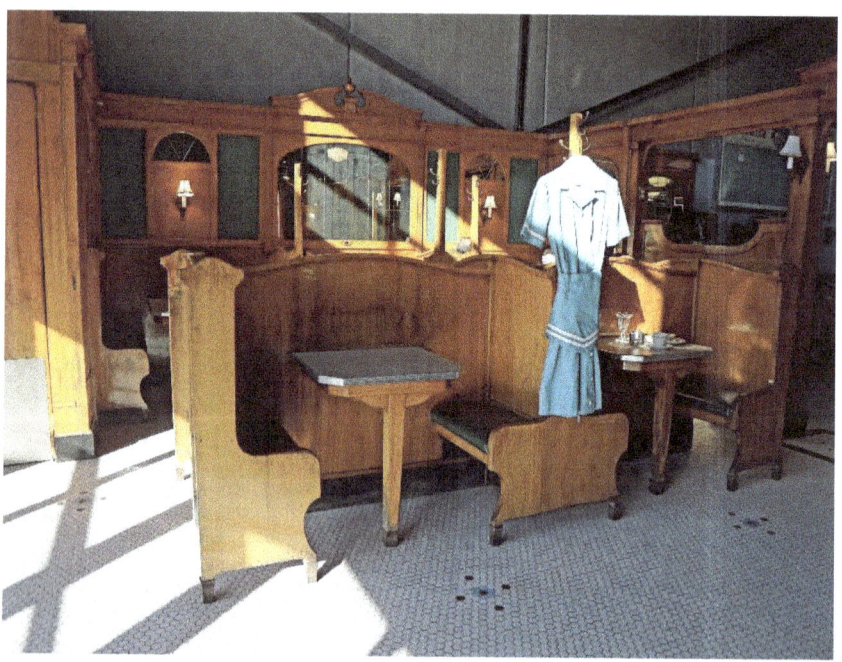

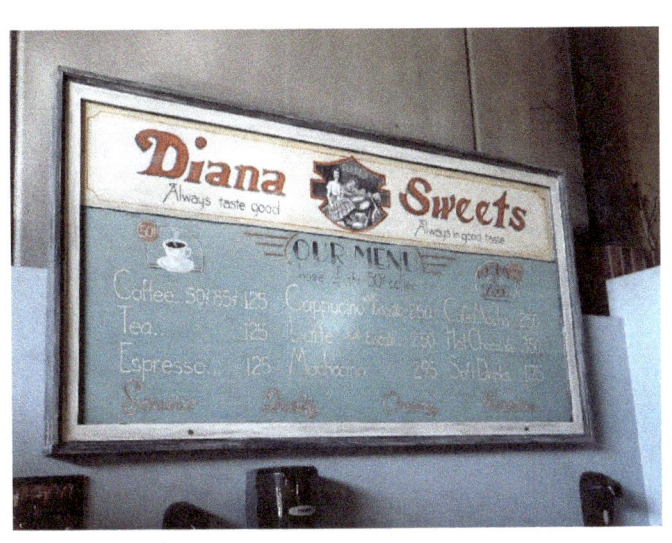

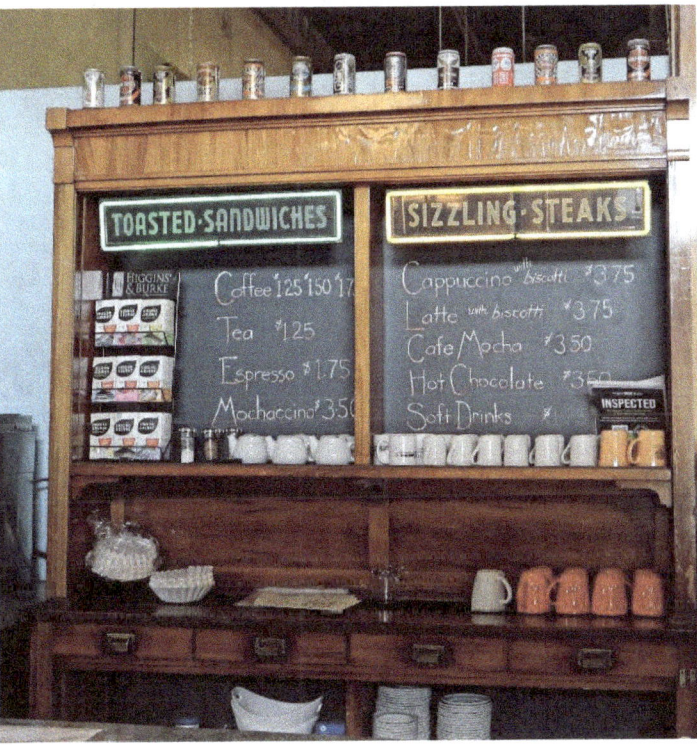

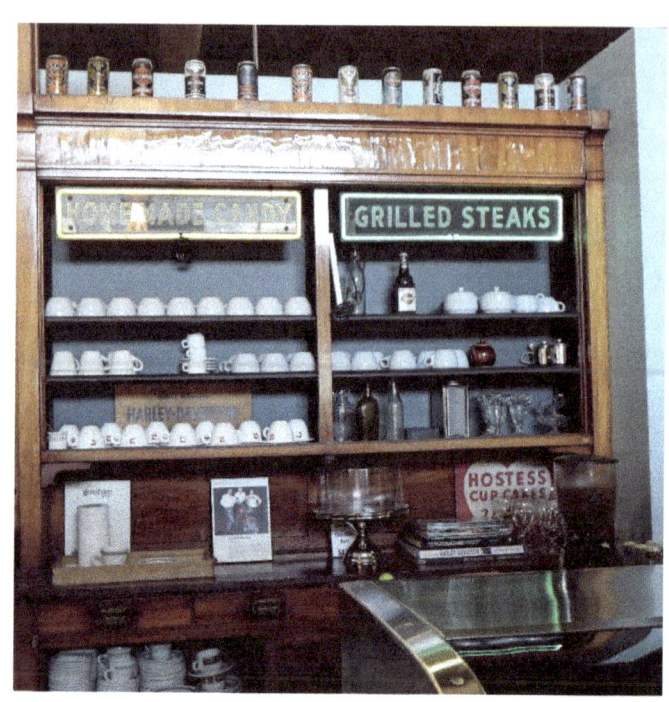

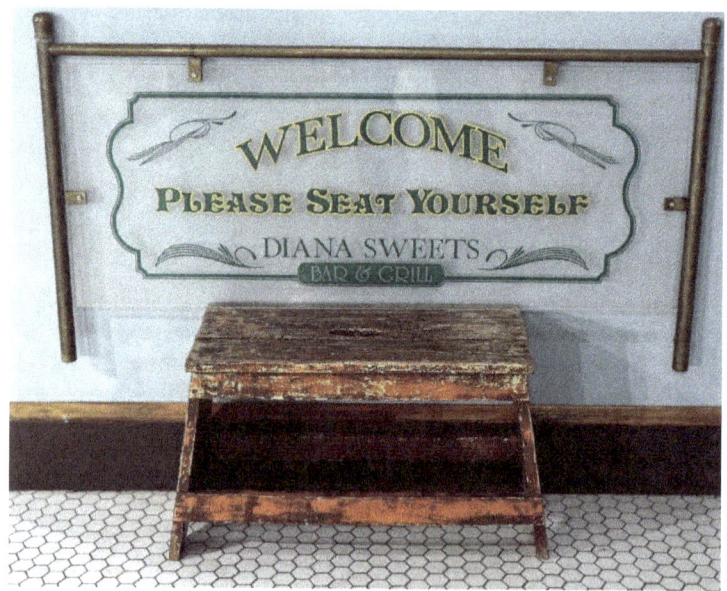

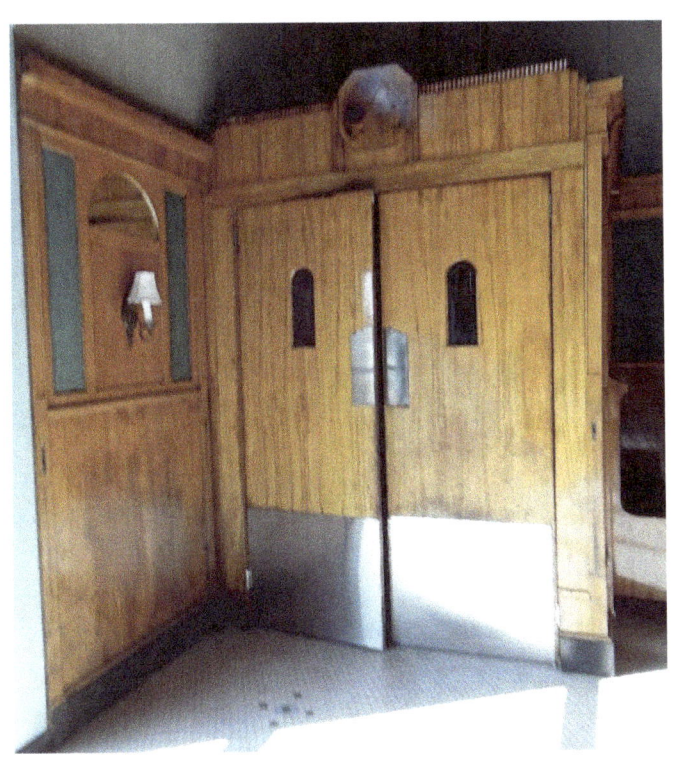

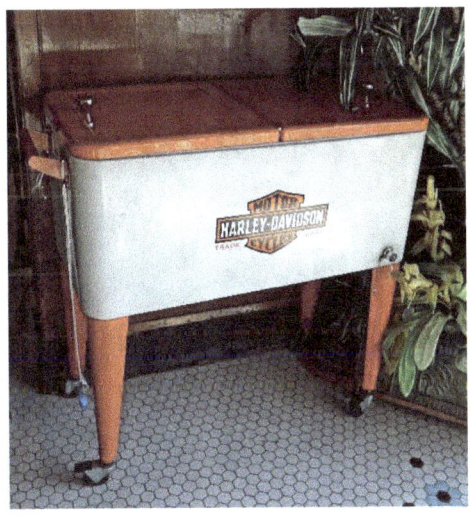

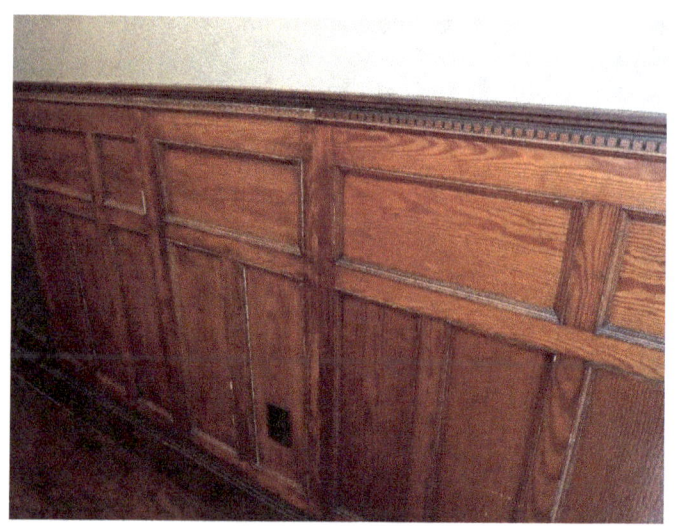

Vintage woodwork

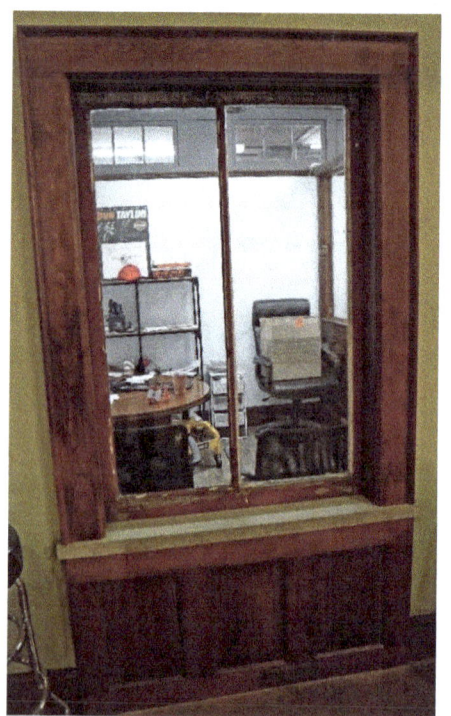

Vintage window

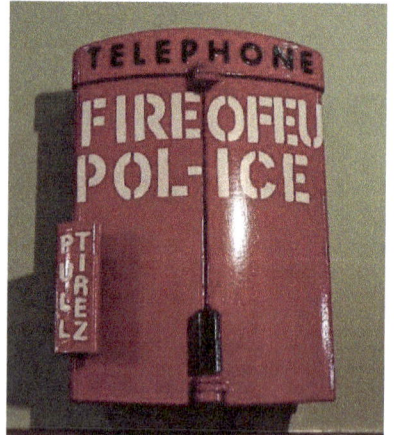

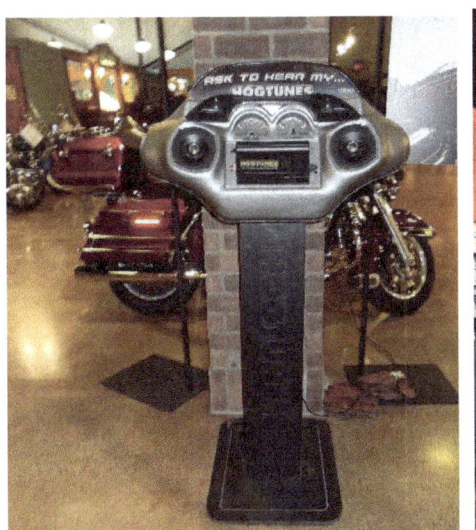

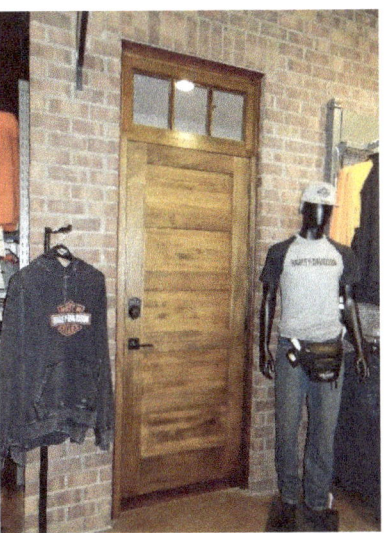

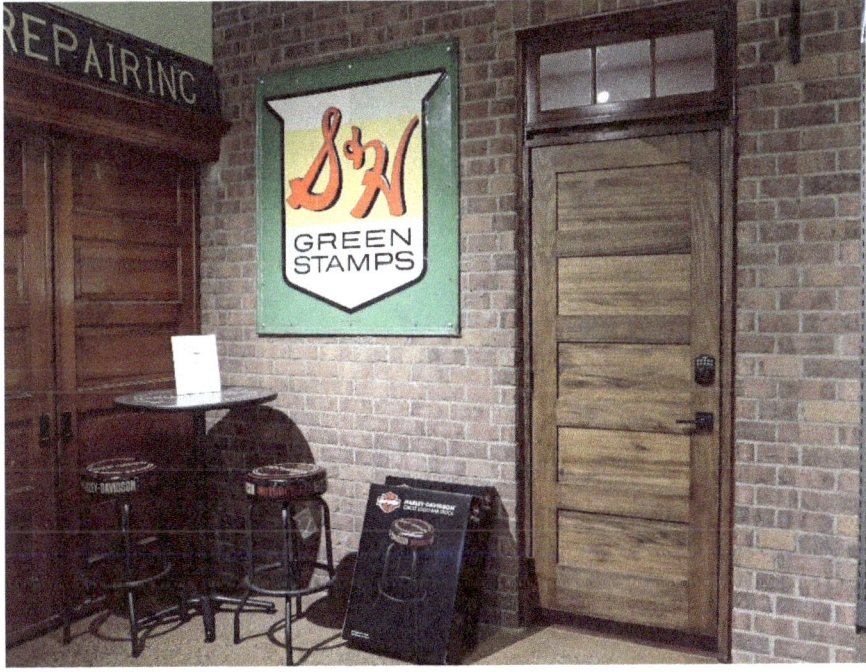

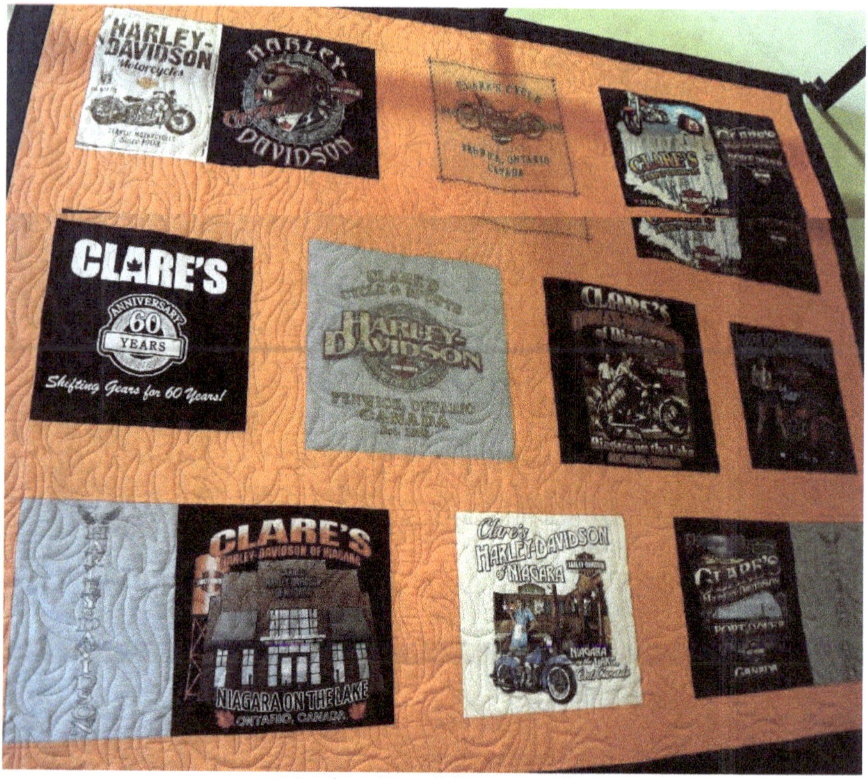

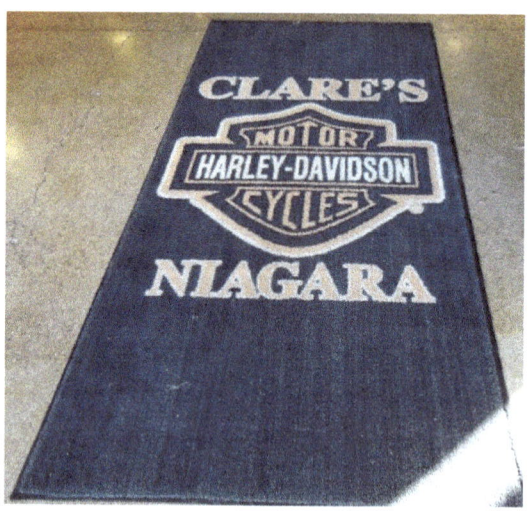

Harley Davidson quilt

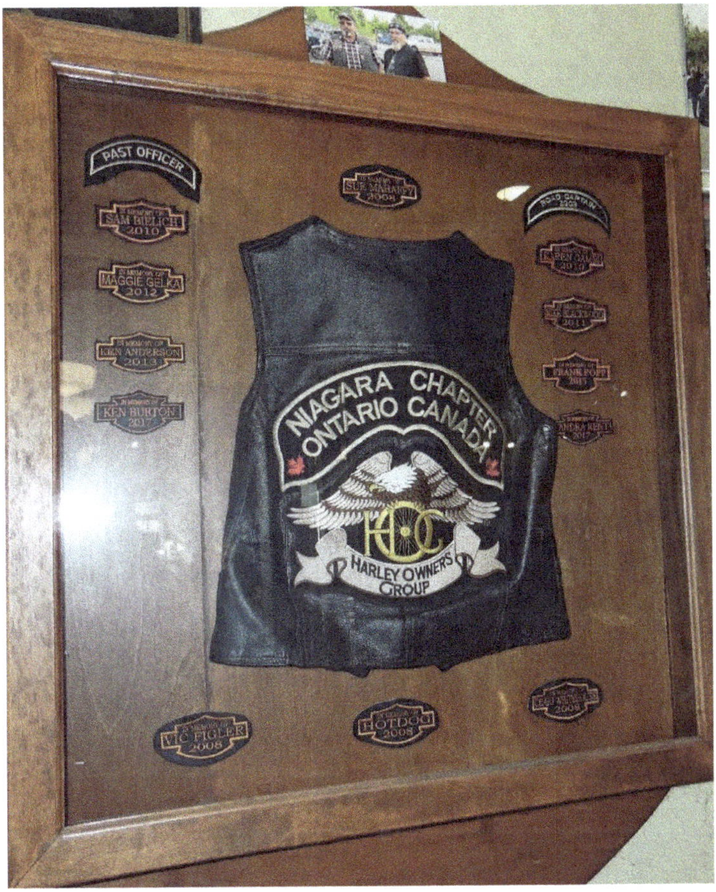

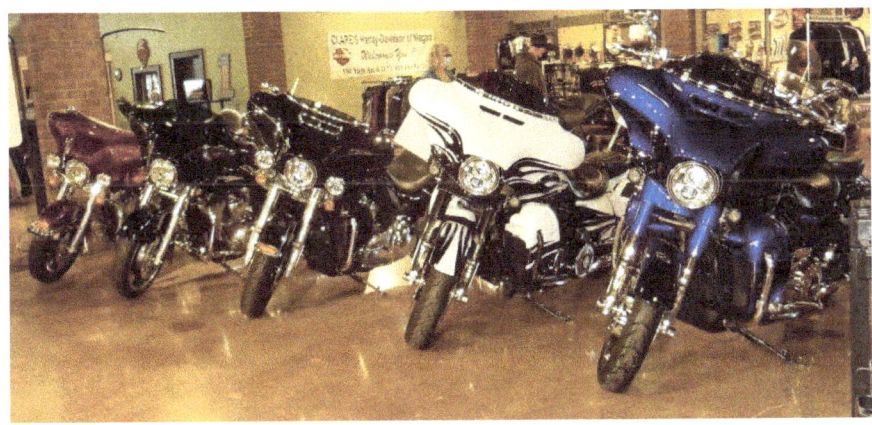

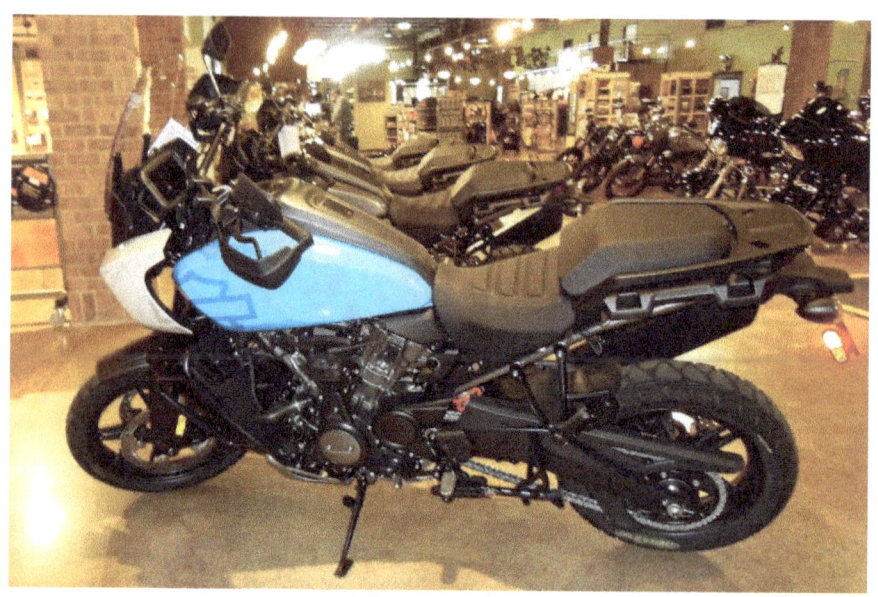

Motorcycles

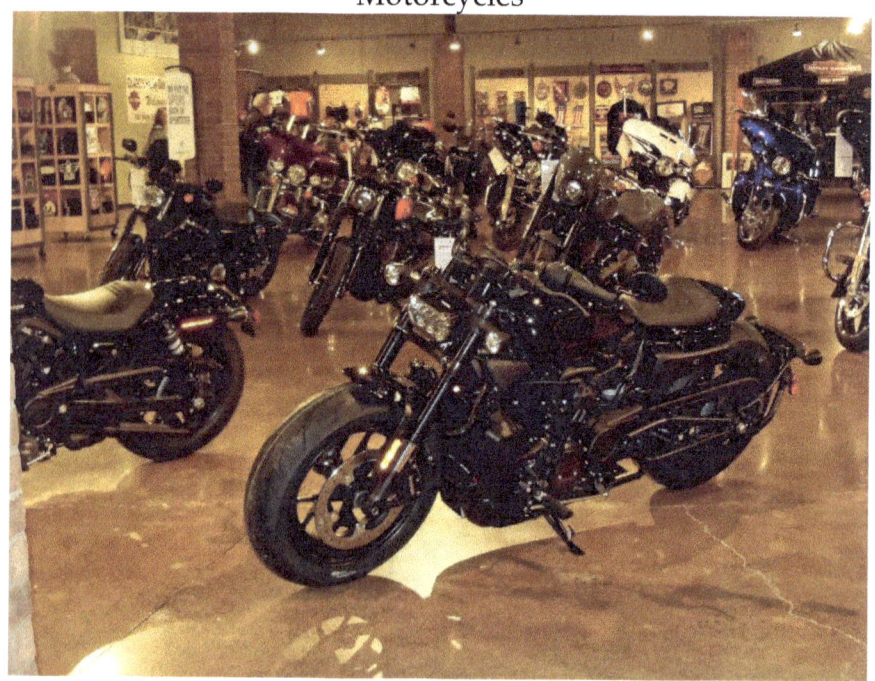

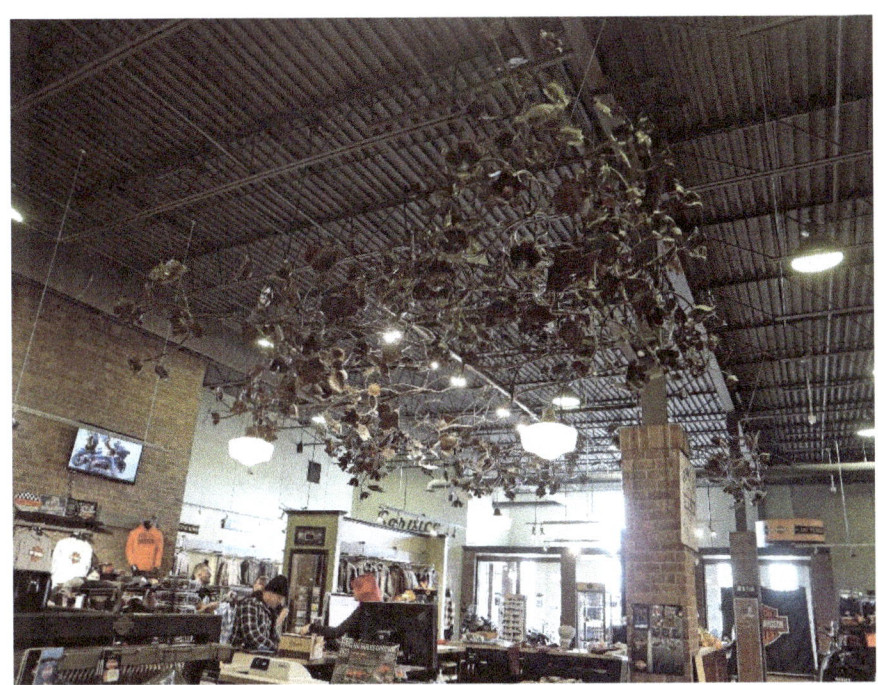

Unique chandelier

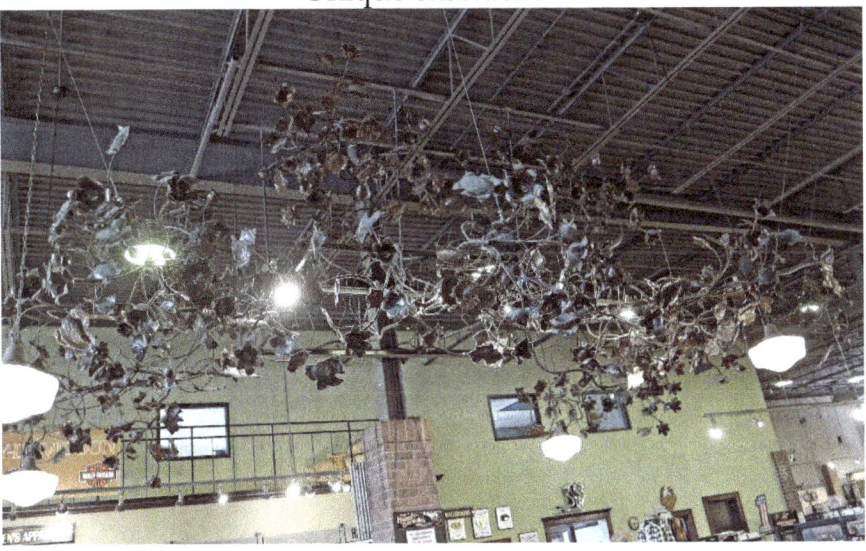

St. Andrew's Presbyterian Church
323 Simcoe Street

Presbyterians formed a congregation at Niagara in 1794 with John Dun as resident minister. Within a year, a church was built, and by 1802 a school house was added. The original 1794 church was burned by the American army during the War of 1812; the Americans claimed British soldiers used the steeple as an observation post. For eighteen years after its destruction, the congregation held services in the school house (circa 1802) until 1831 when a new church was built; it was destroyed by a cyclone. In 1855, the current building was constructed. St. Andrew's is a splendid example of Greek Revival architecture. The church's interior, classically Georgian in design, has the original high pulpit and box pews.

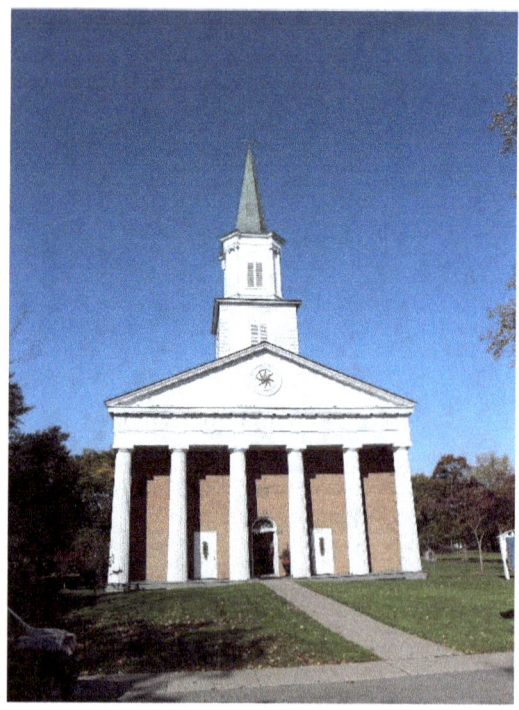

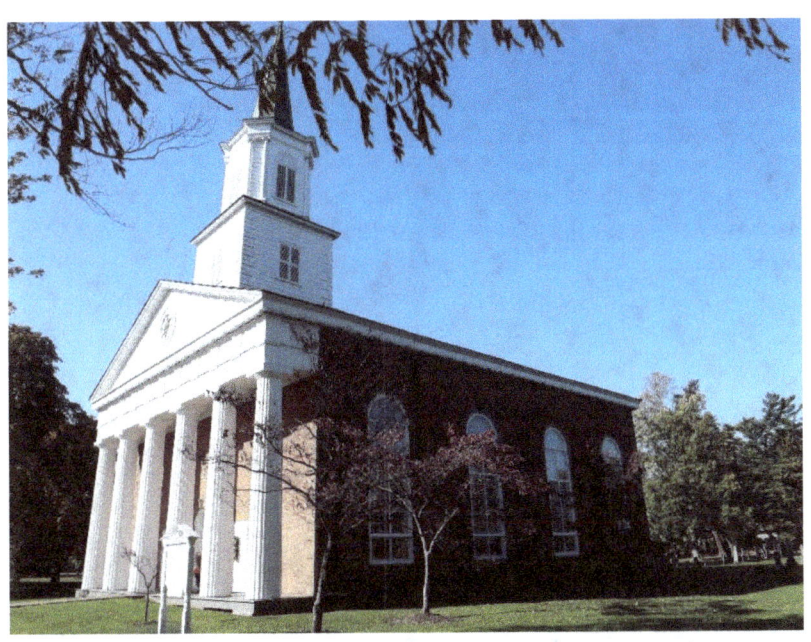

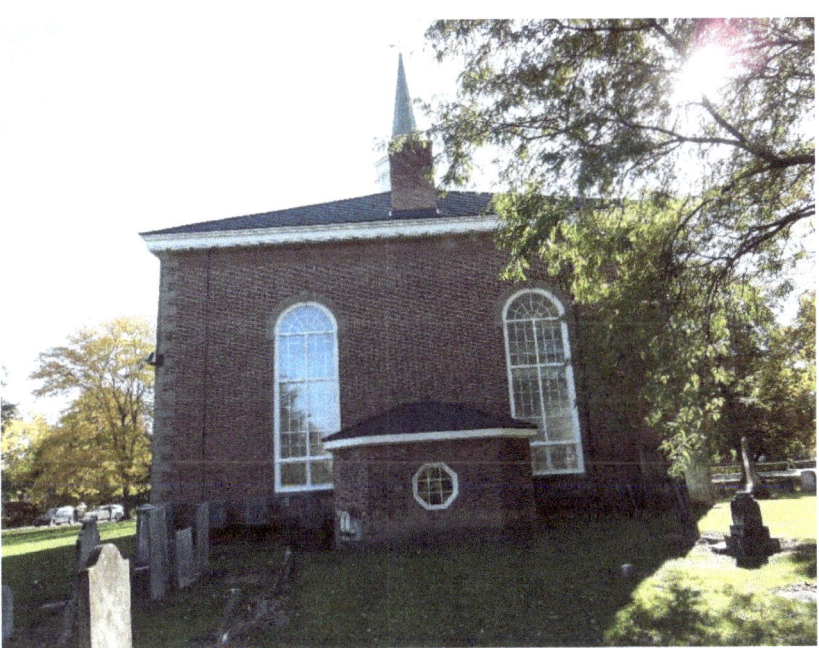

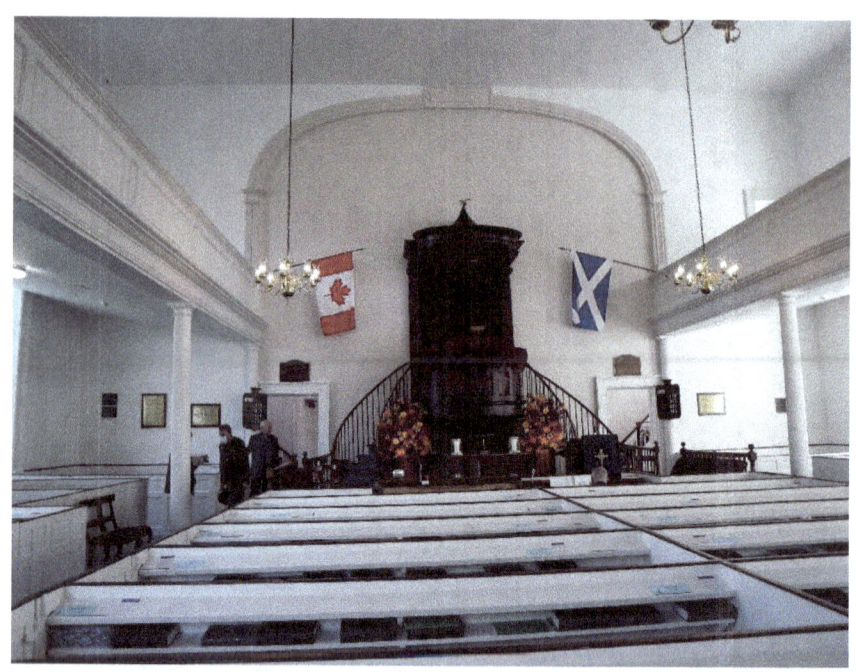

Box pews

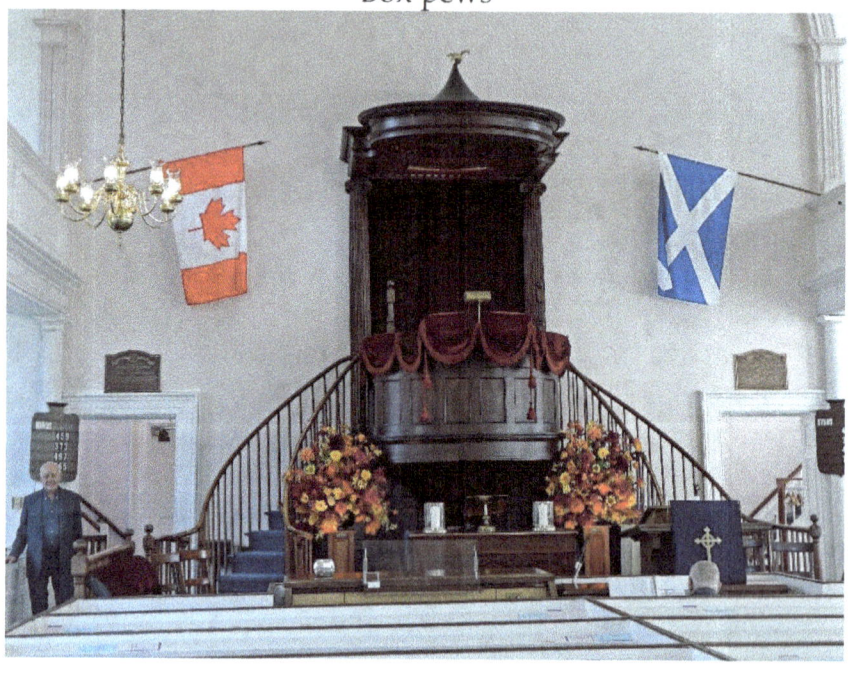

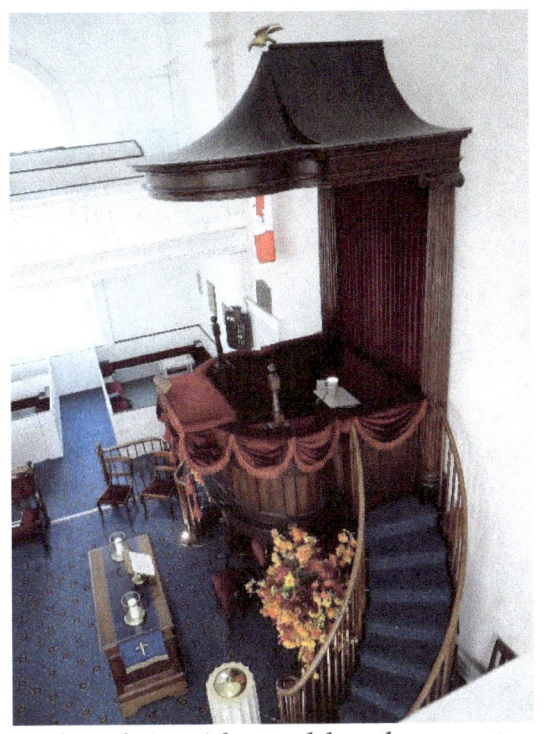

High pulpit with a golden dove on top

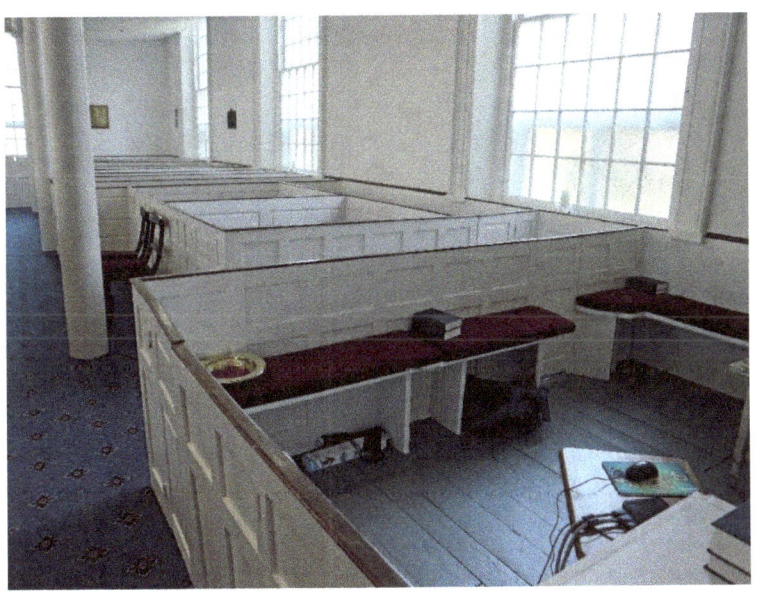

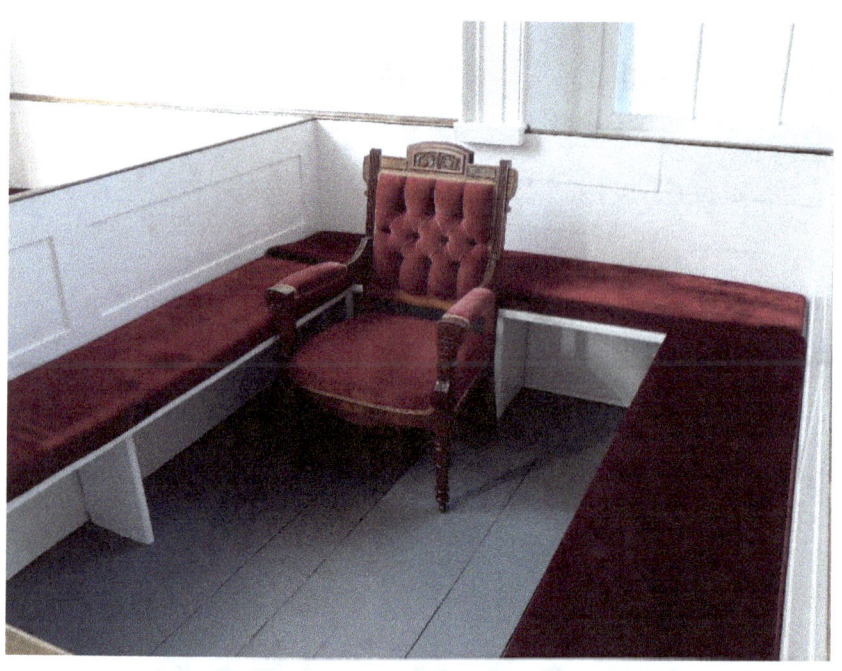

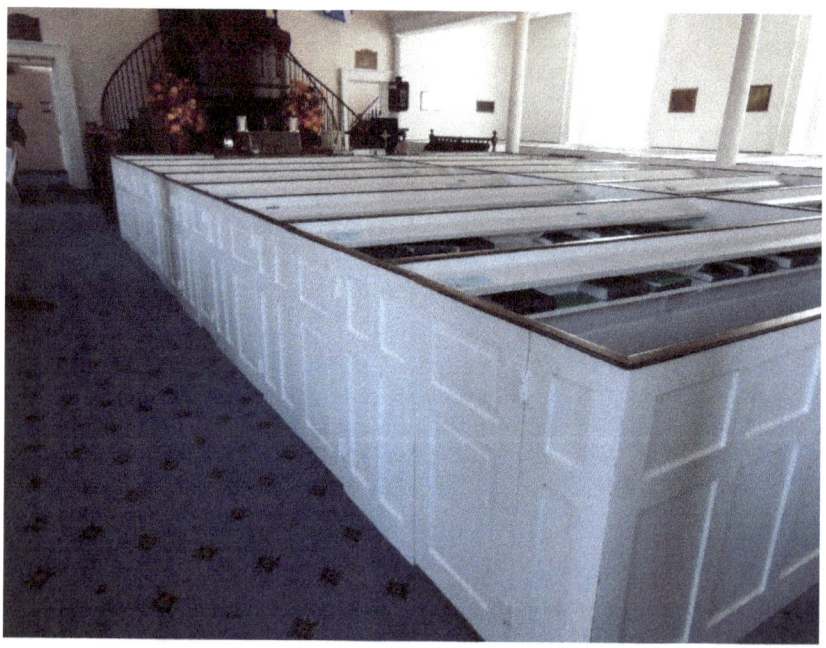

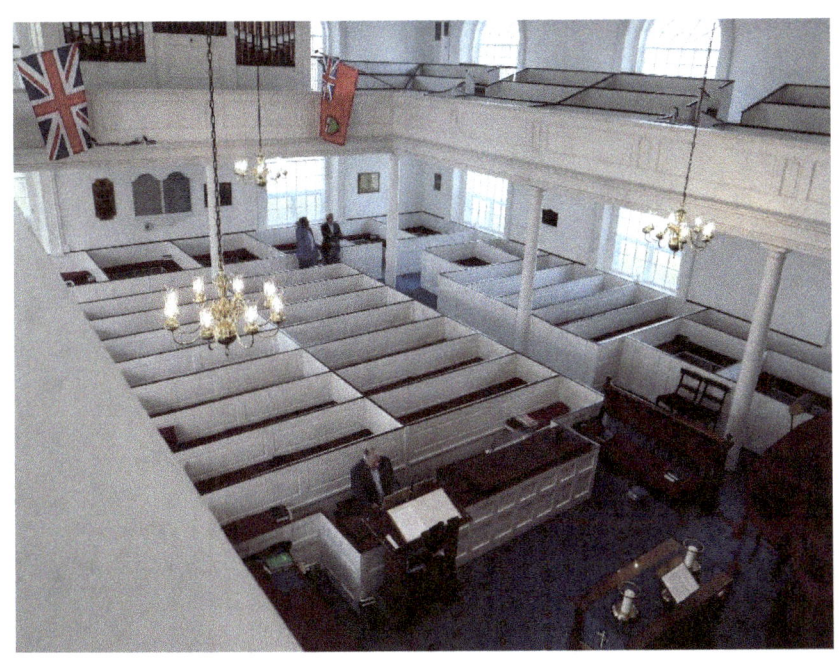

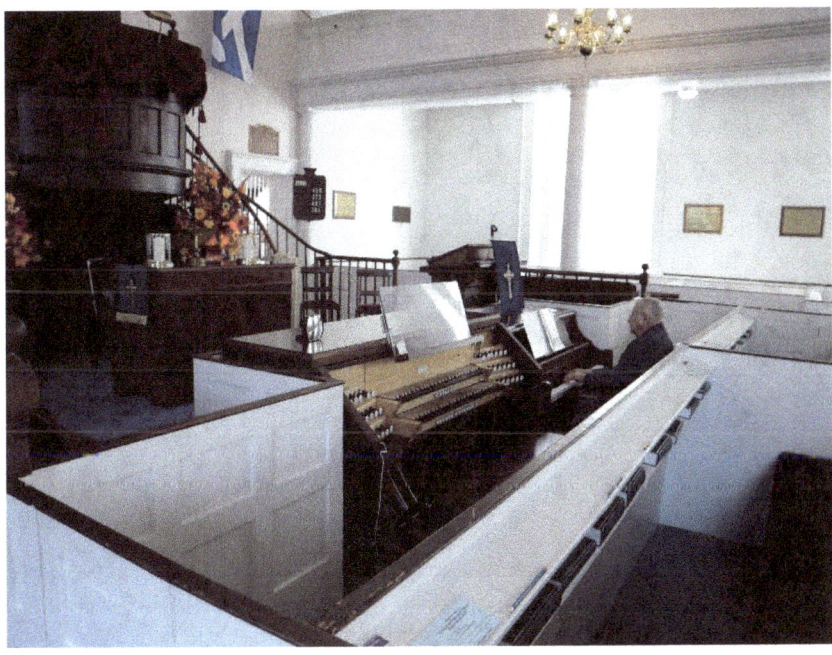

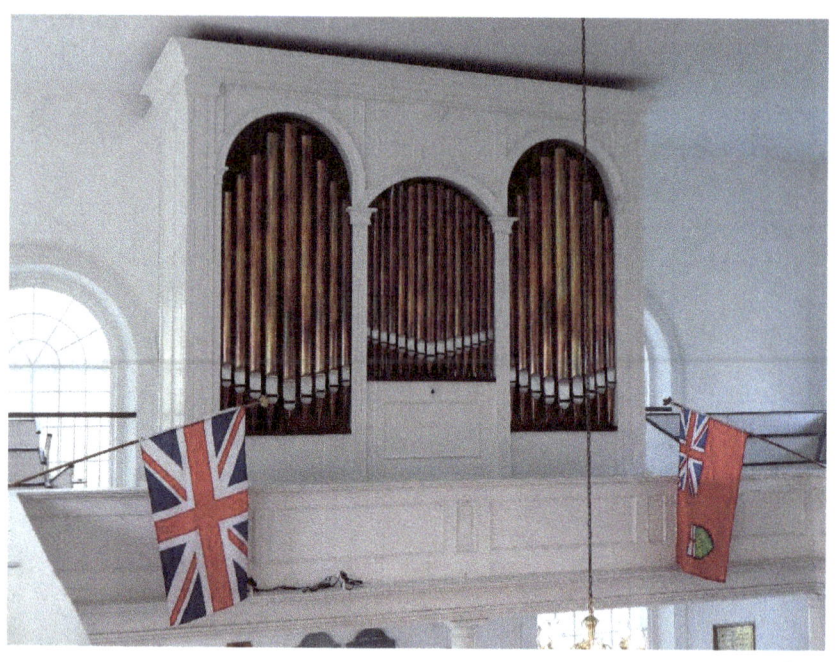

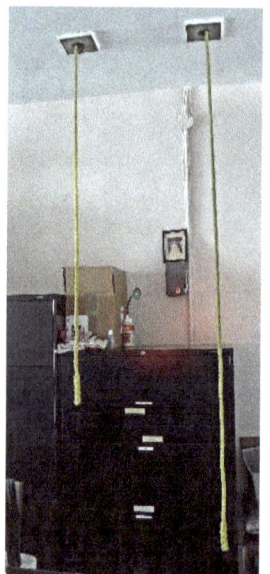

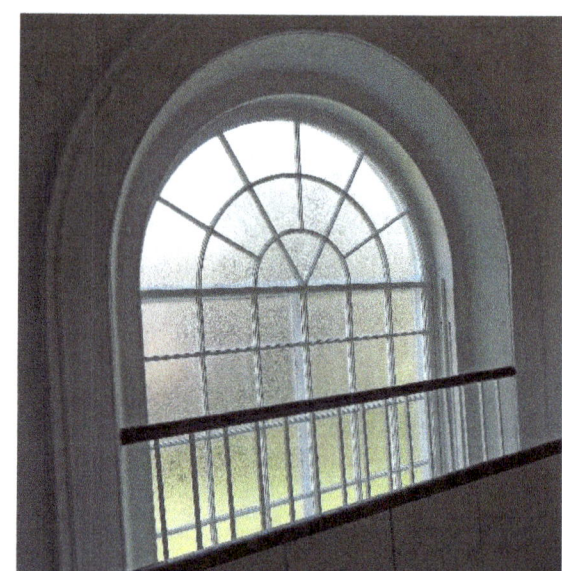

The ropes for playing the bells

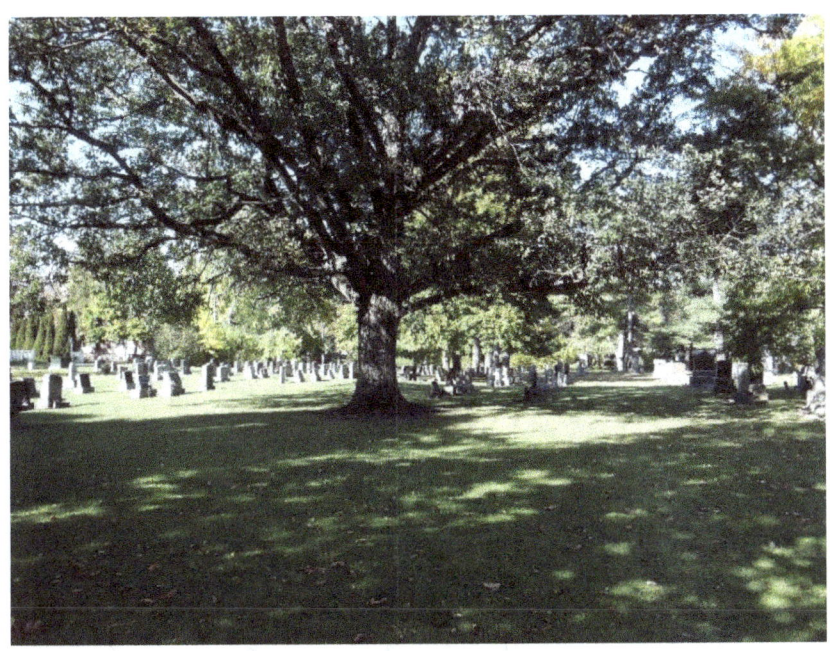

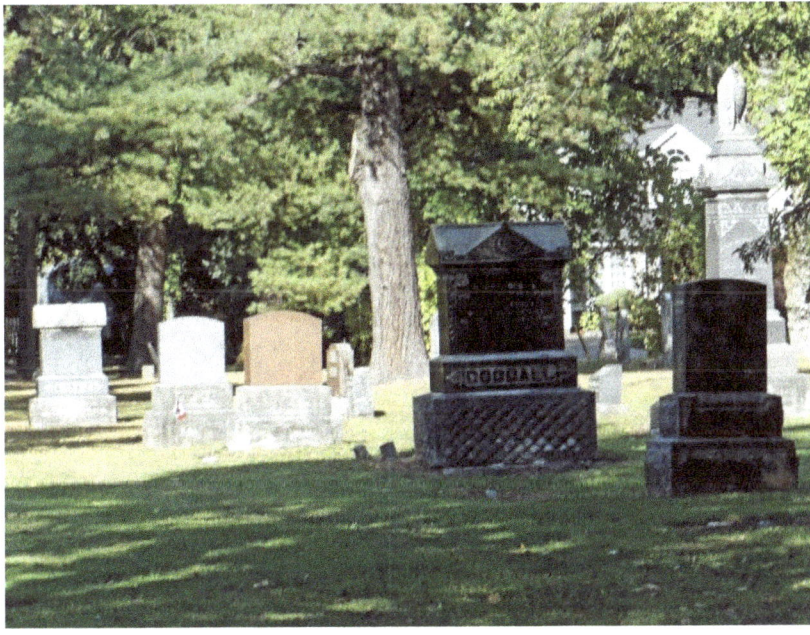

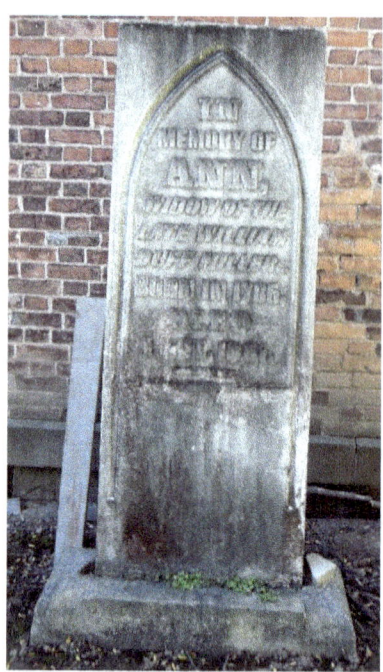

Gravestones of Ann and William Duff – both born in 1786 and died about 1861

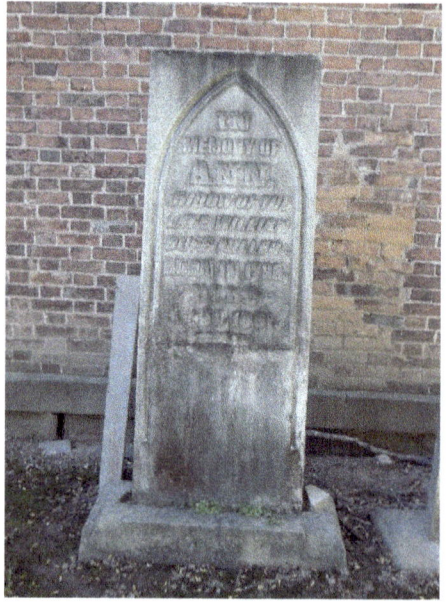

St. Mark's Anglican Church
41 Byron Street

The parish was founded in 1791 when the Reverend Robert Addison was appointed as minister and missionary. Addison was chaplain for parliament for twenty-four years. The first church building was constructed of sandstone and was completed by 1794. St. Mark's is the oldest Anglican church in continuous use in Ontario. The church building was begun in 1804 and completed in 1810. Among its congregants were Lieutenant-Governor John Simcoe, Lieutenant-Colonel John Butler, and Major General Isaac Brock. The church was used by the British as a hospital in 1812 and by the Americans as a barracks in 1813. Burnt by the Americans, the nave was rebuilt by 1822. The transepts were added in 1839 and balconies were placed along three sides to accommodate a growing community. The present Gothic Revival high pulpits and reading desks were added in 1843. The original balconies necessitated the high pulpits. The 1840 East Window is the oldest stained glass in the province and, with the other windows, form the finest collection of stained glass in Ontario. In 1892, the balconies and the box pews were removed.

The earliest marker in the cemetery is dated 1794 and is that of Elizabeth Kerr, daughter of Molly Brant and Sir William Johnson.

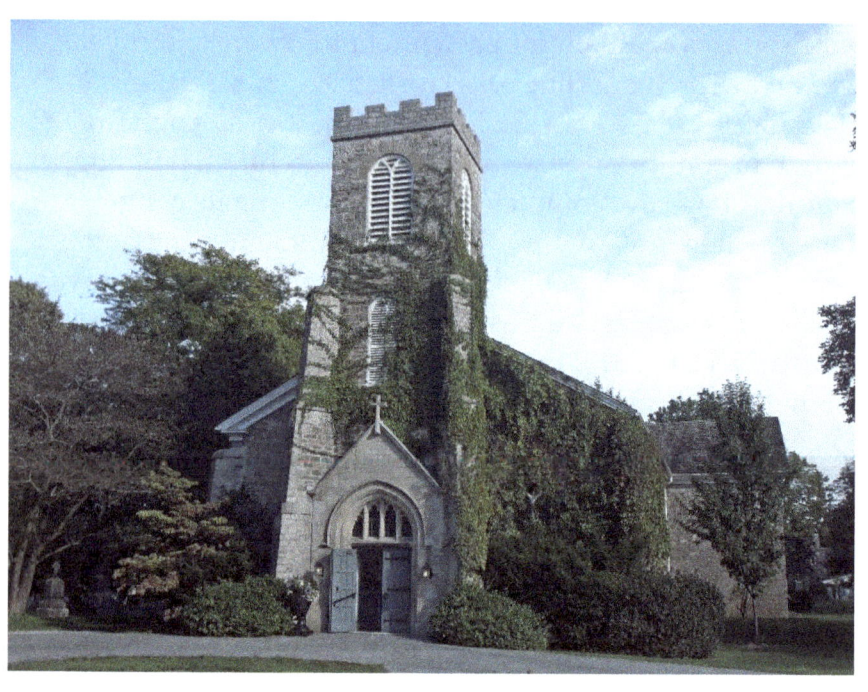

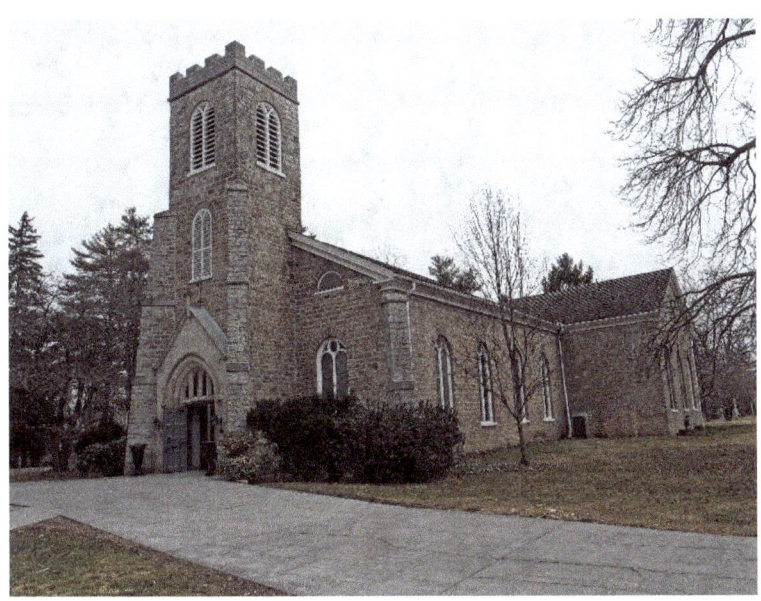

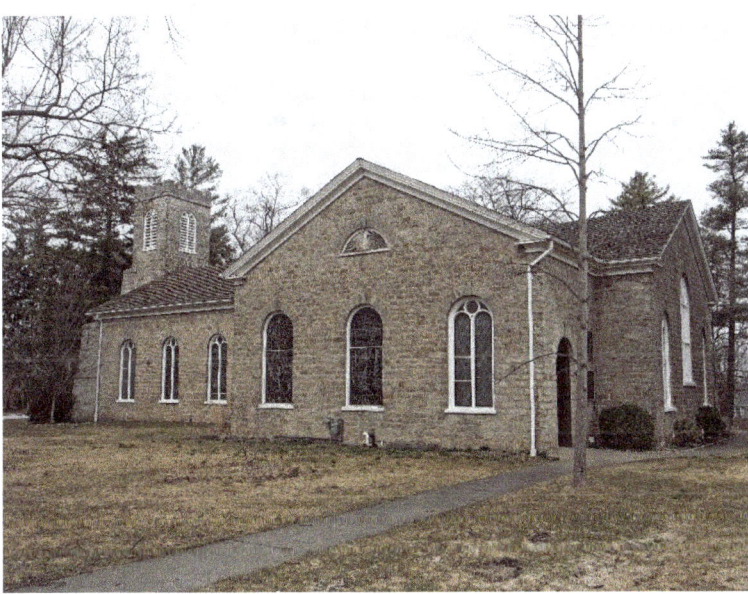

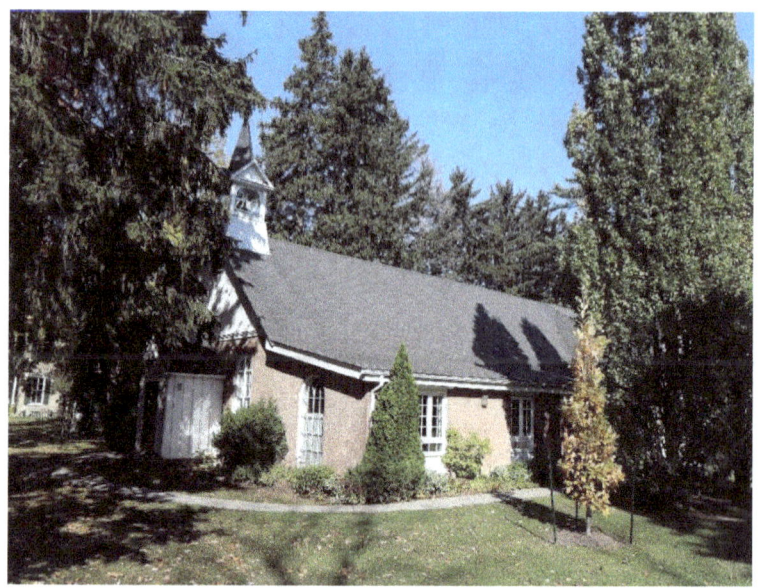

Addison Parish Hall – built as a Sunday Schoolhouse in 1886, with additions to both sides of the original building made in 1966.

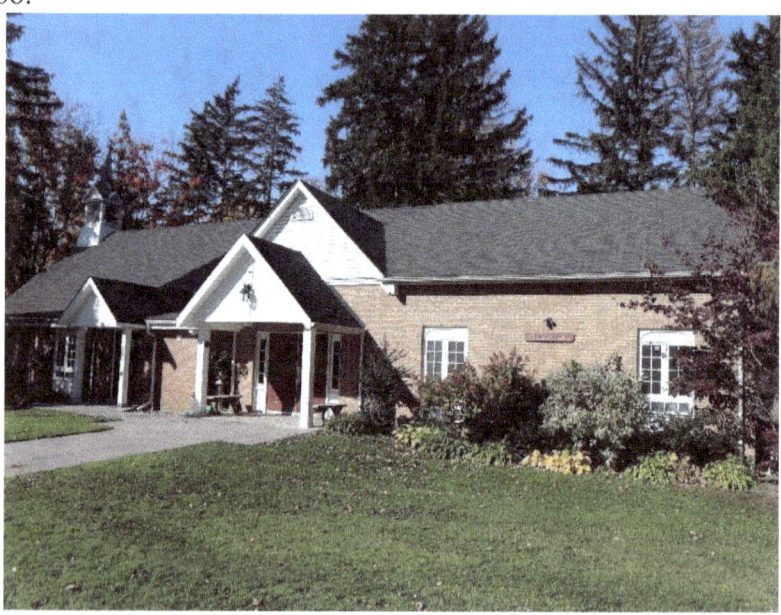

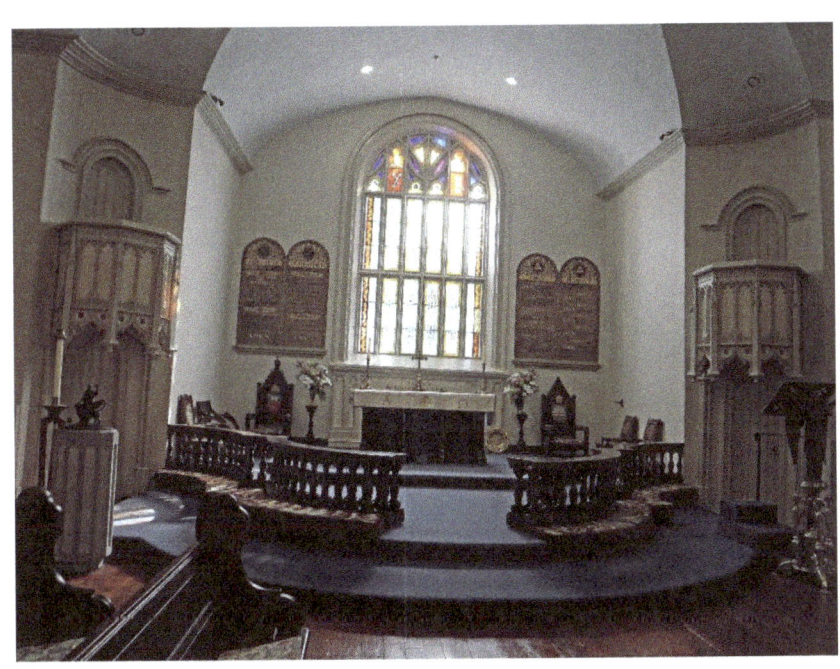

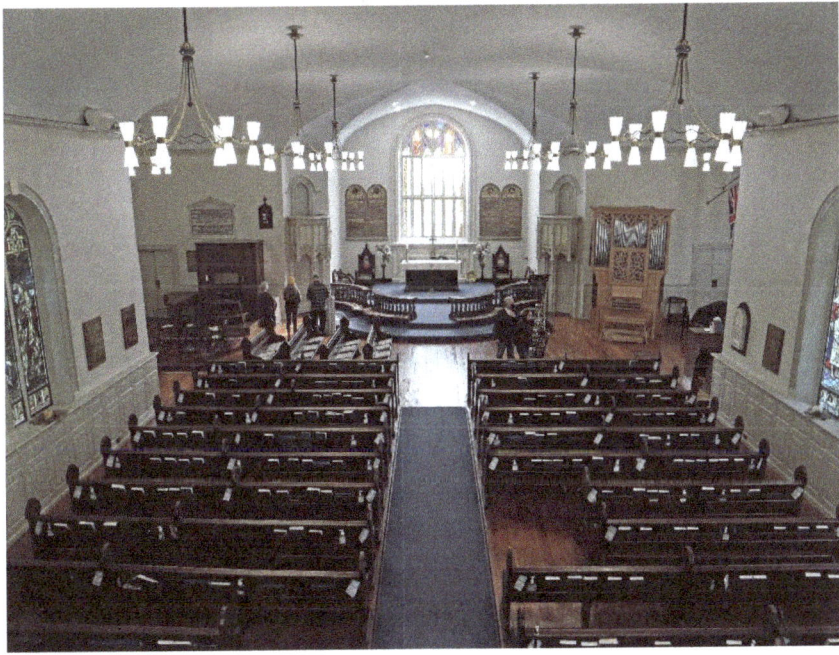

The bells of St. Marks – six bells were presented to the church in 1877 by Walter Augustus Dickson and John Geale Dickson in memory of their wives, Catherine and Matilda. Three bells were added in 1917 by the Ladies' Parish Guild with the proceeds of a legacy from Emma Josephine Brown in memory of her mother, Mary Jackes Brown. Now there are 19 bells and a tuning and console like a larger carillon. It can play almost any music on its one and a half octaves.

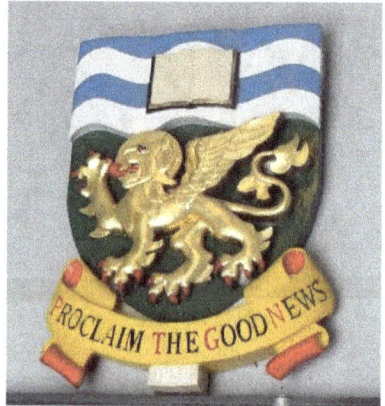

Plaque – 1992 – Proclaim the Good News

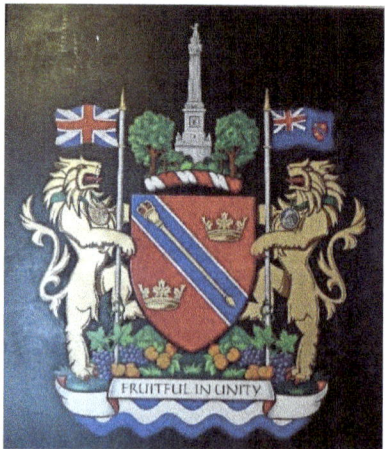

Fruitful in Unity

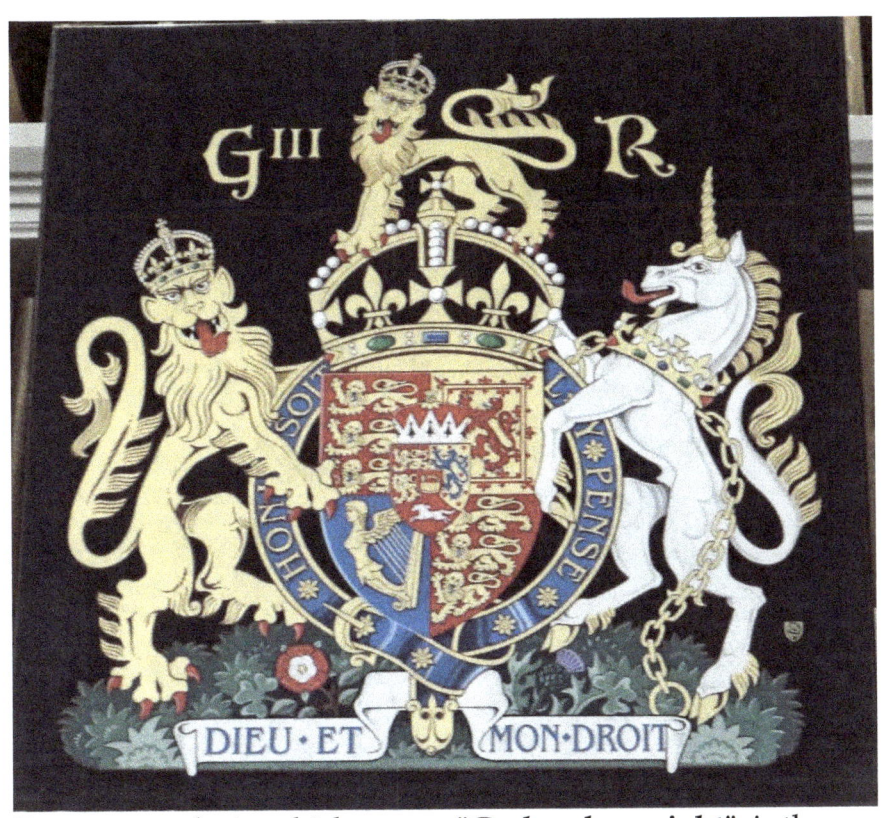

Deu et mon droit, which means **"God and my right"**, is the motto of the monarch of the United Kingdom. It appears on a scroll beneath the shield of the version of the coat of arms of the United Kingdom. The motto is said to have first been used by Richard I (1157–1199) as a battle cry and presumed to be a reference to his French ancestry and the concept of the divine right of the monarch to govern. It was adopted as the royal motto of England by King Henry V (1386–1422) with the phrase "and my right" referring to his claim by descent to the French crown.

The windows of St. Mark's enhance the interior.

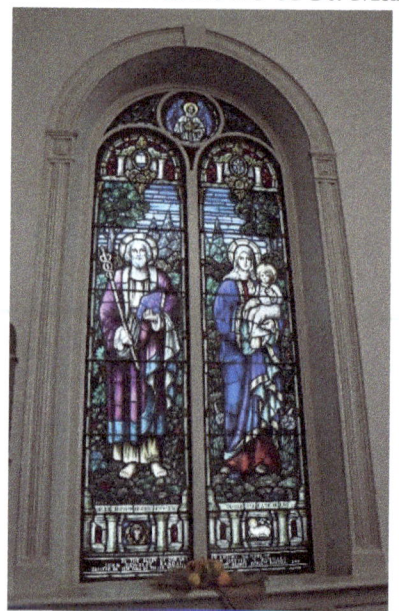

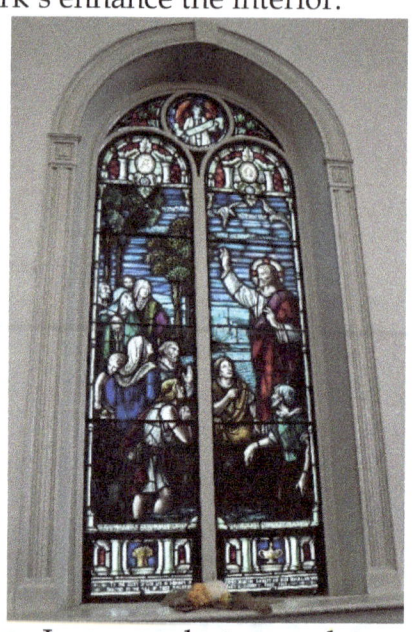

Moses / Mary and Jesus

Jesus speaks to people

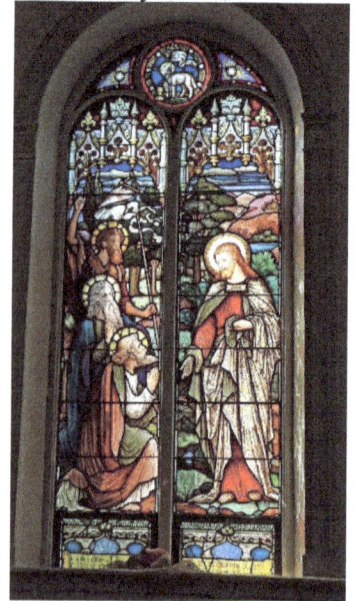

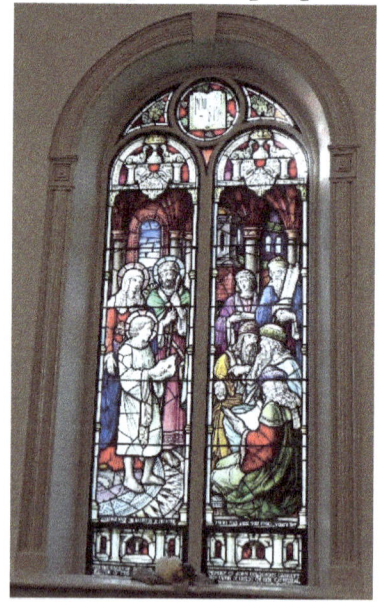

Disciples and Jesus

Jesus age 12 teaching in synagogue

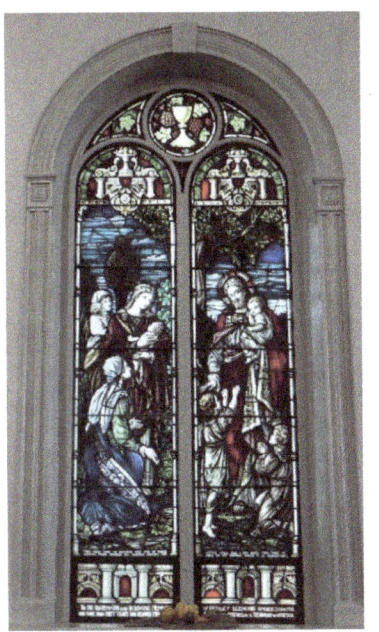

Jesus blessing little children

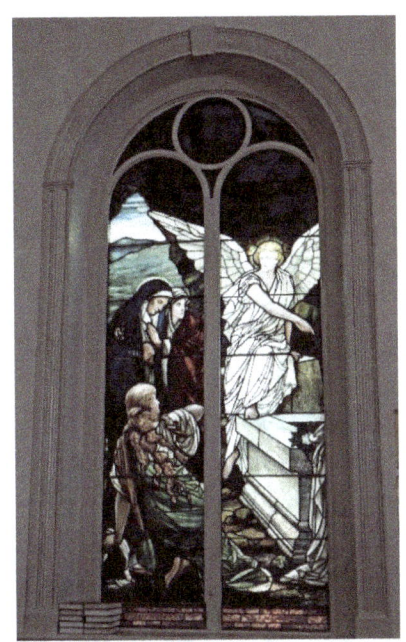

Angel at tomb, Jesus gone

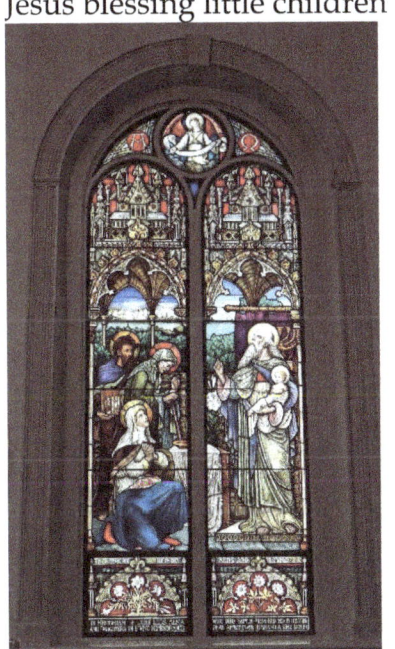

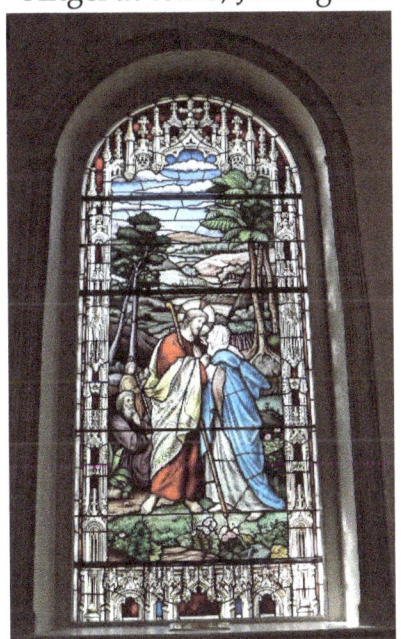

Mary Joseph present Jesus at temple   Mary Jesus in garden

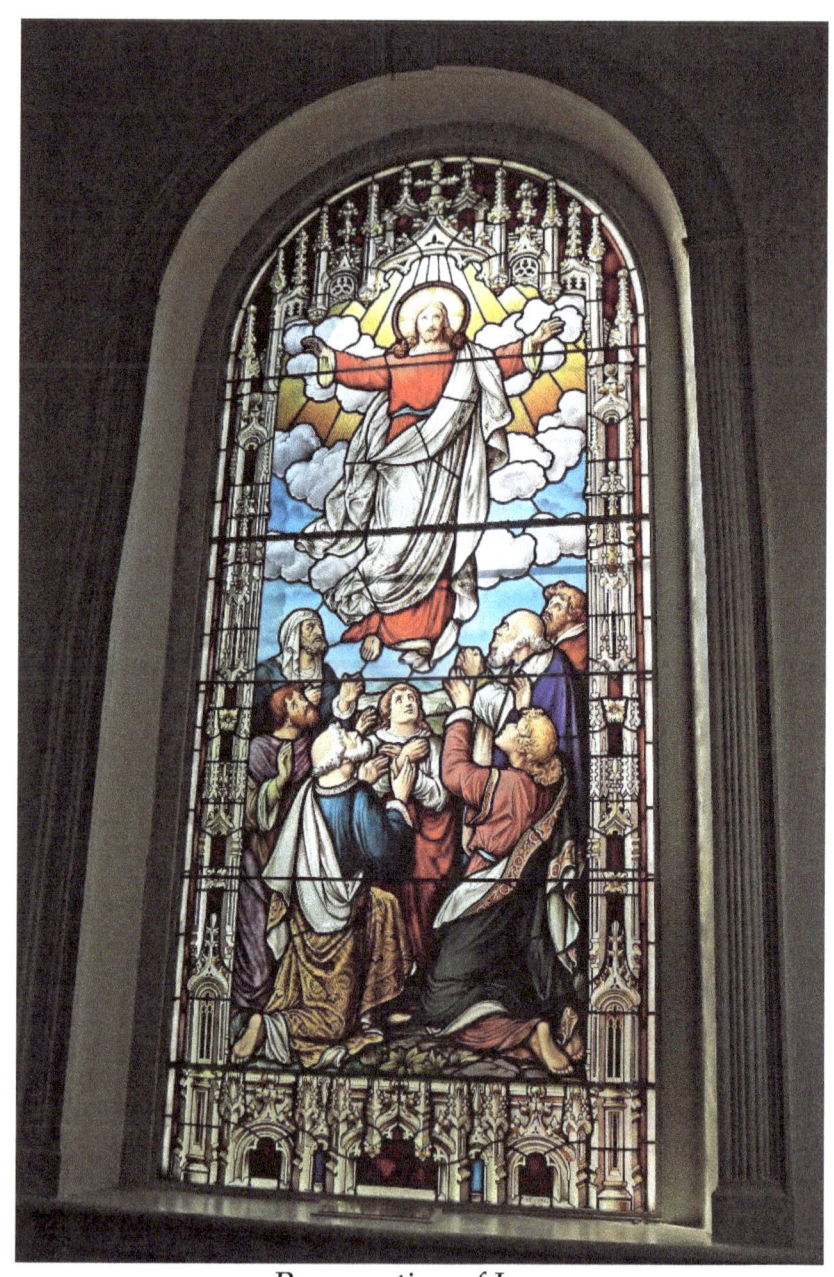

Resurrection of Jesus

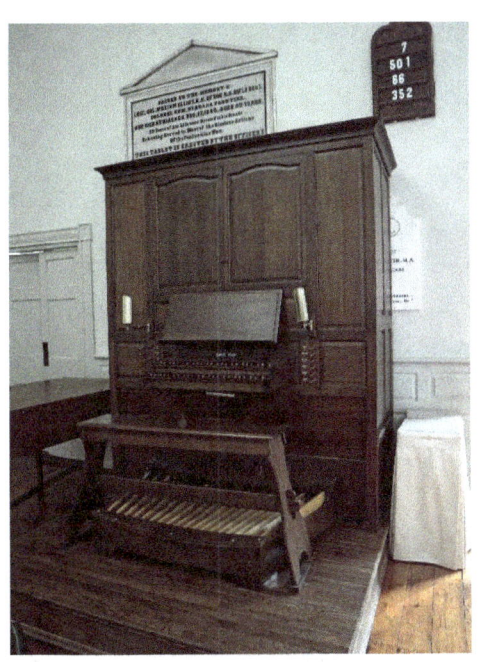

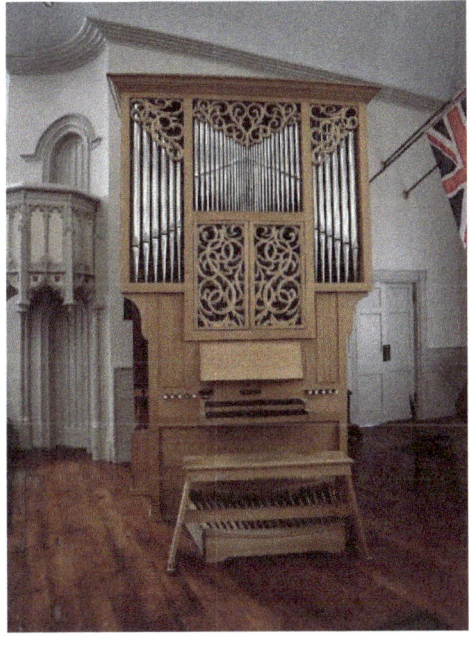

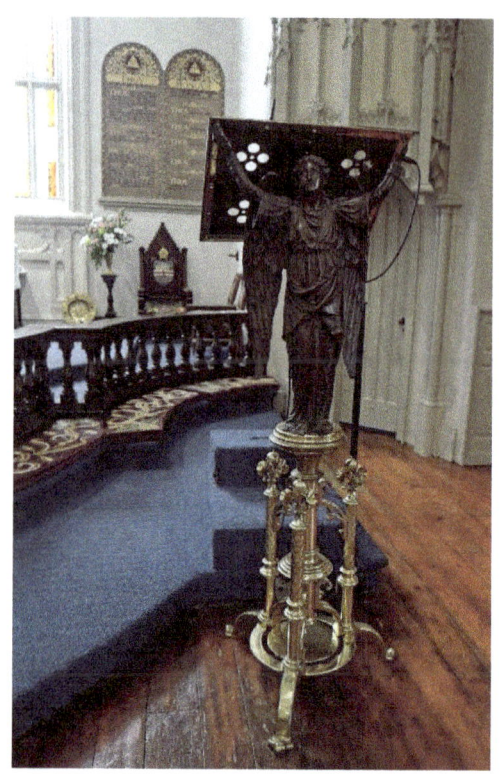

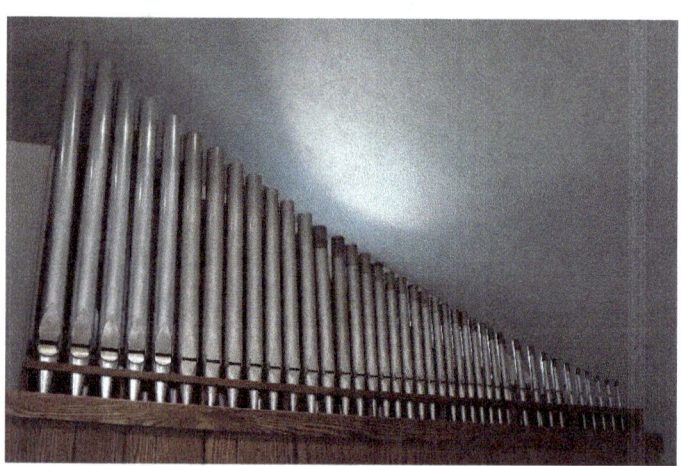

Organ pipes

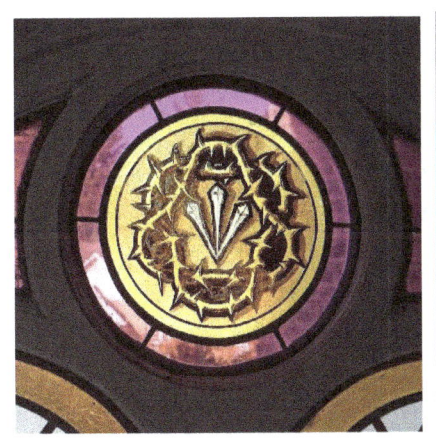

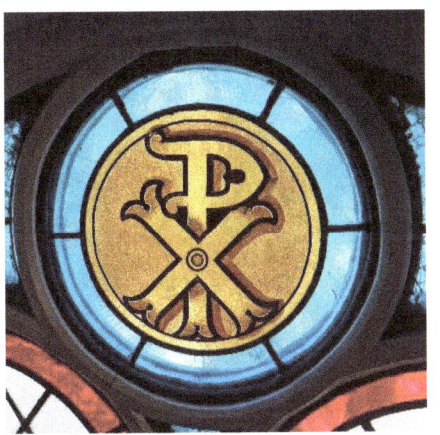

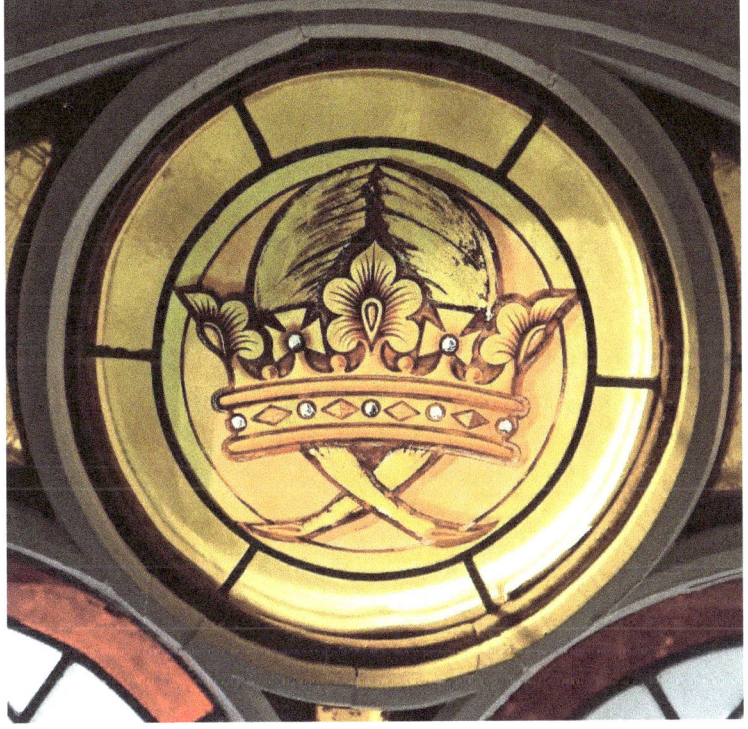

Fear God.
Honour the King.

IN MEMORY OF

COLONEL JOHN BUTLER,

HIS MAJESTY'S COMMISSIONER
FOR INDIAN AFFAIRS.

BORN IN NEW LONDON, PROVINCE OF
CONNECTICUT, 1728, HIS LIFE WAS SPENT
HONORABLY IN THE SERVICE OF THE CROWN.

IN THE WAR WITH FRANCE FOR THE CONQUEST
OF CANADA HE WAS DISTINGUISHED AT THE
BATTLE OF LAKE GEORGE 8, SEPT. 1755, AND
AT THE SIEGE OF FORT NIAGARA AND ITS
CAPITULATION 25 JULY, 1759.

IN THE WAR OF 1776 HE TOOK UP ARMS IN
DEFENCE OF THE UNITY OF THE EMPIRE, AND
RAISED AND COMMANDED THE LOYAL
AMERICAN REGIMENT OF

BUTLER'S RANGERS.

A SINCERE CHRISTIAN AS WELL AS A BRAVE
SOLDIER, HE WAS ONE OF THE FOUNDERS AND
THE FIRST PATRON OF THIS PARISH.

HE DIED AT NIAGARA MAY 1796, AND IS INTERRED
IN THE FAMILY BURIAL GROUND NEAR THIS TOWN.

ERECTED 1880.

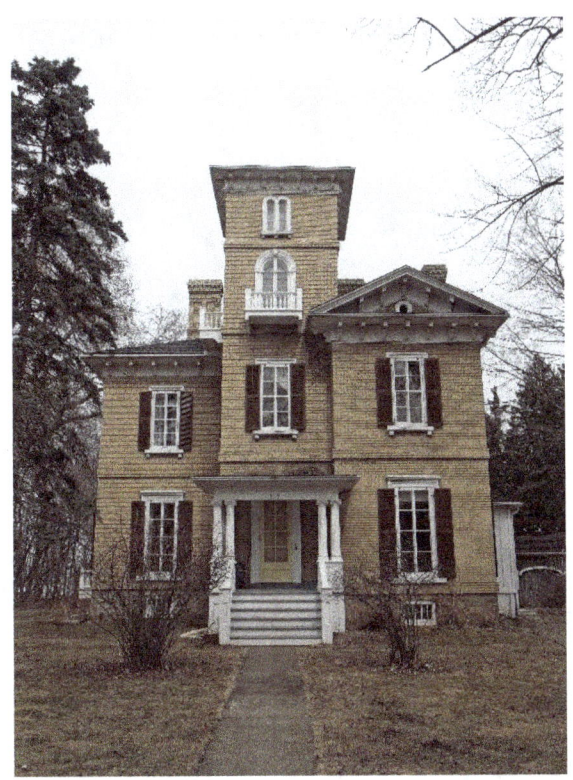

Rectory of St. Mark's Anglican Church - 17 Byron Street – Italian Tuscan Villa style, built in 1858. The upper windows on the tower have Roman arches; the highest windows are paired. The cornice brackets are large and ornate. Within the pediment there is a roundel. The windows on the first and second storey are rectangular with simple window surrounds and cornices. Both storeys have elegant shutters. Like many shutters on older buildings, these would probably have been working shutters that would close in winter for heat retention. The portico on the front door is of a Classical design with Ionic clustered columns and a simple architrave. There is a string course or band separating the first and second storeys.

Niagara Pumphouse Arts Centre
247 Ricardo Street

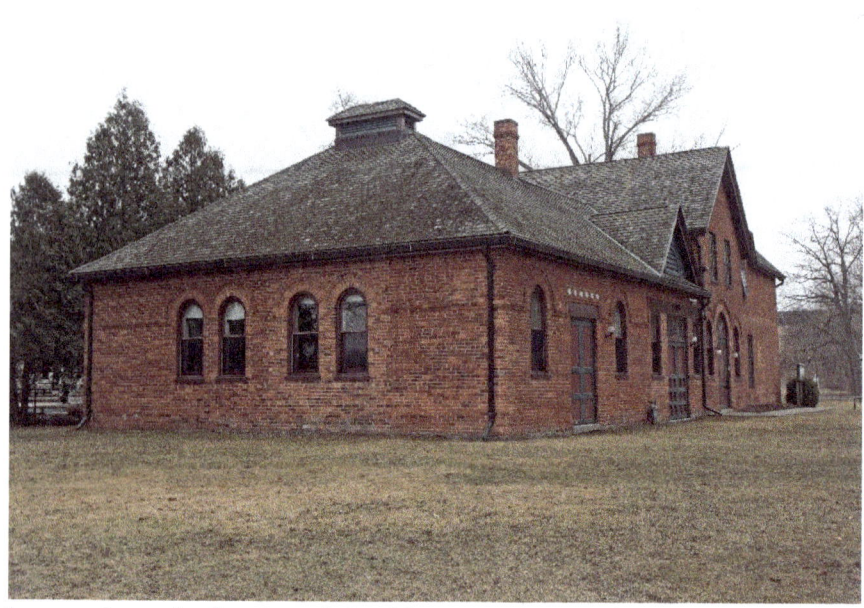

Located on the banks of the Niagara River, the Waterworks Pump House was built in 1891 and served as a pumping station that supplied the town with water from the Niagara River until 1983. The original building contained a steam engine, water pumps, and a boiler with a 75-foot chimney. The building was constructed of brick and shows an asymmetrical composition of Romanesque character. In 1994 the exterior was restored to its original appearance; and interior renovations were designed to accommodate the Niagara Pump House Visual Art Centre.

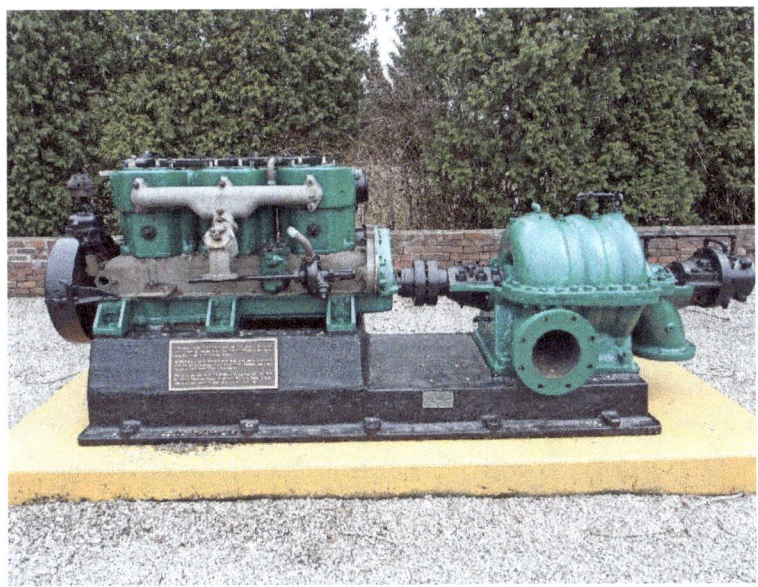

This gasoline engine standby pump was built in 1919 by
Morris Machine Works, Baldwinsville, New York, U.S.A. The
operating panel is located inside the building.

The Niagara Harbour and Dock Company, formed by local
businessmen in 1831, created a shipping basin on the Niagara
River by hiring hundreds of labourers to excavate a riverside
marsh. By the late 1830s, the company employed about 400
workers and operated a busy port and shipyard in Upper
Canada. The company's industrial complex was used to build
railway cars and steamboats in the 1850s and 1860s.

Niagara District Court House
26 Queen Street

The Niagara District Court House is significant for its association with the development of the judicial system and the functioning of courthouses and local governments in the Province of Ontario. When Upper and Lower Canada were established in 1791, courthouses became centers for judicial and civil administration. Courthouses were an embodiment of moral, social and economic values of middle-class Upper Canadians. The courthouse symbolized the authority of the district or county, and the functions that the courthouse served were indicative of the increased responsibility of local governments. As professional architects started to design courthouses, the buildings became more sophisticated and often had classically-inspired ornamentation. Courthouses, like the Niagara District Court House, were examples of monumental public architecture. The Niagara District Court House had a courtroom, offices, a jail, and space for a town hall and market area. Courthouses were community buildings that often housed other government or private offices which increased their public accessibility.

The Niagara District Court House marked the beginning of the dominance of metropolitan architects in courthouse design in Ontario. Architect William Thomas's design for this building began a trend in courthouse architecture all over the province. The courthouse served as the Town Hall after the county seat moved from Niagara to St. Catharine's in 1865. In 1962 The Shaw Festival Theatre started performing in the courthouse and converted the courtroom to a 327-seat auditorium; the Shaw Festival used the building until 1973. Today, Parks Canada and the Chamber of Commerce have offices here. It was designated a National Historic Site in 1981.

William Thomas (1799-1860) was one of the founders of the Canadian architectural profession. During Thomas' seventeen-year career in Canada, over one hundred of his building designs were constructed across the country. This three-storey structure was built by Garvie and Co. from 1846-1848. It is in the Neo-Classical architectural style. The courthouse is distinguished by the projecting frontispiece and a heavily bracketed cornice and pediment. The main entrance is framed by Doric columns that support a portico with a stone balustrade. There are decorative quoins on the corners. The front of the courthouse is enhanced by rectangular windows in the second storey with pedimented hoods, and arched windows on the third storey. The courthouse is at the front of the property and the market hall is at the back of the property and is accessed via a service corridor.

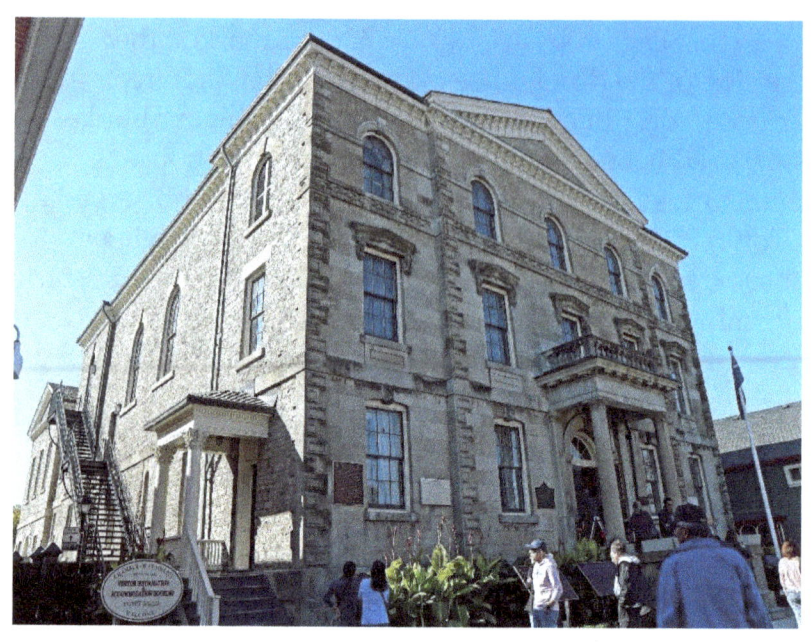

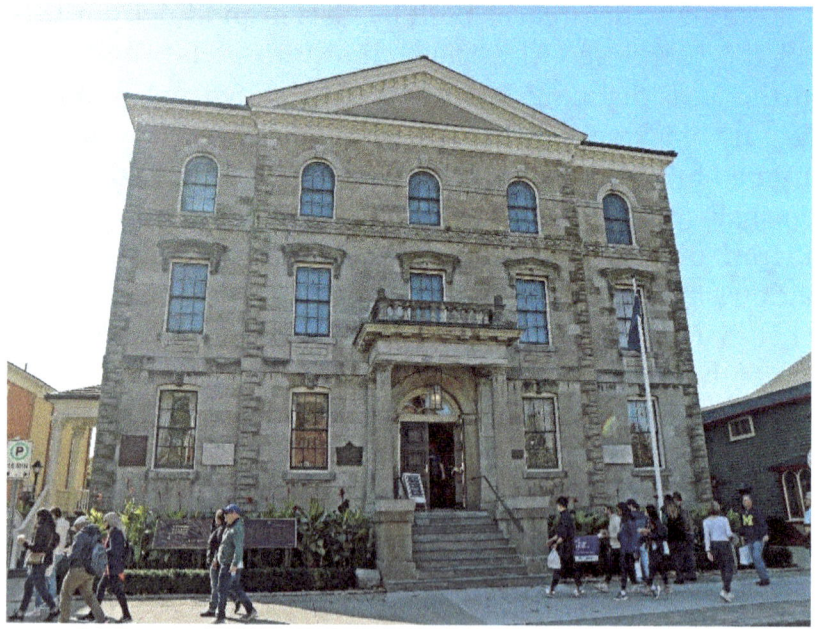

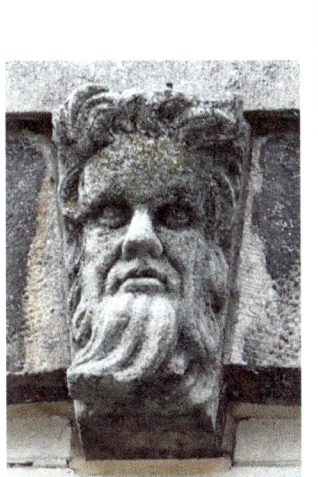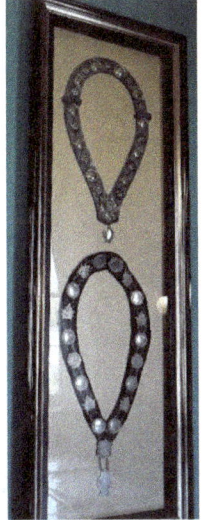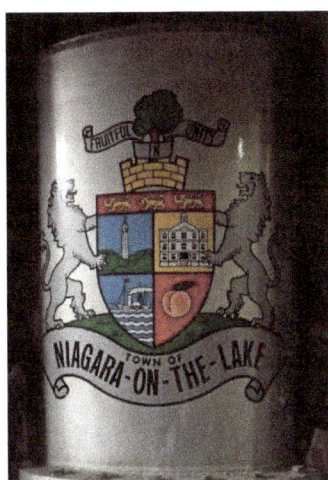

Keystone above window

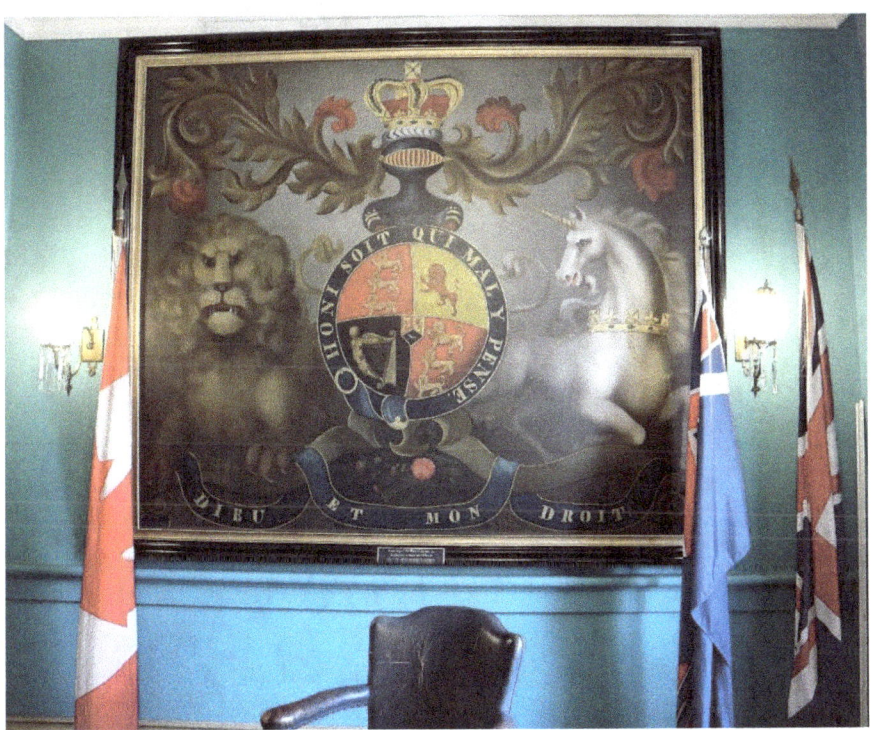

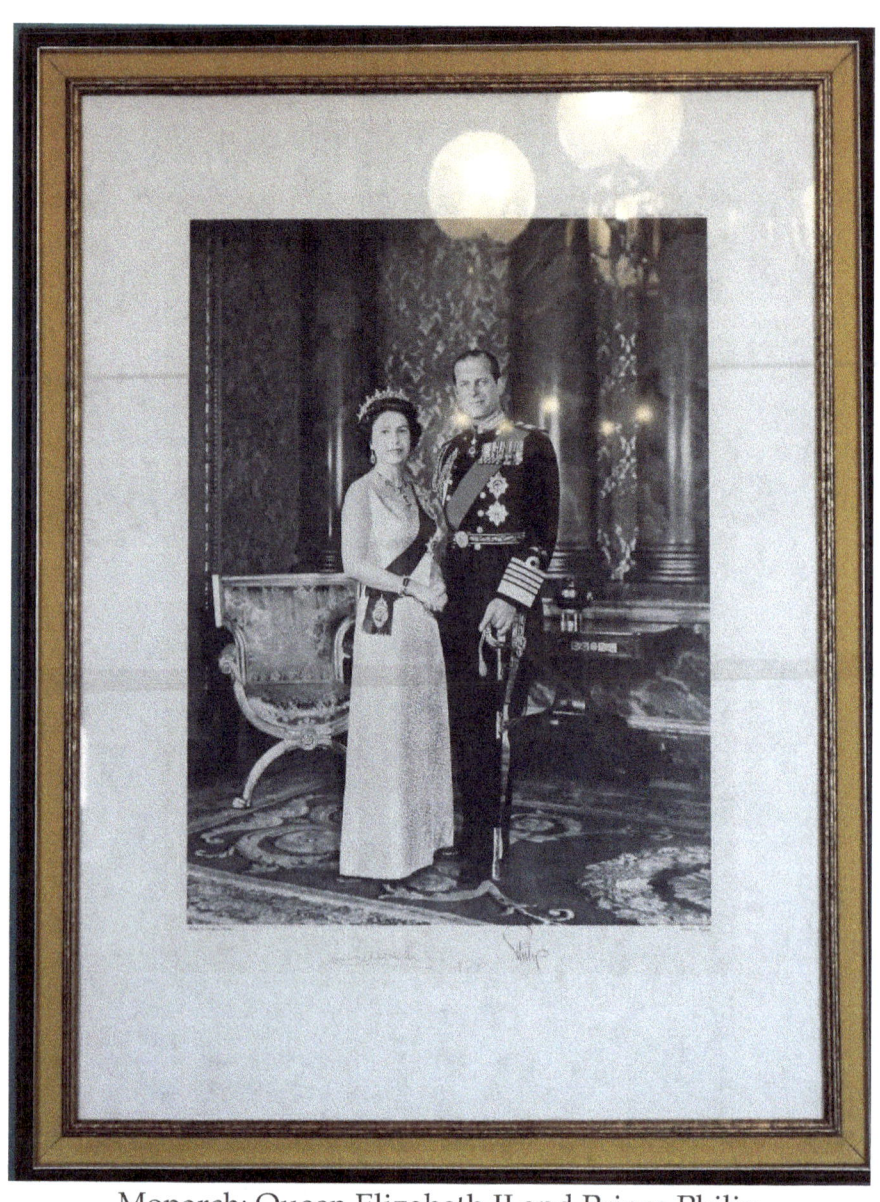

Monarch: Queen Elizabeth II and Prince Philip

Governor Generals of Canada

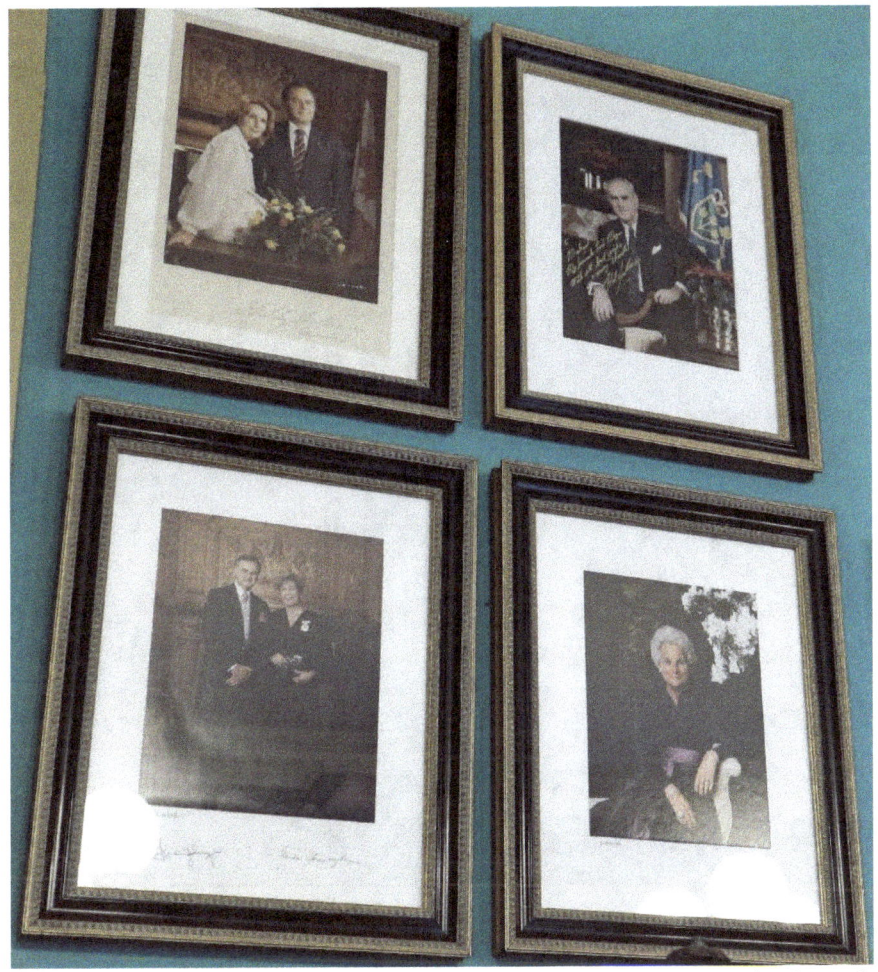

Ed & Lily Schreyer 1979-1984 – Prime Ministers: Joe Clark and
Pierre Trudeau
(2nd picture – unknown)
Ray & Gerda Hnatyshyn 1990-1995 – Prime Ministers: Brian
Mulroney, Kim Campbell and Jean Chretien

Jeanne Sauvé 1984-1990 – Prime Ministers: Pierre Trudeau,
John Turner and Brian Mulroney

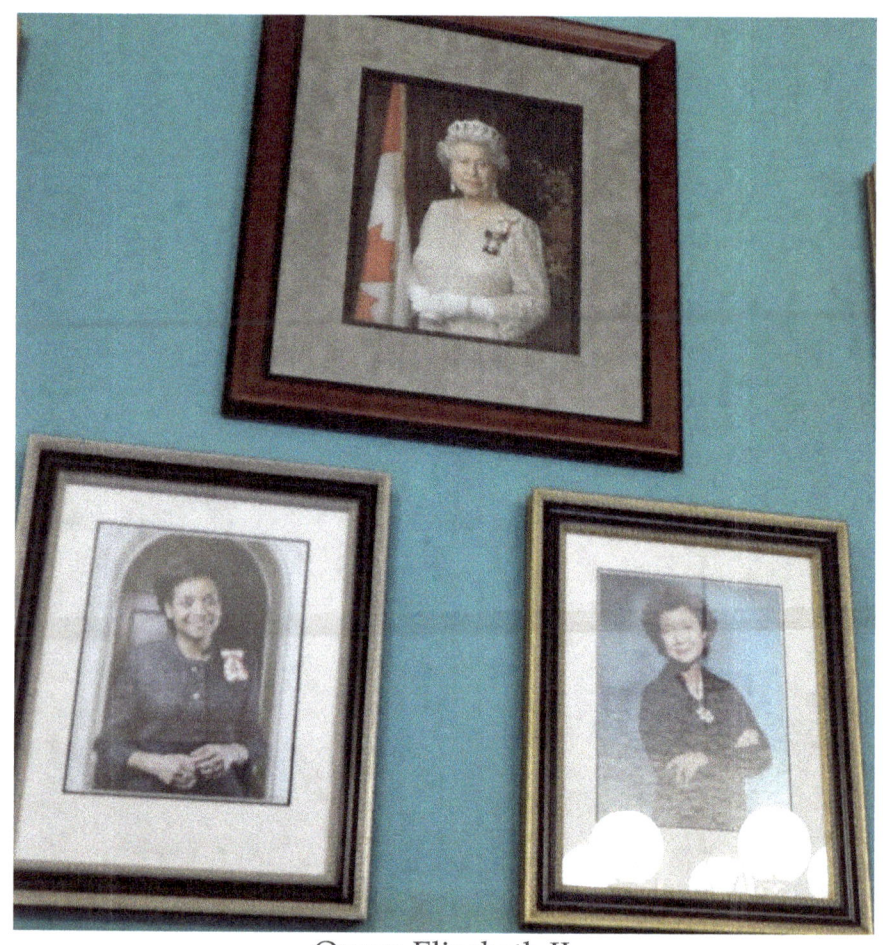

Queen Elizabeth II

Michaelle Jean 2005-2010 – Prime Ministers: Paul Martin and Stephen Harper

Adrienne Clarkson 1999-2005 – Prime Ministers: Jean Chretien and Paul Martin

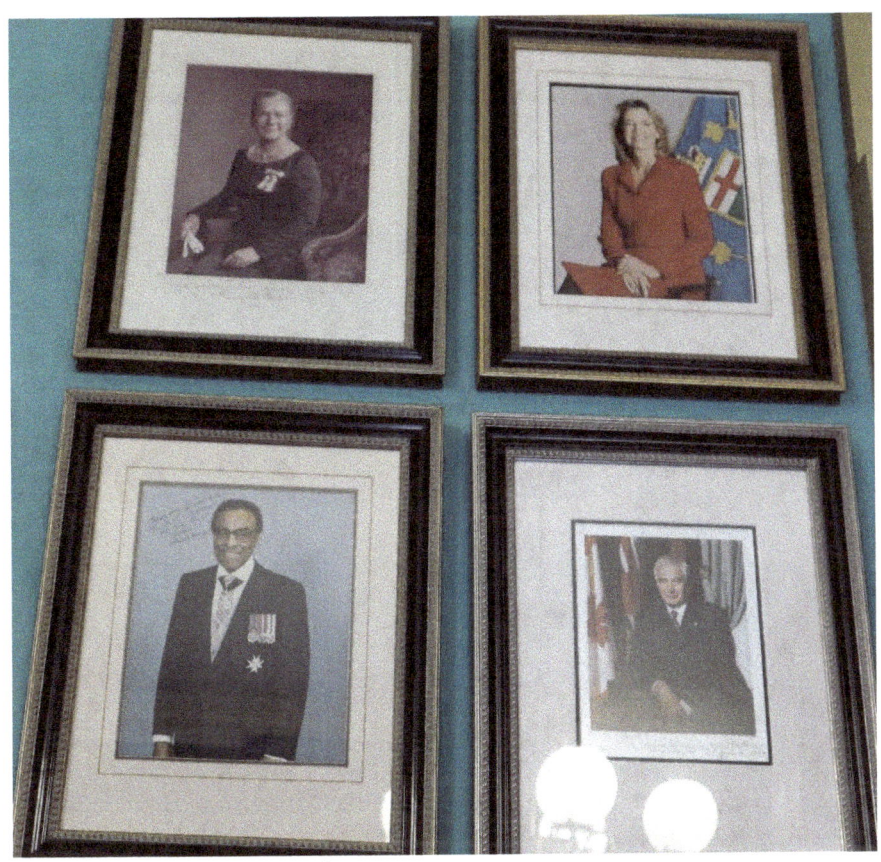

(1st picture – unknown)

Julie Payette 2017-2021 – Prime Minister: Justin Trudeau

Lincoln Alexander 1985-1991 – Lieutenant-Governor of Ontario - Premiers: David Peterson and Bob Rae

David Johnston 2010-2017 – Prime Ministers: Stephen Harper and Justin Trudeau

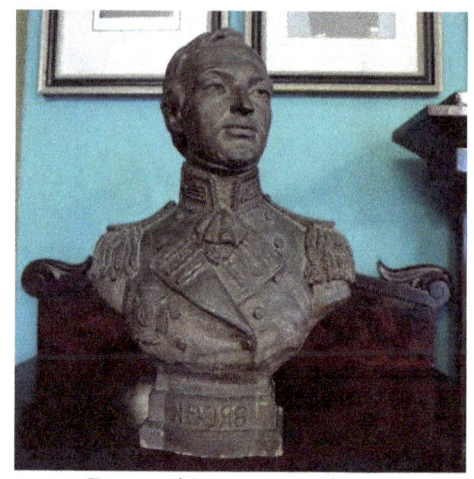
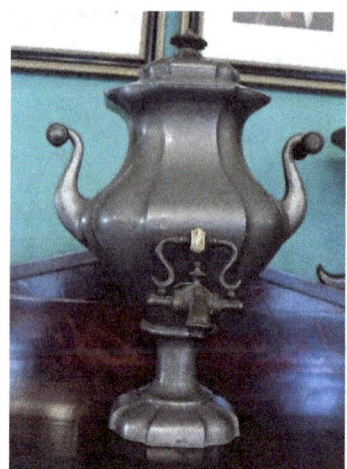

Bust of Isaac Brock

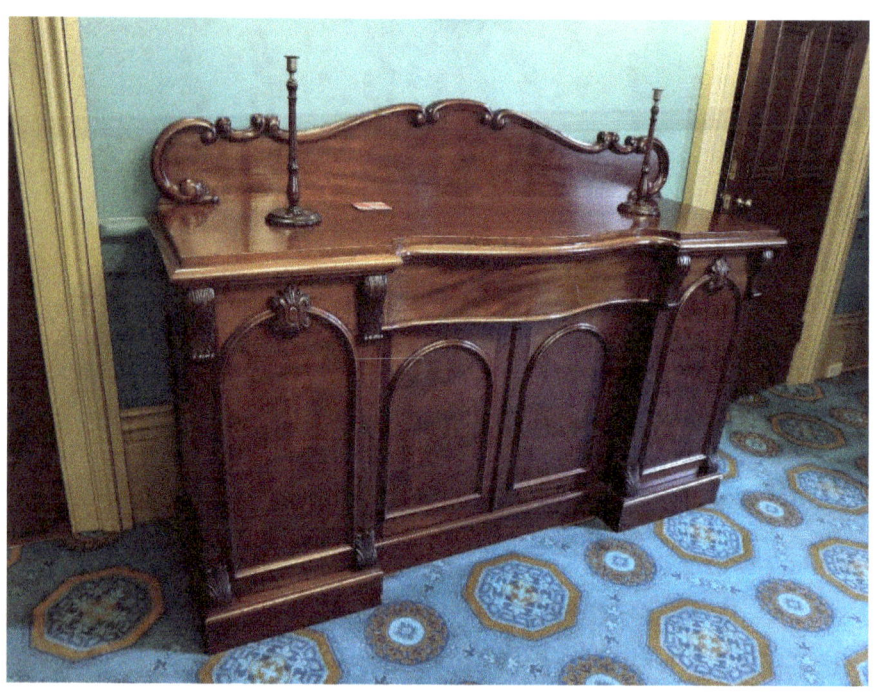

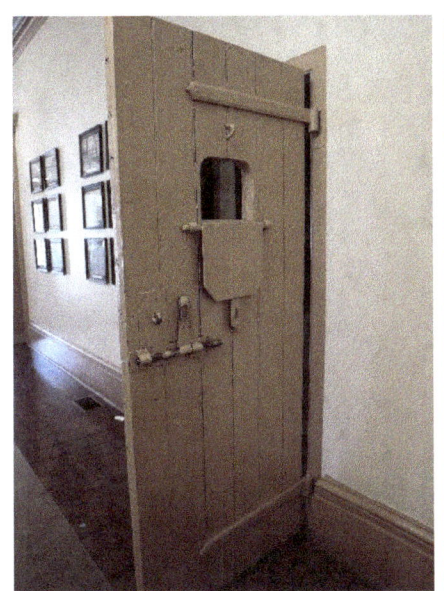
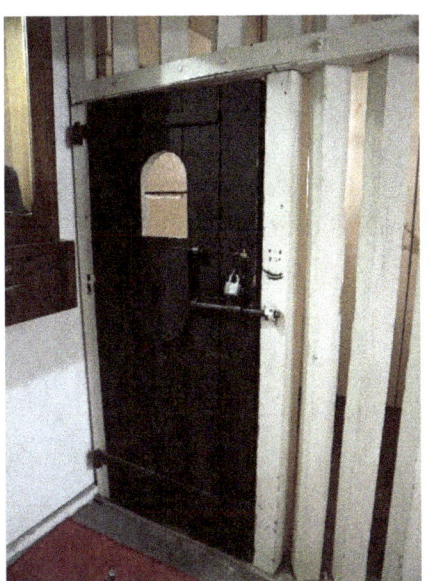

Jail

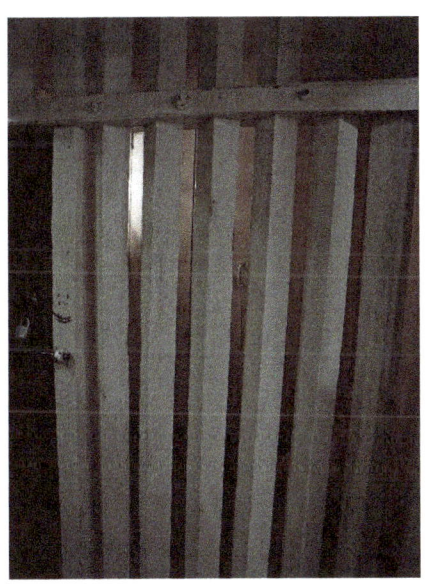

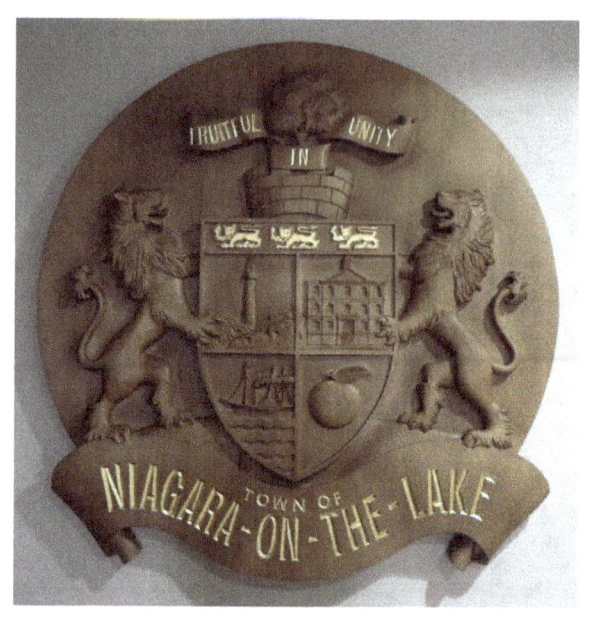

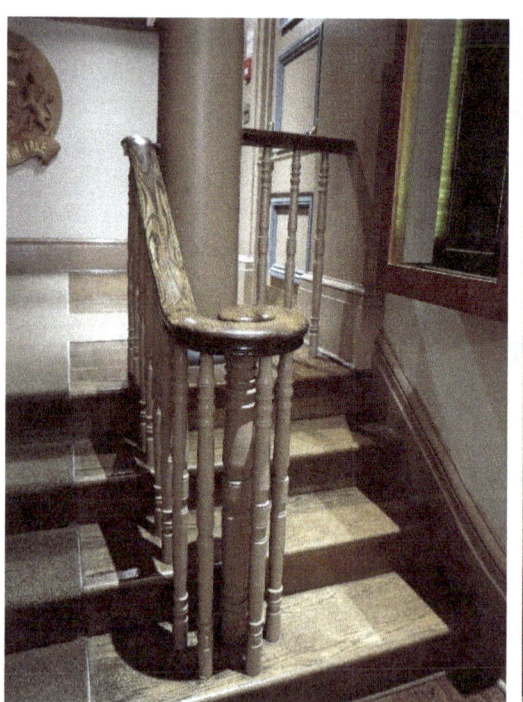

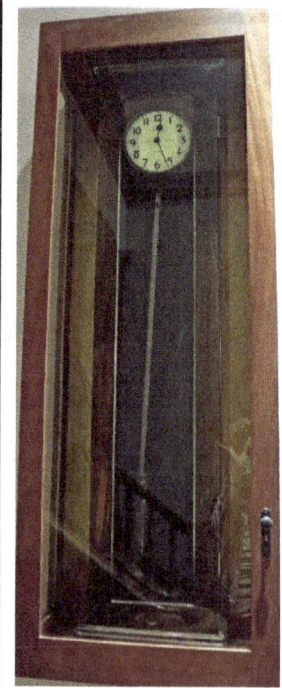

The Exchange Brewery
7 Queen Street

The brewery site was the first telephone exchange building in the Niagara region. Pieces from the original interior were repurposed to create a bar and tables within the current brewery. The building was constructed in 1880.

The Exchange is a new premium brewery and tasting room located in Niagara-on-the-Lake's Old Town heritage district. The town is known as the scene of a burgeoning craft-brewing industry. With brewing and agricultural roots that stretch back to the late 1700s, Niagara-on-the-Lake is the perfect home for The Exchange's approach to brewing, which blends traditional and modern techniques and equipment.

Exceptional craft beers are made using high quality ingredients, including local Niagara fruits. The selection includes a range of American styles along with sour and funky Belgian-style beers and ales.

The brewery houses a brewhouse with five large fermenters and eight serving vessels running to their draft lines. The cellar is equipped with two large German-made Hungarian oak Foeders and fifty French oak wine barrels obtained from the Pearl Morissette Winery in Jordan. The Belgian-style ales spend a range of time maturing in this oak to develop their distinctive and complex flavors.

The tasting room has two eight-tap bars: one on the main level and one in an intimate event space upstairs. Each bar features a selection of flagship brews along with seasonal and specialty limited-release beers.

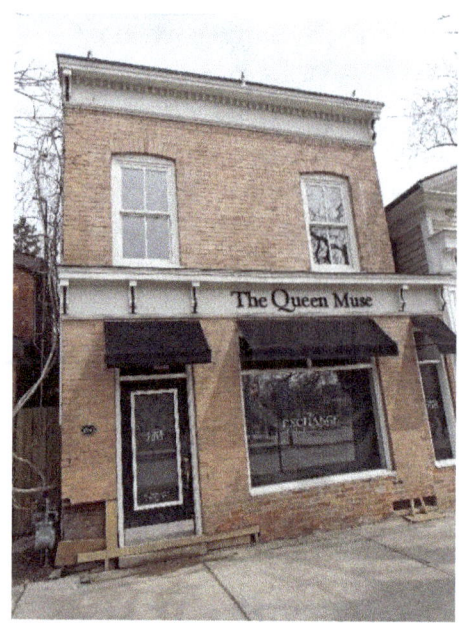

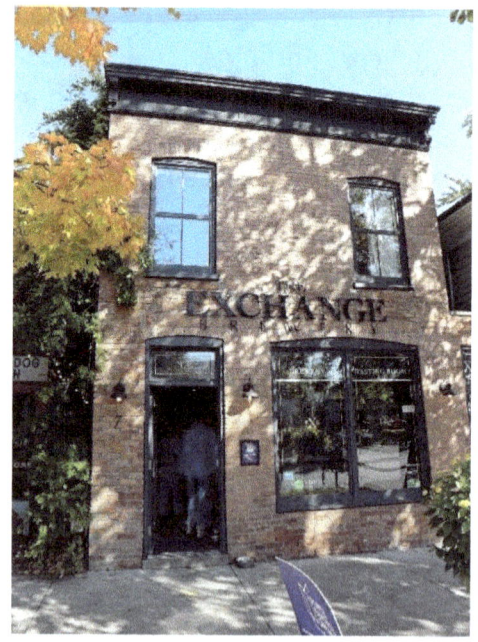

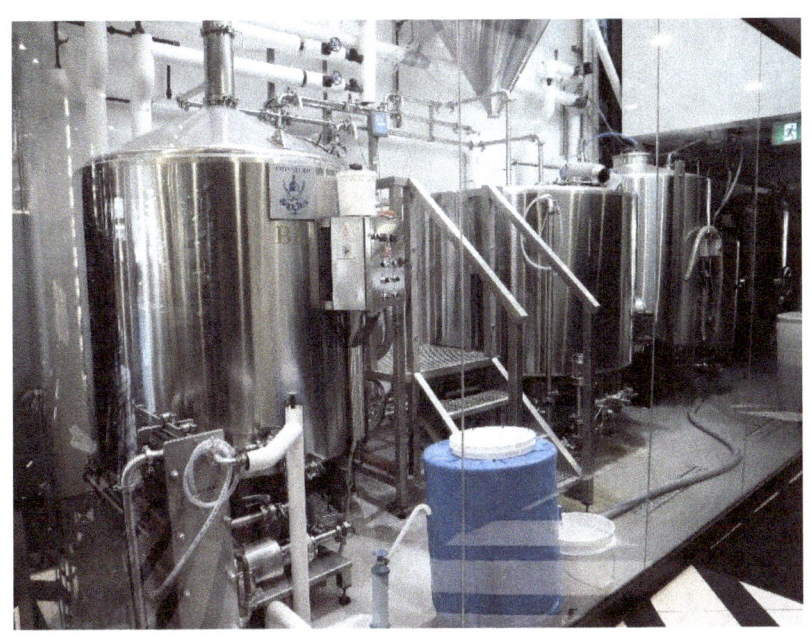

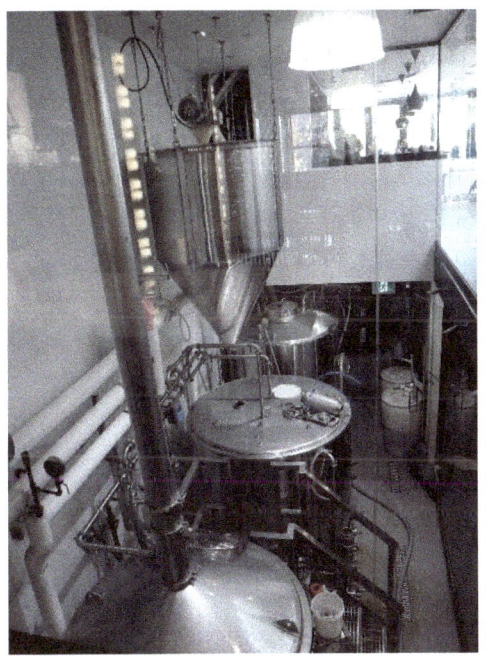

The Niagara Apothecary

The Niagara Apothecary is an authentic museum restoration of an 1869 pharmacy as part of a practice that operated in Niagara-on-the-Lake from 1820 to 1964.

The Niagara Apothecary at the Sign of the Golden Mortar is an excellent example of high style, eclectic mid-Victorian commercial architecture. The building dates to the 1820s. It was extensively renovated in 1866 when taken over by an apothecary. It was at this time the Italianate façade featuring arched glazed double doors and two arched plate glass show windows with accents of a Florentine "twisted rope" treatment were installed, and the interior was fitted up as a drug store.

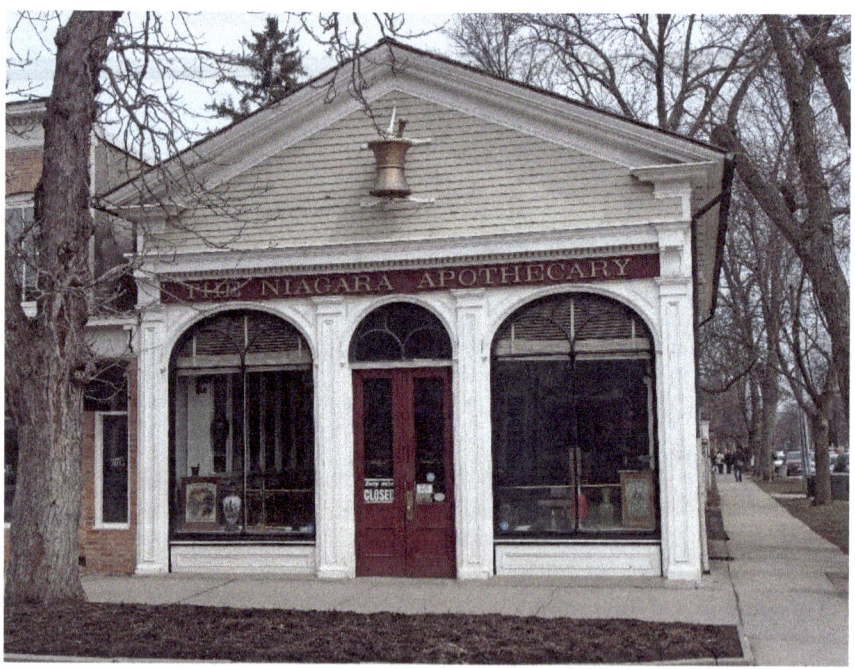

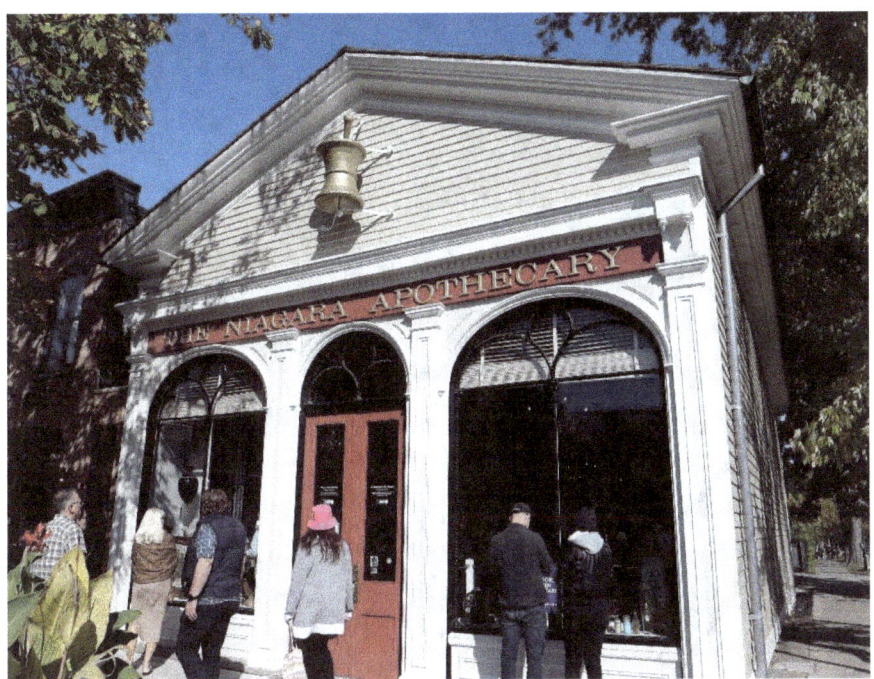

The interior with its lustrous black walnut and butternut fixtures, elaborate plaster rosettes to anchor three crystal chandeliers (gasoliers in their time) projected an impression of nineteenth-century well-being and financial stability. This was especially grand for a small town in a rural setting, but it was intended by its owner to offer a boost to a community experiencing difficult financial and political problems beyond its control.

The original interior fittings of the Apothecary, all in use for nearly a century from 1869 to 1964, have been painstakingly restored. The hub of the Apothecary was the ornately carved dispensary which dominates the rear of the main room. Except for certain proprietary or patent and non-prescription remedies, even pills and other compounded medications were made in the dispensary during the nineteenth and early twentieth century.

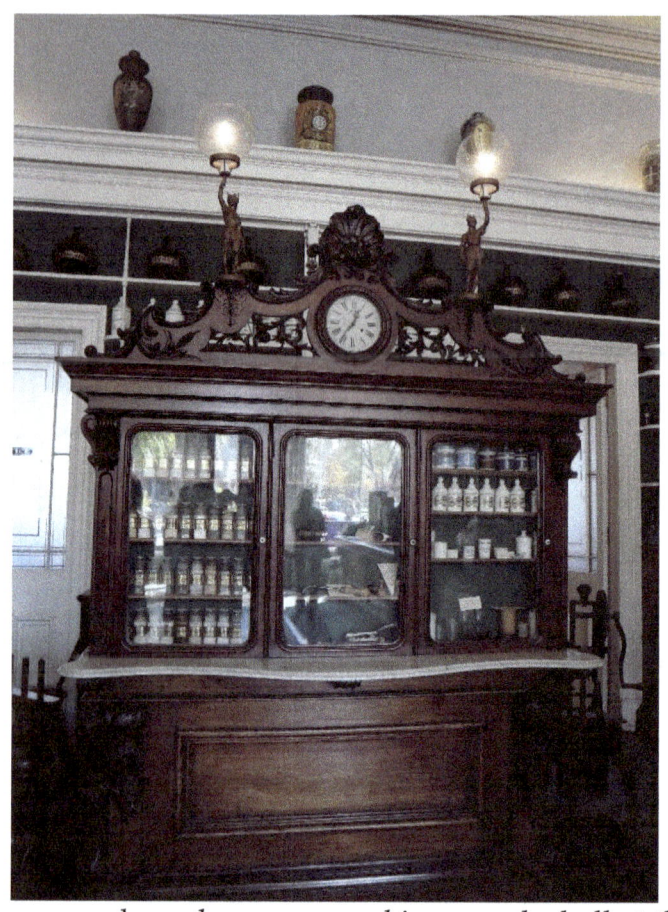

The dispensary has a beaver carved in a conch shell at the top center. Below the conch shell is a clock, dated 1866, made in Albany, New York, which remains in working order, but now battery operated rather than hand wound. On either side of the above are exotic gilded figures that appear to be Amazon women warriors who hold aloft lighted globes. In Paffard's time, the globes were of colored glass, most likely green and red.

All the pharmacist-owners during the history of the practice from 1818 to 1964 contributed to the health needs of the citizens and to the community of what is now Niagara-on-the-Lake. All of them remain a part in various ways of what was restored and re-opened as a museum in 1971. Many of them also played active roles as contributors to the institutions of the town, from the positions of mayor to various roles with the library, historical society, fire department, Simcoe Park, the shade trees that still grace the streets, the introduction of the system of electric lights, and the paved sidewalks.

The Niagara Apothecary opened its doors at its present location in 1869 (during the Canadian Confederation period). It is the only surviving building of that time in the town. The Niagara Apothecary operated for nearly 150 years under a succession of six owners, starting about 1818/1820 (at another location in town), and it closed in 1964 due to the ill health of the last pharmacist owner.

Rodman Starkwather established a pharmacy practice sometime between 1818 and 1820 on Prideaux Street - which runs parallel to Queen Street (the town's main street) - one block north to Lake Ontario.

In the early 1820s, soon after Starkwather moved to Queen Street, he took on a partner named Brown and the practice became "Starkwather and Brown." The professional character of the practice obviously also changed, since it then became the "Niagara Apothecary and Cheap Cash Store." Their advertisements offered whiskey by the barrel, dry goods, crockery, paints and varnish, and a variety of patent remedies.

They discontinued their dry goods and reverted to the more professional "Niagara Apothecary" name and practice. In 1829, Starkwather returned to solo practice. In 1833, Starkwather sold the practice to James Harvey.

During Starkwather's time and that of the other pharmacist owners in the early nineteenth century, before shipments of needed pharmaceutical and other necessary supplies could be readily made from the Atlantic seaboard or upper great lake cities like Chicago, supplies had to come from Britain or other European sources by ship. Given the length of time for, and the uncertainties of Atlantic crossings, pharmacists had to buy large quantities of needed supplies well in advance.

During the years he operated the pharmacy, James Harvey was active in the affairs of Niagara. He was a judge, and in 1845 was elected to Niagara's first Council after its incorporation. He was one of the five members of the Board of Police. In 1848, he became a charter member of the Board of Directors of the Niagara Mechanics Institute that later became the town's public library. In addition, he was a member of the committee to erect the new fire bell and later became secretary of the Niagara Fire Company. James Harvey also owned another pharmacy in St. Catharines nearby, not an unusual situation at the time.

In October 1851, James Harvey died suddenly of tuberculosis, at the early age of 44 years. Henry Paffard, who had served as an apprentice with Harvey, operated the pharmacy briefly for the Harvey family, then purchased and assumed the practice, January 1, 1852.

Despite the short time during which Harvey operated his pharmacy, the most relevant artifacts in the present museum are attributed to him, as well as the surviving archival records, particularly the prescriptions of his era. Early in his practice, Harvey imported from Britain all the containers on the shelves along the wall to the right and some along the back that first catch the eyes of the visitors who enter the Niagara Apothecary Museum. They include the large green demijohns along the upper shelves, the attractive cobalt blue jars on the next shelves below, and the smaller clear glass tinctures and salt mouths on the two rows of shelves below.

Henry Paffard had those shelves, bins, and drawers installed as part of his grand vision when he moved the practice to its present location in 1869. The containers remained when Paffard sold the pharmacy in 1898 to his apprentice, James deW. Randall, and he in turn to Arthur James Coyne in 1914. Coyne, like Harvey, also owned a pharmacy in St. Catharines, to which he returned in 1922, when he in turn sold the practice to the last owner, Erland Field. Those wonderful containers left with Coyne were carefully preserved until they were returned at the time of the restoration of the Niagara Apothecary and its re-opening in 1971.

Prior to moving his practice, Paffard made major changes by extending the building to the street line, lowering its floor to street level, and raising its ceiling. In other words, Paffard expanded the structure in every dimension. Paffard was determined to provide an imposing structure, interior and exterior in mid-Victorian Eclectic style.

The Ontario College of Pharmacy (now Pharmacists) (OCP) achieved official status--with the first Ontario Pharmacy Act of 1871--to serve as a licensing body, professional association, and operate a school of pharmacy.

Prescription and business records from the Niagara Apothecary survive from 1833 to 1964. Those records show that Harvey's practice was a profitable one and remained so when Paffard first acquired the pharmacy. Paffard continued to serve a clientele that included in addition to the townsfolk, members of the military, as well as those in other professions and businesses, area farmers, and others from the surrounding area.

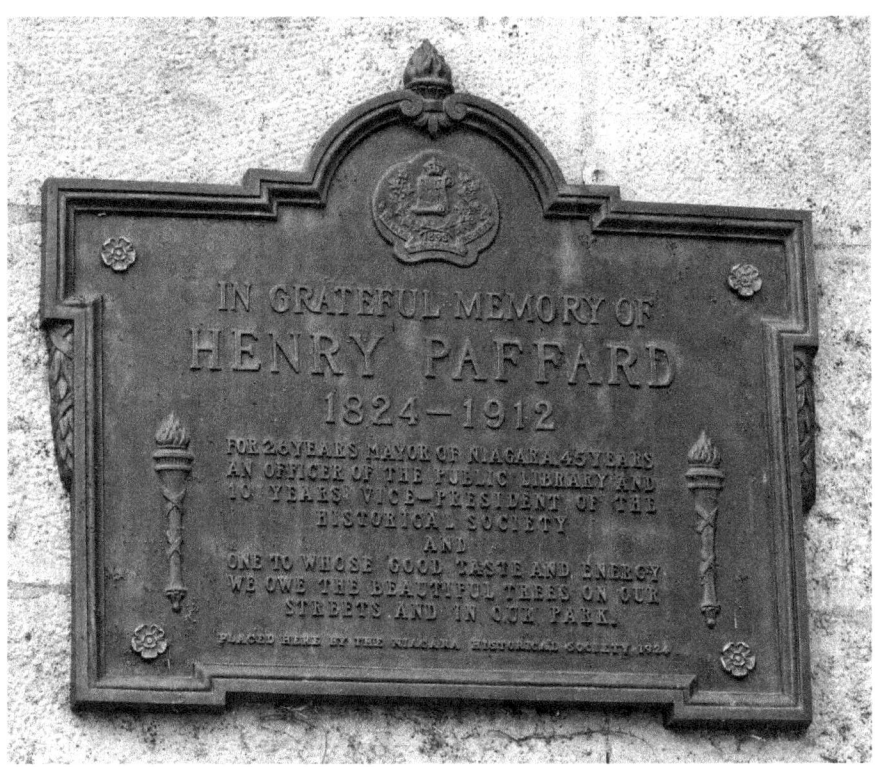

In grateful memory of Henry Paffard (1824-1912)
For 25 years as Mayor of Niagara, 45 years as an officer of the
public library, and 10 years as vice-president of the Historical
Society, and one to whose good taste and energy we owe the
beautiful trees on our streets and in our park

In 1857, Queen Victoria selected Bytown (on the Ottawa River) to be the capital of the Province of Canada. In previous years the location of the capital was a matter of dispute. It had moved among Toronto, Kingston, Montreal, and Quebec City at great expense and confusion. One year later, in 1858, Canada adopted the dollars and cents decimal system. This was a striking example of the growing influence of the United States over Great Britain.

The most important moment in Canadian history to that point was July 1, 1867, when Canada East (Québec), Canada West (Ontario), New Brunswick and Nova Scotia became the first British territories in North America to come together as the Dominion of Canada and by a peaceful democratic process. Ottawa remained the capital and John Alexander Macdonald became Canada's first prime minister.

In 1873, the Royal Northwest Mounted Police, predecessor to the Royal Canadian Mounted Police, were established to maintain order in western Canada.

Lucy Maude Montgomery, one of Canada's most famous writers--the author of Anne of Green Gables and many other works--was born in 1874 in Clifton, Prince Edward Island. In February 1876, Alexander Graham Bell made the world's first telephone call in Brantford Ontario.

During the 1850s and through the remainder of the nineteenth century, a frenzy of railroad construction and speculation gripped Canada along with the rest of the world. The arrival of the railroad profoundly changed life everywhere. No longer were people so isolated. Methods of doing business changed and accelerated as firms were able to send travelling salesmen from town to town, even in far-flung areas to make calls.

An important year for the young Dominion was 1885, when Donald Smith, later Lord Strathcona, ceremoniously drove the last spike November 7th to complete the Canadian Pacific Railway's transcontinental track at Craigellachie, British Columbia.

Throughout the time of Henry Paffard's nearly half a century as pharmacist owner, 1852-1898, Queen Victoria was the only British monarch. During her reign of 64 years, from 1837 to 1901, her domain expanded throughout the world - The sun never set on the British Empire.

The Crimean War (1853-1856), the U.S. Civil War (1861-1865), and the Spanish American War (1898) were fought during this time. Science and technology witnessed Charles Darwin's publication of *The Origin of Species* (1859) and *The Descent of Man* (1865), Gregor Mendel's primal work on genetics (1865), laying of the Atlantic Cable (1860s), and eventual world-wide benefits of Graham Bell's discovery in Canada of the telephone (1876), Thomas Edison's electric light bulb (1879), and Eastman's photographic film (1889).

Medical or Pharmaceutical Highlights
1850s
Chloroform in childbirth for Victoria in 1853; first blood pressure measures by Marey in 1858; Salicylic acid synthesized by Kolbe in 1859; and Cocaine isolated by Niemann in 1859

1860s
Carbolic acid as disinfectant; Pasteur's work with bacteria; Lister with antisepsis in surgery; and the use of clinical thermometer by Wunderlich in 1868

1870s
Smallpox vaccination compulsory in Britain; Digitoxin extract for cardiac problems; and Nitroglycerin used for angina

1880s
Cocaine used as local anesthetic; Ampoules for hypodermic injection; and the term "antibiosis" was coined

1890s
Thyroid extract; Diphtheria antitoxin used by Behring in Germany; Aspirin for rheumatism by Bayer in 1893; and X-rays and radium discovered

Randall's period at 5 Queen Street occurred during the Boer War (1899-1902), part of the Chinese-Japanese wars, World War I (1914-1918), which was followed by the founding of the League of Nations, and the British Commonwealth of Nations. It also saw the beginning of the application of the telegraph and the sinking of the "unsinkable" Titanic in 1912.

Queen Victoria ruled since 1837, and was succeeded from 1901 to 1910 by Edward VII, and then by George V from 1910 onward. Randall's practice had begun with Wilfred Laurier as Prime Minister of Canada (1896-1911), followed by Robert L. Borden (1911-1920).

Randall's successor, A. J. Coyne, was a short one, during the period of World War I, plus a few years post war. Coyne had an earlier and second pharmacy at 116 Lake Street in nearby St. Catharines. His practice was very busy in the summer, but very slow in the winter.

The British introduced the use of tetanus antitoxin for wounded soldiers in 1915 during World War I; modern plastic surgery began to develop in Britain; vitamins D & E were discovered along with recognition that D promoted bone growth and combated rickets; the first birth control clinic was established in Britain; in Canada, Banting and Best discovered insulin to treat diabetes; the influenza pandemic of 1918-1919 killed fifteen million people.

George V was the British monarch; Robert L. Borden was the Canadian prime minister, succeeded by Arthur Meighen, then Mackenzie King (1921 to 1948). World War I with the end of Kaiser William's rule in 1918 occupied the first half of Coyne's practice in Niagara-on-the-Lake. The League of Nations and British Commonwealth of Nations followed, along with the International Court in the Hague and the International Labour Organization.

Erland ("Earl") Field assumed the practice from Coyne in 1922 and maintained it until 1964 (42 years), when declining health persuaded him to close the pharmacy after a continuous practice in the town of just under 150 years.

Field's time as pharmacist-owner of the practice saw huge changes in the practice of pharmacy, as well as advances in pharmaceutical and medical spheres and social and political events: from the first discovery of insulin; discovery of vitamins C, D, and E, with the role of D to promote proper bone growth and combat rickets; the first birth control clinics, heart and kidney transplants, oral insulin, and tranquilizers. Alexander Fleming discovered penicillin, the first antibiotic. The first female hormones were isolated and a usable pregnancy test emerged. The iron lung was developed. BCG vaccine was used against tuberculosis.

The 1930s saw the discovery of the first sulfa drugs, radioactive drugs, cortisone, vitamin K, the male hormone, the first electron microscope, artificial heart, barbiturate anesthesia, the first synthesis of estrogen, and the antimalarial drug, atebrin, as well as the definition of "antihistamine."

The 1940s saw the active use of penicillin after stable production methods were developed and it had widespread use to treat wound infections during World War II (1939-1945). Also new were cortisone, streptomycin, and antihistamines (such as Benadryl). The period also saw the first kidney dialysis machine, the first fluoridated water, and the first successful heart operation in a newborn.

The 1950s brought the first modern diuretics, the first heart pacemaker implanted, anticoagulants, the first successful kidney transplants, oral insulin, tranquilizers, contraceptive tablets ("the Pill"), polio (Salk) vaccine. The same period also suffered the horrors of birth defects caused by thalidomides, as well as recognition of the close association between smoking and cancer.

The 1960s witnessed chemotherapy used to attack plasma lipids and smallpox.

Miscellaneous Science and Technology
Developments 1922-1964

1922 – Tutankhamen's tomb discovered
1925 – frozen food process developed by Birds Eye
1925-26 – invention of television by Baird
1928 – electric razor developed by Schick
1929 – decompression chamber invented by Davis
1935 – radar invented by Watson-Watt
1938 – xerography invented by Carbon
1955 - optical fibers invented by Kapany

1957 – Sputnik I first orbiting satellite launched
1958 – microchip invented by Kiley
1959 – first pictures of far side of the moon
1960 – laser invented by Maiman
1961 – Yuri Gagarin is first man in space

Canadian and World Social and Political Events
1920s – Hague International Court; International Labour Organization; Great Depression begins 1929; Canadian prime ministers: Robert Borden, Arthur Meighen, Mackenzie King

1930s - CBC established; Edward VIII succeeds George V, but abdicated and was replaced by George VI; Canadian prime ministers Mackenzie King, followed by Richard Bennett; Abyssinian War (1935-1936); Spanish Civil War (1936-1939); World War II (1939-1945)

1940s – World Health Organization (WHO). United Nations (UN) and NATO established; Newfoundland joined Canadian Confederation; Mackenzie King retired and was succeeded by Louis St. Laurent; Truman succeeded Roosevelt who dies in 4th term; USA drops atomic bombs on Japan

1950s – Elizabeth II succeeds George VI in 1952; John Diefenbaker succeeds St. Laurent; St. Lawrence Seaway opens; Korean War (1950-1953); Vietnam War (1957-1975); hydrogen bomb tested (1952)

1960s – Lester B. Pearson succeeded John Diefenbaker in 1963 as prime minister of Canada

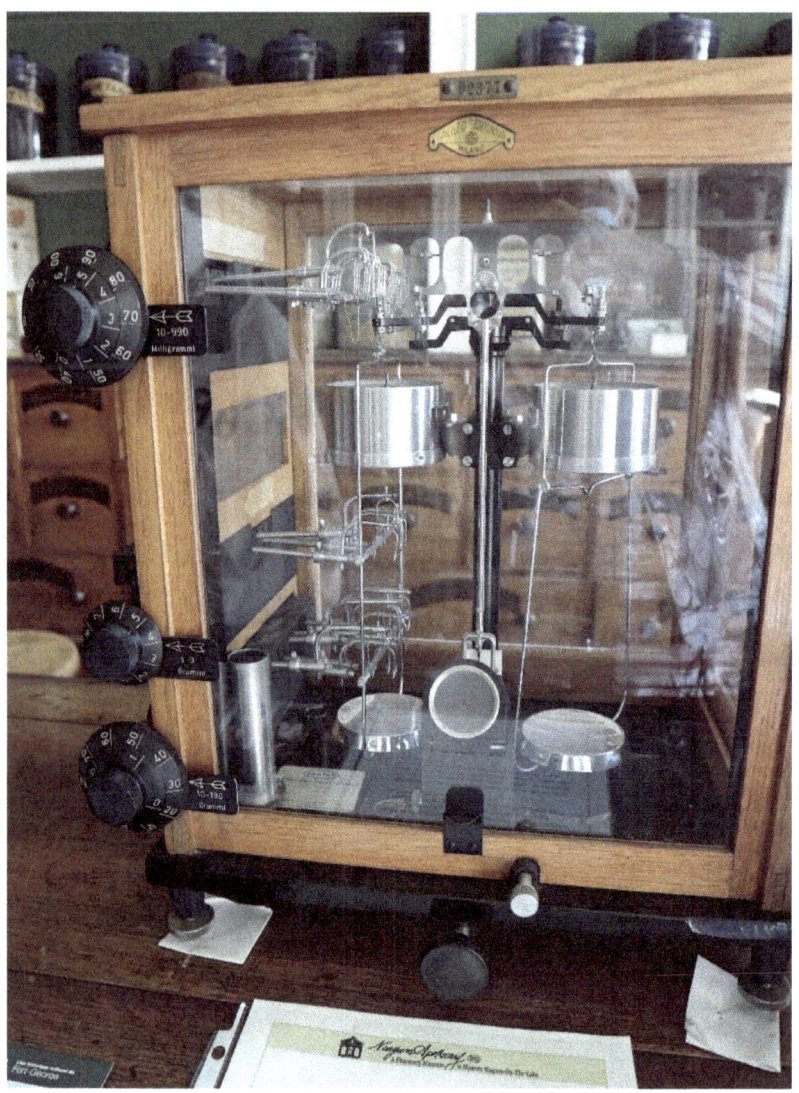

The Analytic Balance was in common use through the late 1950s. It featured greater sensitivity than Class A or B prescription balances. They were sensitive to 1/10 of a milligram (1/100th of a grain), with a 200 gram capacity.

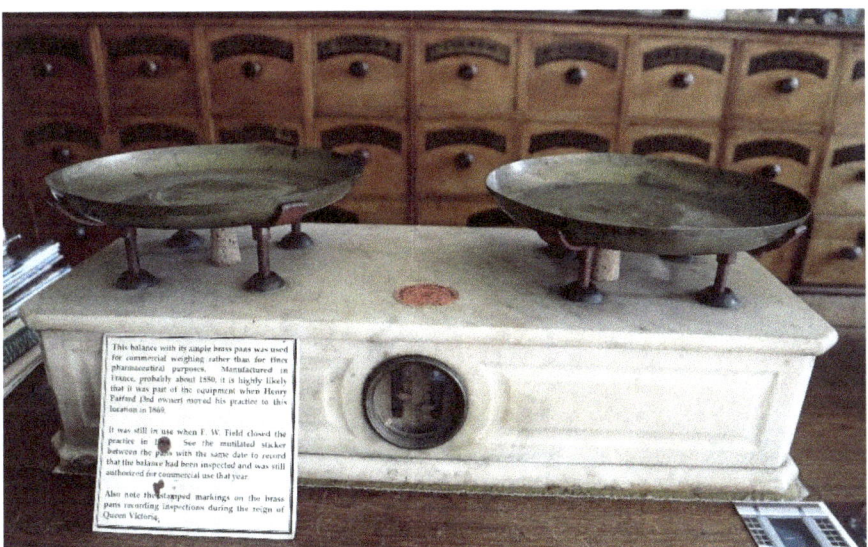

The scales remained in active use until Erland Field closed the practice in 1964, as indicated by the official red government seal between the two brass weights. Such scales, with ample brass pans, were normally used to weigh larger quantities than would have been needed for more precise weighing for prescriptions.

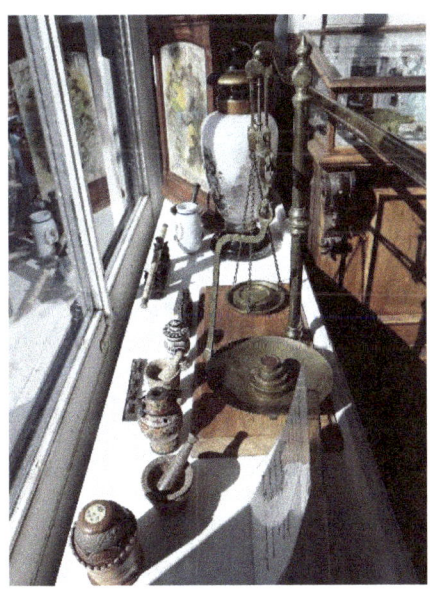

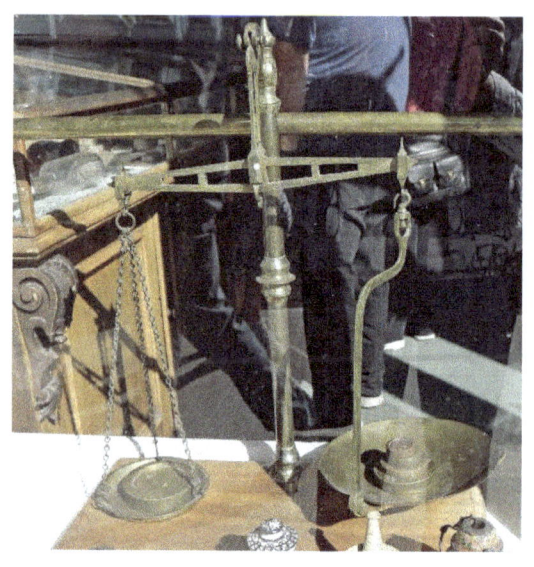

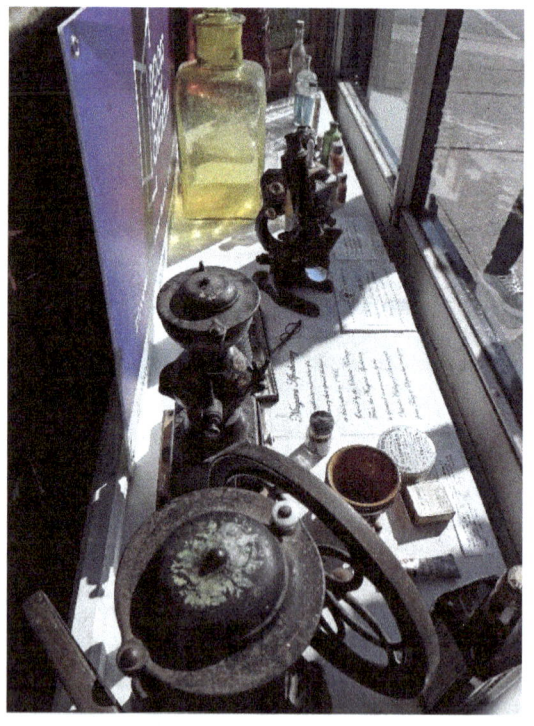

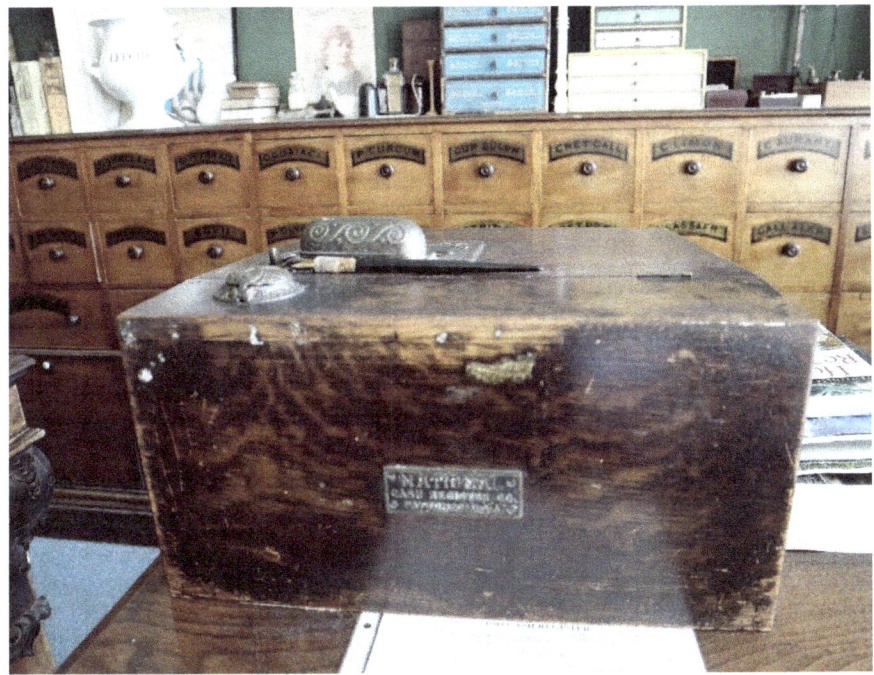

John de Witt Randall, the fourth pharmacist-owner (1898-1914), installed a new-fangled oak cash register manufactured by National Cash Register of Dayton Ohio in 1903. A sale was recorded by writing the amount on the exposed paper with a steel pen using the ink from its inkwell. When the cash drawer opened, a bell rang and the recording paper ratcheted up one notch. The money was taken, and change counted out. Customers did not get a receipt, but likely they did get a "Thank You!" At the end of the day, sales were added manually. The calculated total and the amount of cash in the drawer were expected to balance, just like today.

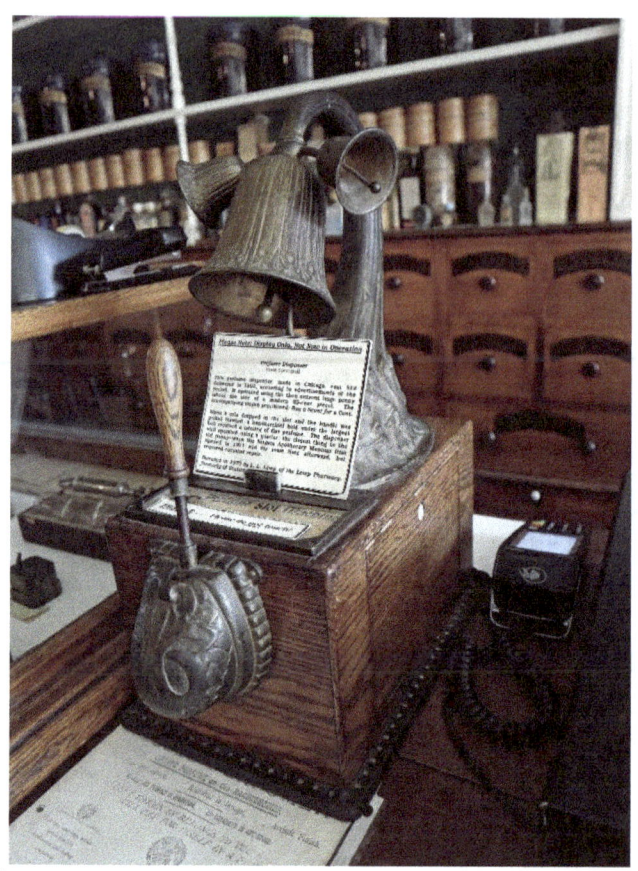

The Perfume Dispenser dates from 1892. The customer inserted a large-as-a-quarter in those days one-cent coin into the slot, sharply pulled the lever and a spray of "the finest Paris" perfume came through a large flower as a bell tinkled into the recipient's hand or on to her handkerchief. The claim, "a scent for a cent," was visibly displayed on its front.

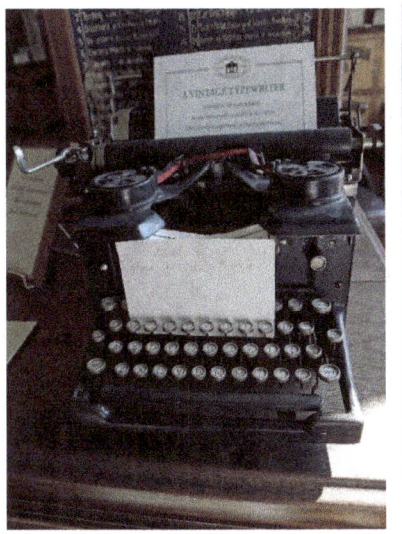
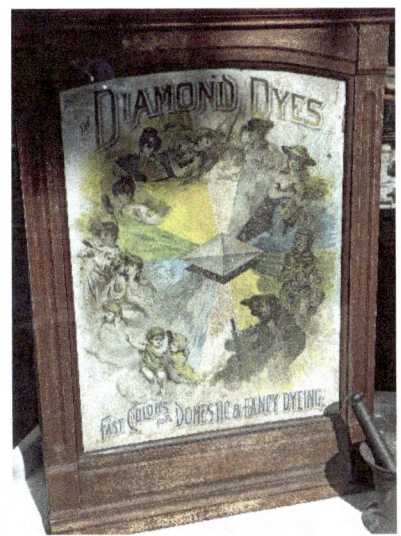

A vintage typewriter

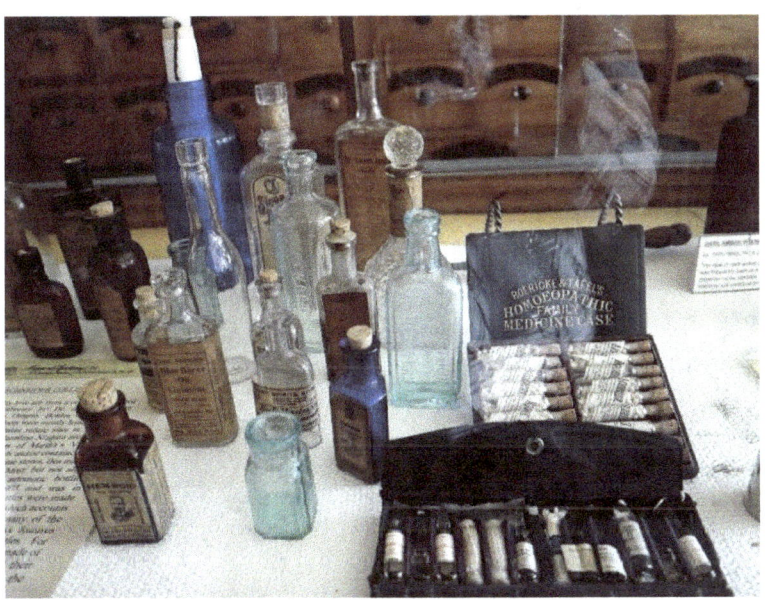

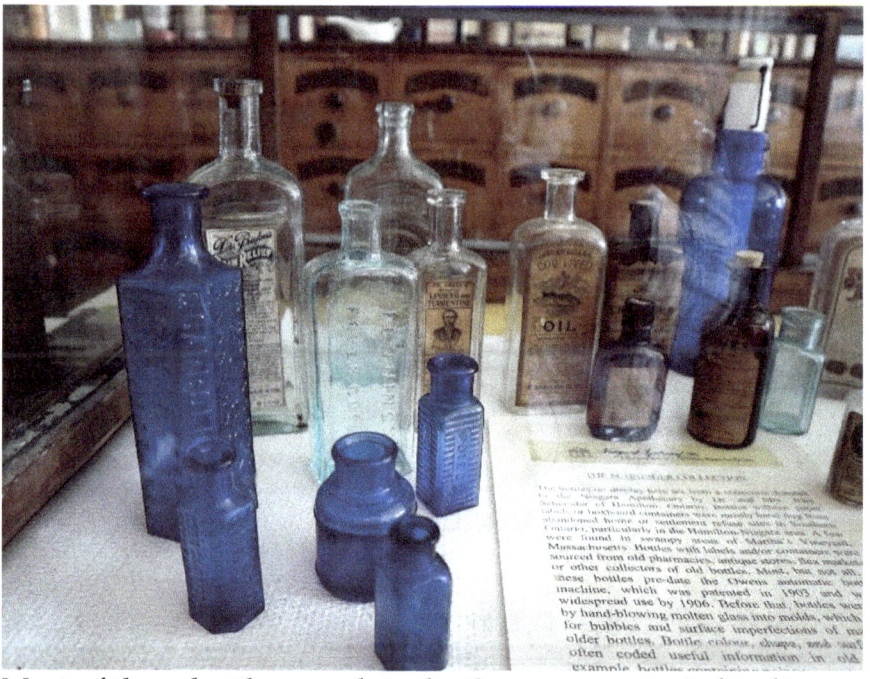

Most of these bottles pre-date the Owens automatic bottling machine which was patented in 1903 and in widespread use by 1906. Before that bottles were made by hand-blowing glass into molds, which accounts for bubbles and surface imperfections of many of the older bottles. Bottle color, shape, and surface features often coded useful information in old bottles. For example, bottles containing poison were typically made of blue glass for easy identification in daylight, and their surface had many raised x's which could be felt in the dark.

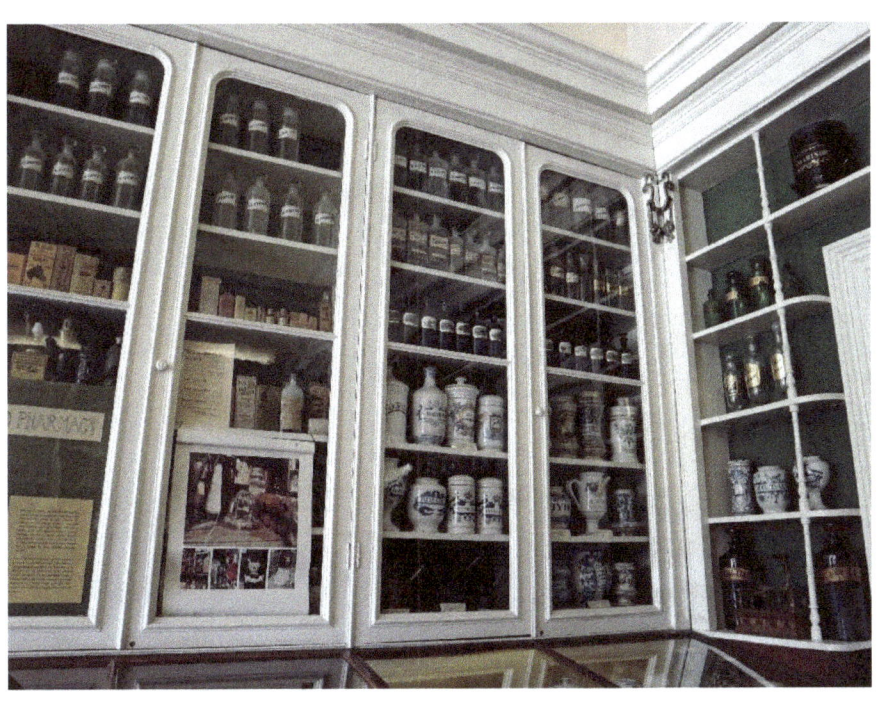

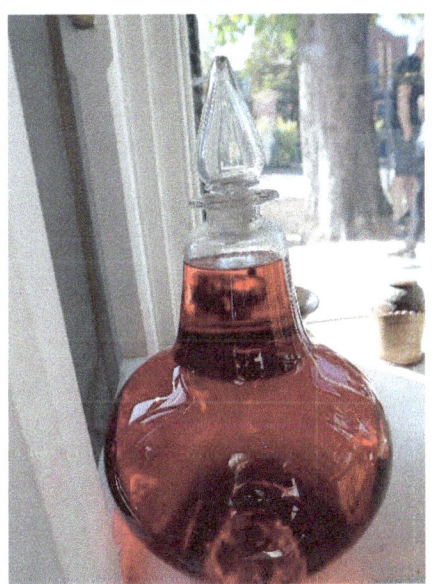

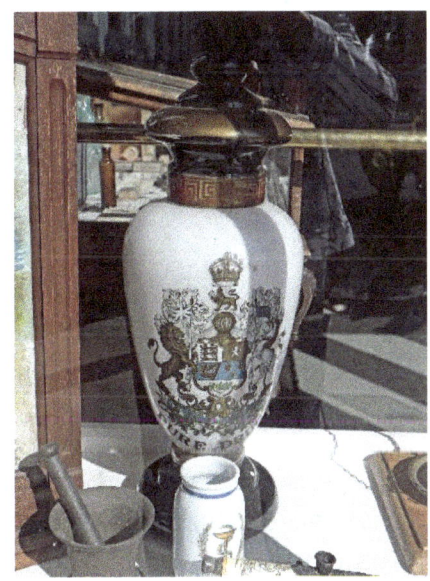

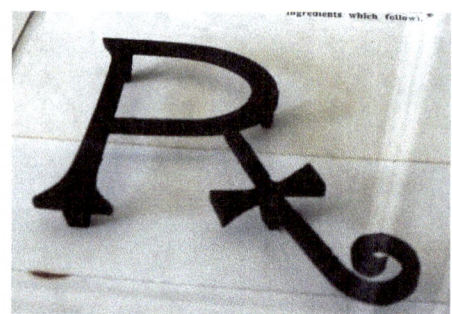

The prescription sign – the symbol more likely derives from "Re" – short for *Recipe* – Latin for "Take" (of the ingredients which follow)

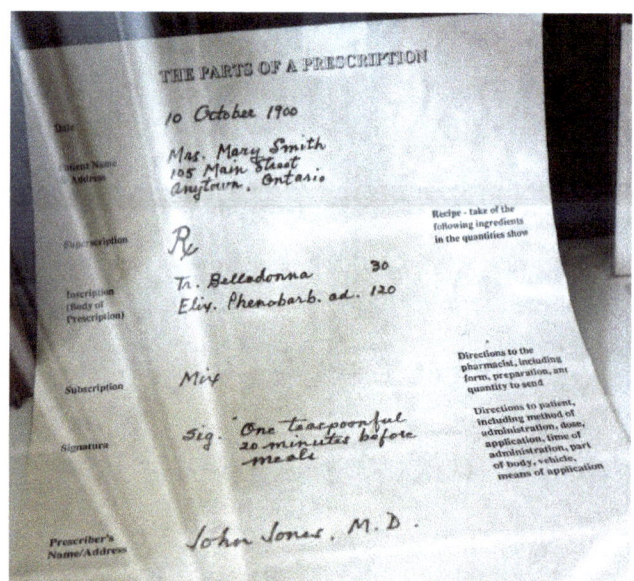

Recipe – take of the following ingredients in the quantities shown

Subscription – directions to the pharmacist including form, preparation, and quantity to send

Signatura – direction to patient, including method of administration, dose, application, time of administration, part of body, vehicle, means of application

Niagara-on-the-Lake Museum
43 Castlereagh Street

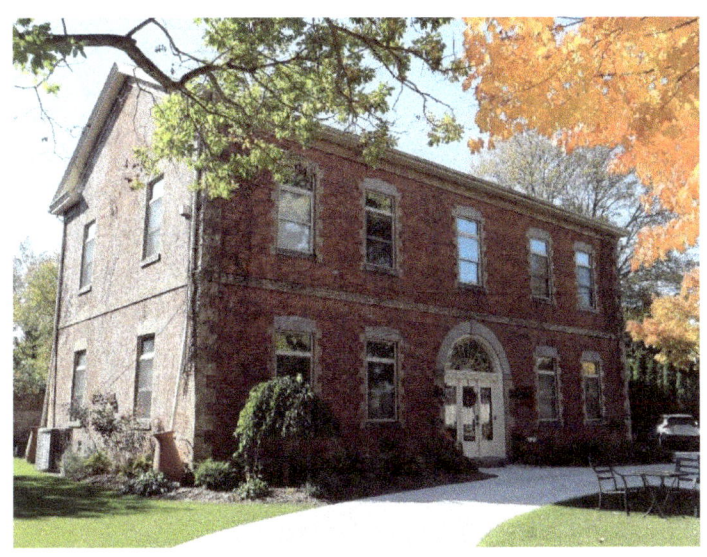

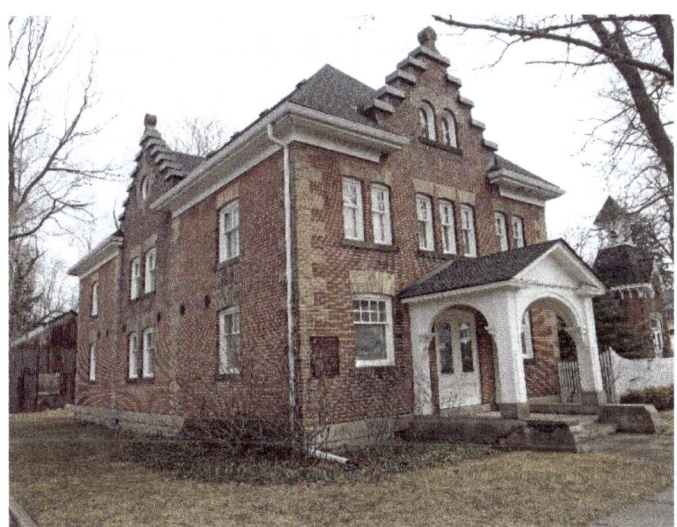

43 Castlereagh Street

The Niagara Historical Society, founded in 1895, opened the Niagara-on-the-Lake Museum in 1907. The museum collects, preserves, researches, educates and promotes the history of Niagara-on-the-Lake and its communities – inspiring an appreciation of local history through engaging programs and exhibitions.. It was a high school building; Memorial Hall was built in 1906; and Link Building was built in 1971.

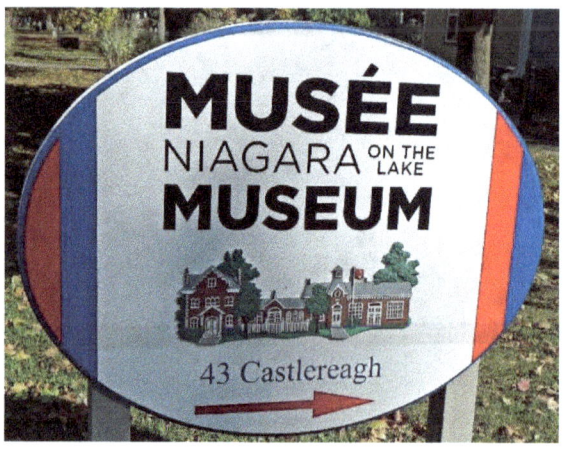

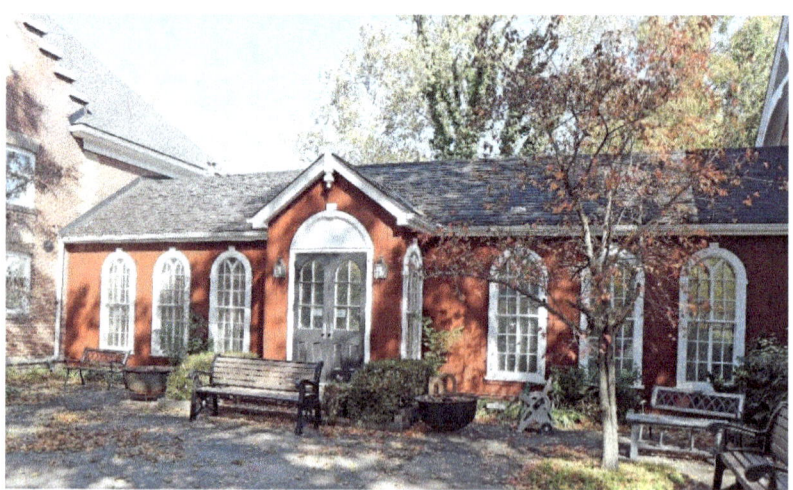

Link Building

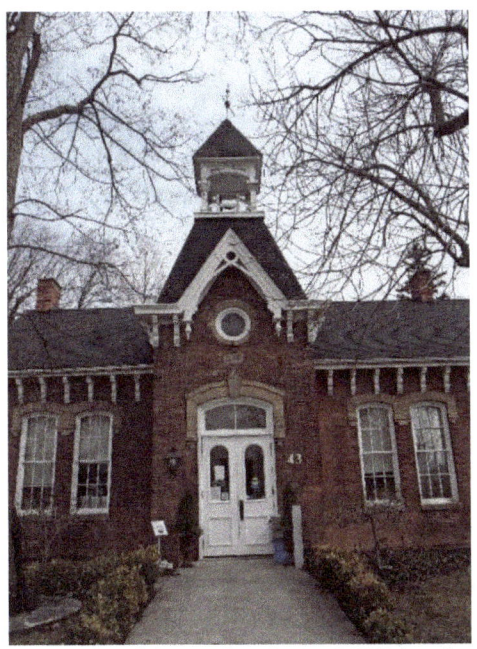

It was a high school building, built in 1875 in the Italianate architectural style

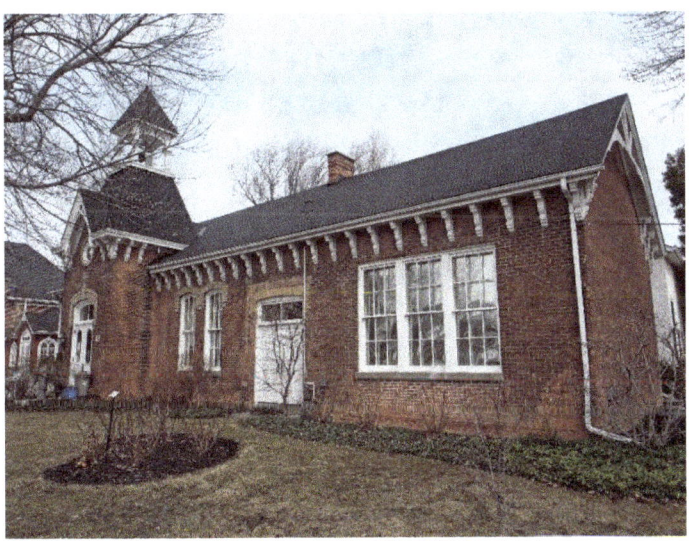

Memorial Hall (the first building in Ontario to be constructed solely as a historical museum) was built in 1906

For thirty years Miss Janet Carnochan (1839-1926) taught elementary and secondary school at Niagara-on-the-Lake. The erection of Memorial Hall was due largely to her efforts when she successfully campaigned for its construction. (She donated the land for the building.) For thirty years, she was the curator of the Niagara Historical Society. She made her greatest contribution to the community as a historian. working tirelessly to safeguard and promote the rich heritage of Niagara. She wrote and edited many historical works including 'The History of Niagara.' In 1949, when the town's former high school was incorporated into this complex, it was renamed Janet Carnochan Hall as a tributed to her efforts and dedication.

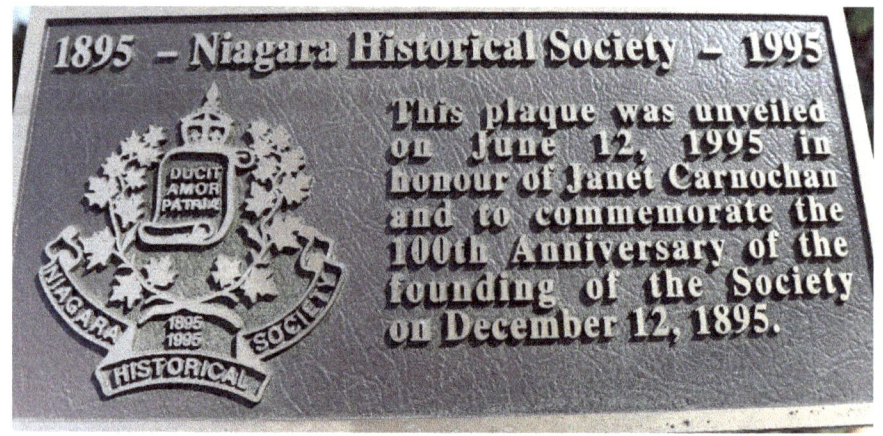

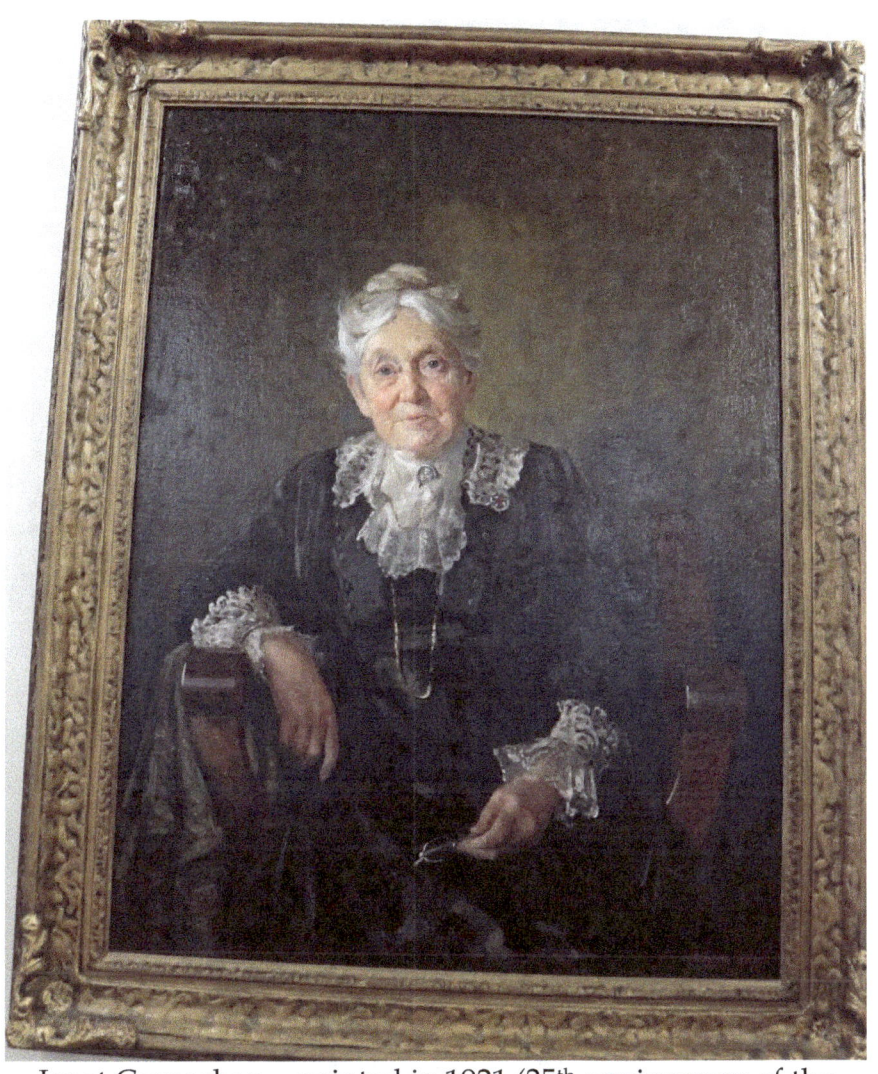

Janet Carnochan – painted in 1921 (25th anniversary of the
Niagara Historical Society) by Sir E. Wyly Grier of Toronto

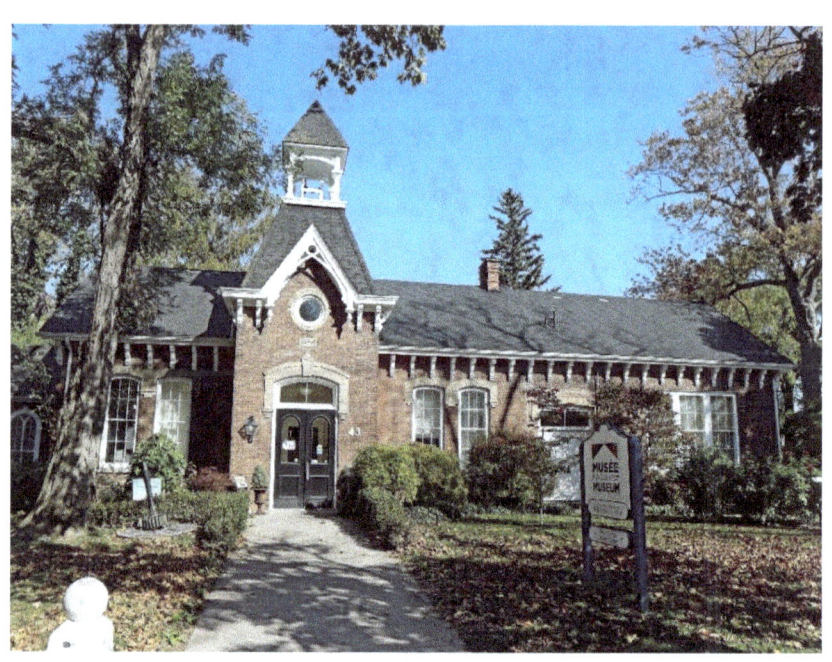

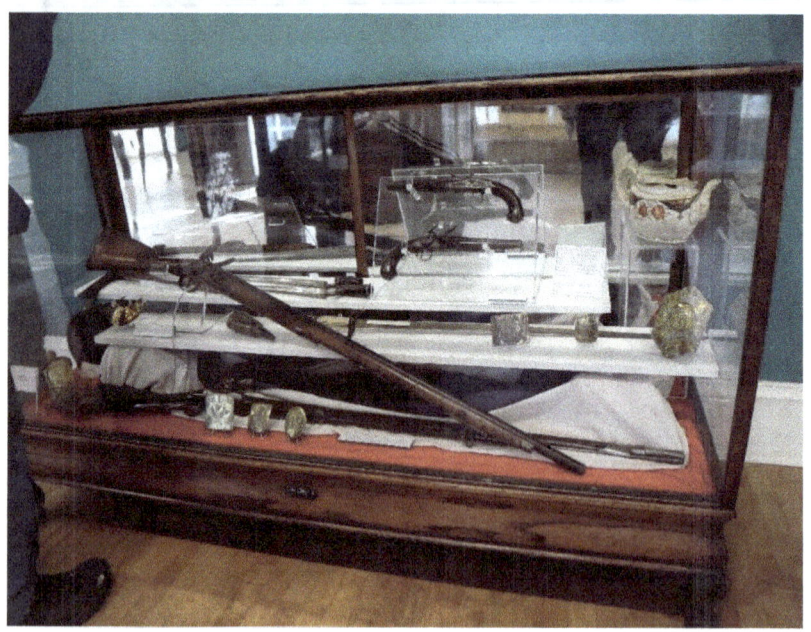

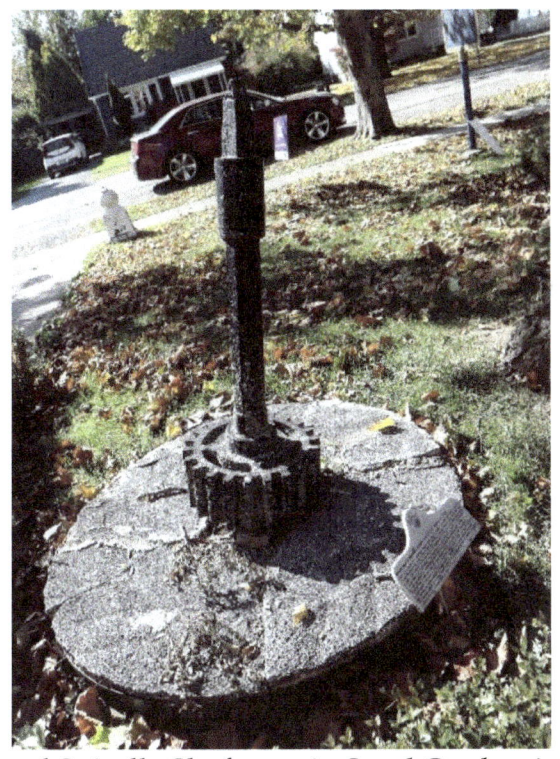

Stone Nut and Spindle Shaft cast in Sorel Quebec in 1782. The cast iron gear is called a 'stone nut.' Its function in the grist mill was to receive power by meshing its iron teeth with the hardwood cogs of a horizontal 'great spur wheel.' This diverted the torque 90 degrees into the iron spindle shaft and up through the eye of the stationary bed stone to the runner stone above, causing the upper stone to rotate whenever the water wheel turned. The iron stone nut, the iron spindle, and runner stone components were supported from below by a bearing under the stone nut that sat in a cup on a heavy but movable beam called a 'bridge tree.' Adjusting the bridge tree either up or down set a thin gap between the millstones in order to produce finer or coarser flour or meal.

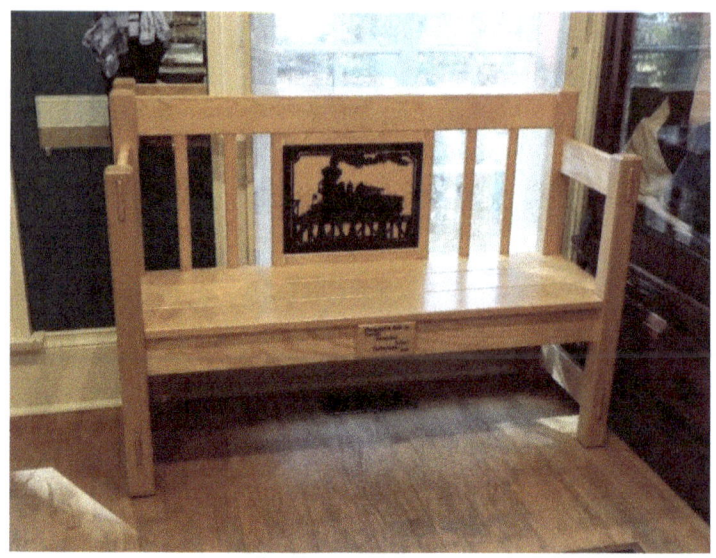

Designed and built by Thorold Secondary School Technologies in 2006

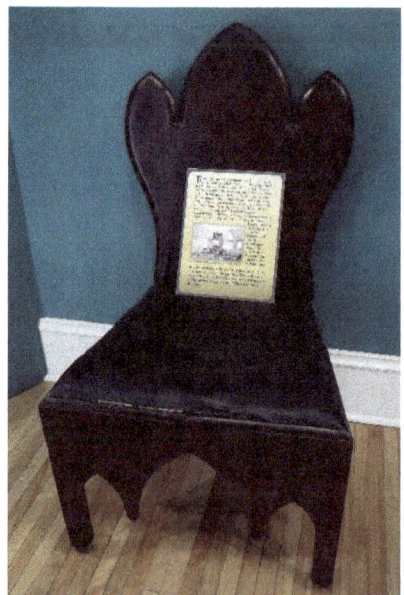

This chair was used in the 1817 and 1847 Court Houses. The mayors of the Town of Niagara continued to use it until at least 1877.

The rebuilding of the town after 1814 included plans to establish a wharf and a sheltered port and to dredge the marsh which bordered the river downstream from the Navy Hall. The town's connection to the water continued to be its greatest strength and the source of its name Niagara-on-the-Lake. Ships carried passengers and freight to and from Niagara into the middle of the twentieth century.

A rail line was constructed from Queenston to Chippawa above the falls on the Niagara River in 1839. The rail line was extended to the Niagara Dock and in 1863 to Fort Erie and Buffalo with connections at Niagara Falls for New York, Albany and Boston.

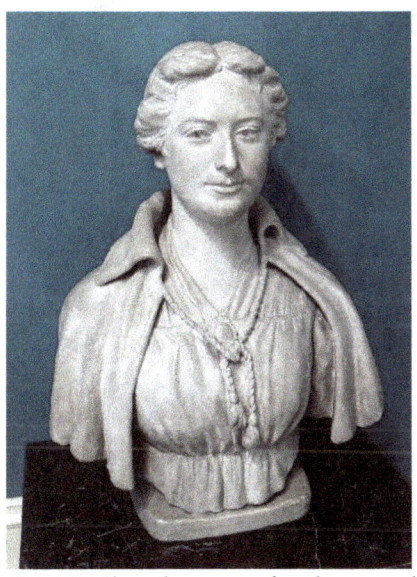

Laura Secord (1775-1868) is known for her walk from Queenston in June 1813 to warn the British troops at Beaver Dams of an impending American attack.

In 1901, anticipating a Royal visit, the Queen's Royal Hotel installed an acetylene gas plant to light the rooms. Unfortunately, on October 12 when the future King George V and Queen Mary were at the hotel, the gas leaked, and the Royal party was forced to sit on the veranda until 3 a.m. Seen here are the future King and Queen with Lord and Lady Minto.

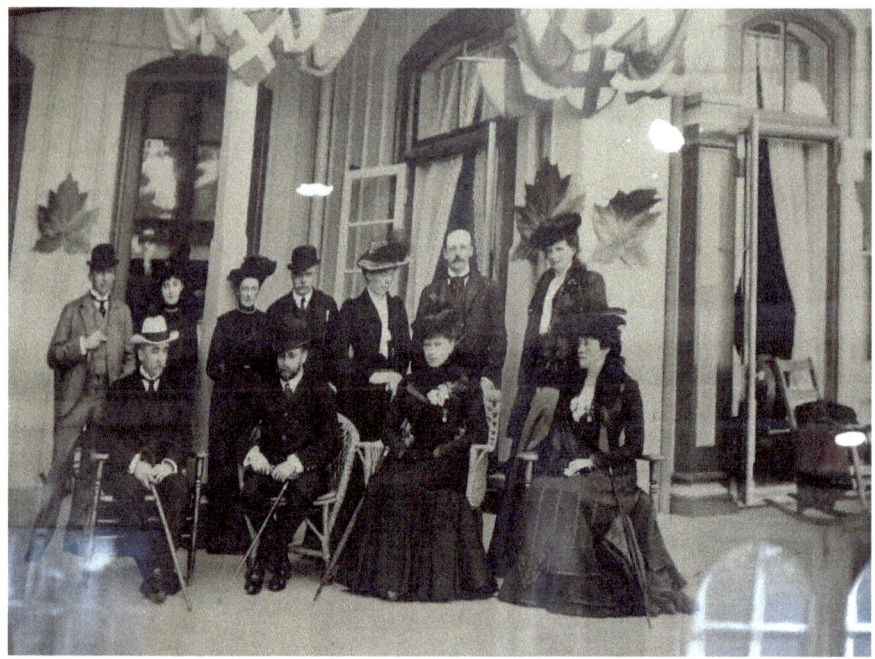

The Dock Area had a harbor, wharves, rail lines, a lumber mill, and axe factory, two hotels, a soap, basket and candle factory, and a lime kiln brickyard. Industry, agriculture and tourism benefited from each other's success. Seasonal fresh fruit from Niagara's orchards were shipped to Toronto markets.

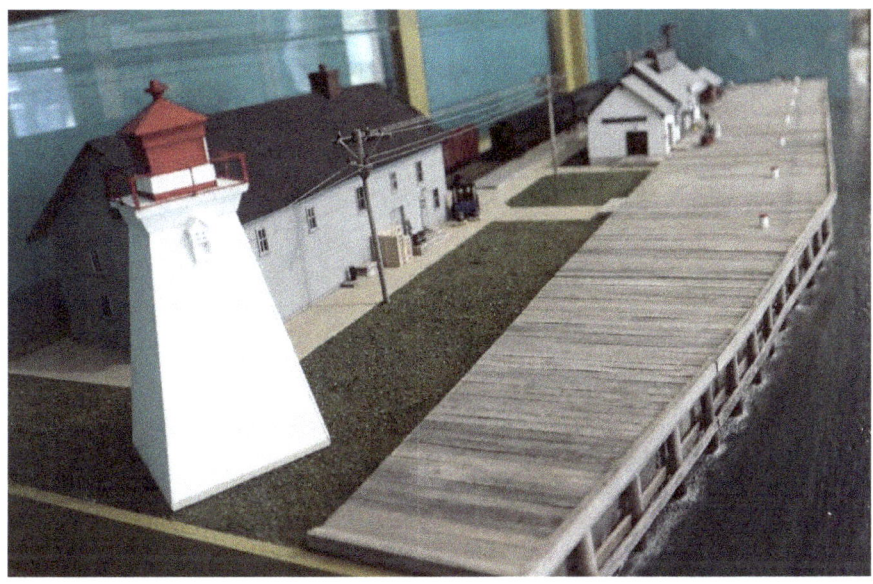

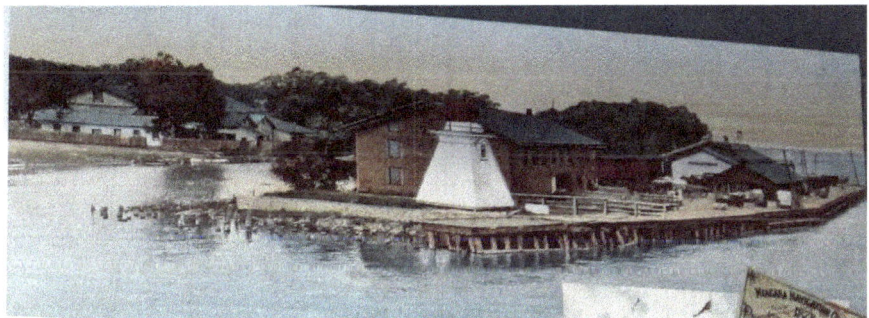

Rivers are natural transportation routes and the Niagara River was the main highway into the Great Lakes and beyond. Niagara Falls and the strong rapids were daunting, natural obstacles that could not be maneuvered easily. Portaging was necessary. The original route around Niagara Falls was on the east side (the American side), but later the main portage route, and the one most crucial to Canadian history, was on the west side.

As early as 1788, the first goods were portaged along the west bank by Queenston resident, Robert Hamilton, and his associates. By 1805, there was likely an average of sixty wagons loaded every day from Queenston to Chippawa. Goods not carried by individuals were loaded into wagons which oxen pulled up the steep slopes. Goods were brought up river and re-loaded onto the boats. Boats heading south, against the current, were assisted with the use of cranks set up along the shoreline to help pull them along.

The opening of the First Welland Canal in 1829 was the beginning of the end for the portage route. The canal system cut through the Niagara region starting in St. Catharines (Lake Ontario) and ending in Port Colborne (Lake Erie). Many ships opted to make the journey through the canal lock system rather than unloading and re-loading goods via the portage route.

Throughout the First World War, ships were instrumental in moving goods and soldiers who were arriving for training at Niagara Camp and then leaving for the front. The Niagara Commons was an attractive spot for military training.

With the Great Depression of the 1930s, passenger traffic was greatly reduced and most of the ships were decommissioned. The last passenger ship left the port in 1957. Commercial shipping continued.

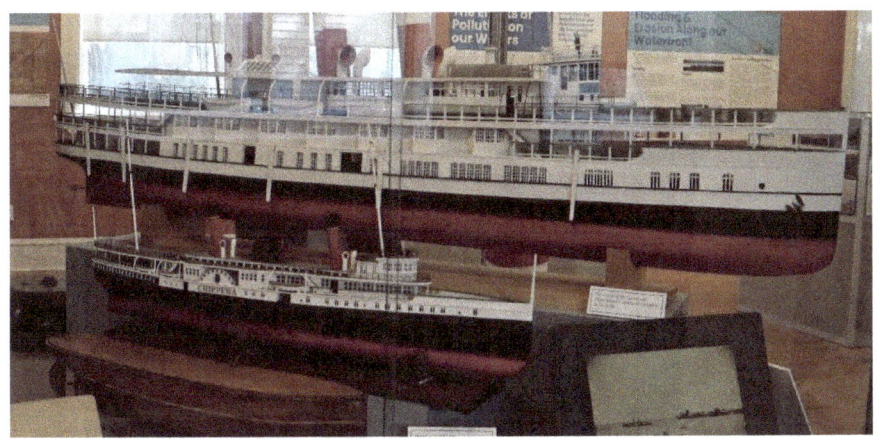

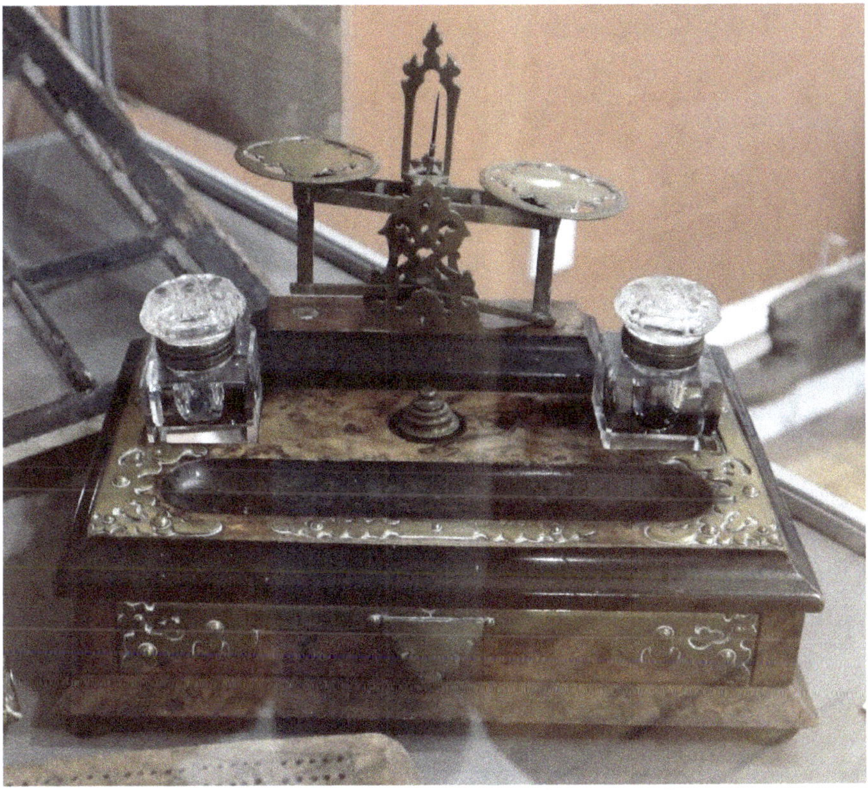

Postage scale to determine shipping fees

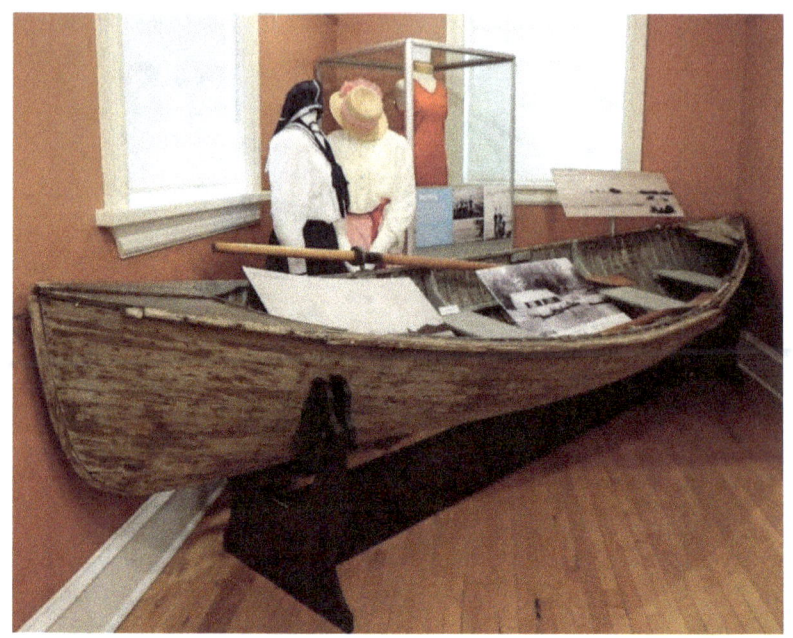

The Dish with One Spoon Wampum is a formal peace agreement between the Anishinaabe and Haudenosaunee peoples that settled in the Great Lakes region and along the St. Lawrence River. The agreement describes how the land and its resources will be shared for the benefit of all: Take only what we need, leave resources behind for others, and make sure that we do not pollute the land.

Even though this agreement was established before the arrival of settlers, it is expected that everyone who comes to this region will abide by these tenets. Instead, settlers conquered and took ownership of the land and its resources, aided in the collapse of entire species, dumped chemicals into the water supply, and destroyed natural habitats.

Today, A Dish with One Spoon allows us to confront the negative impacts we have had on the environment. It can offer lessons on what actions we can take toward the sustainability of our natural resources.

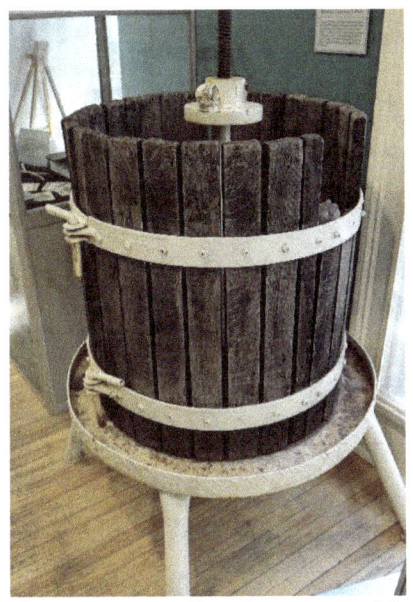

The wine press is known as a 'basket press.' It is a hand-powered mechanical system for wine making. Pressing is done to separate the seeds, skins, and any other non-juice items from the juice of the freshly picked grapes.

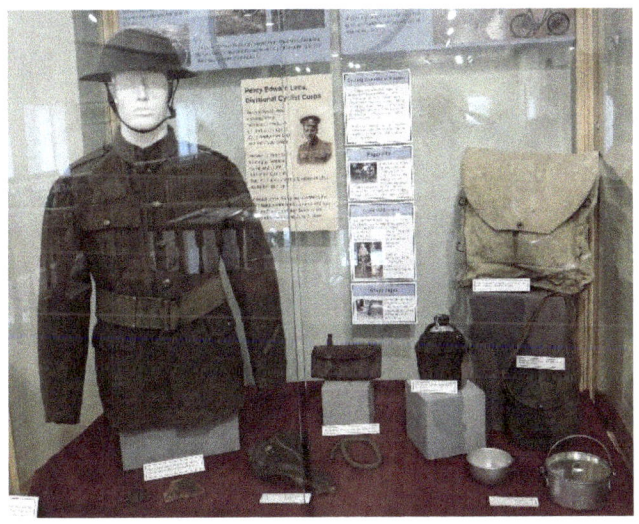

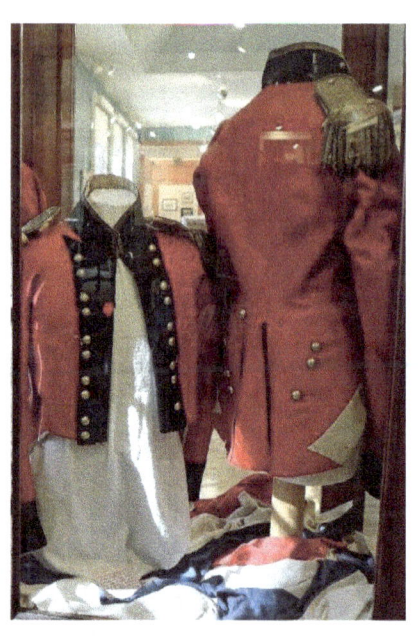

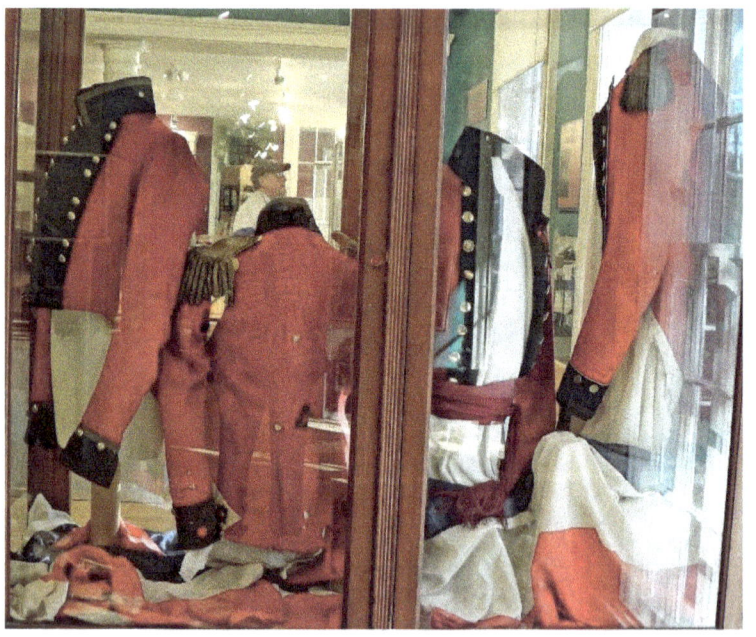

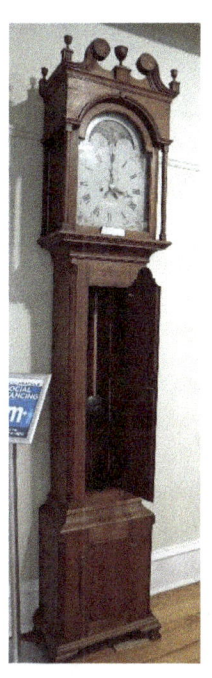

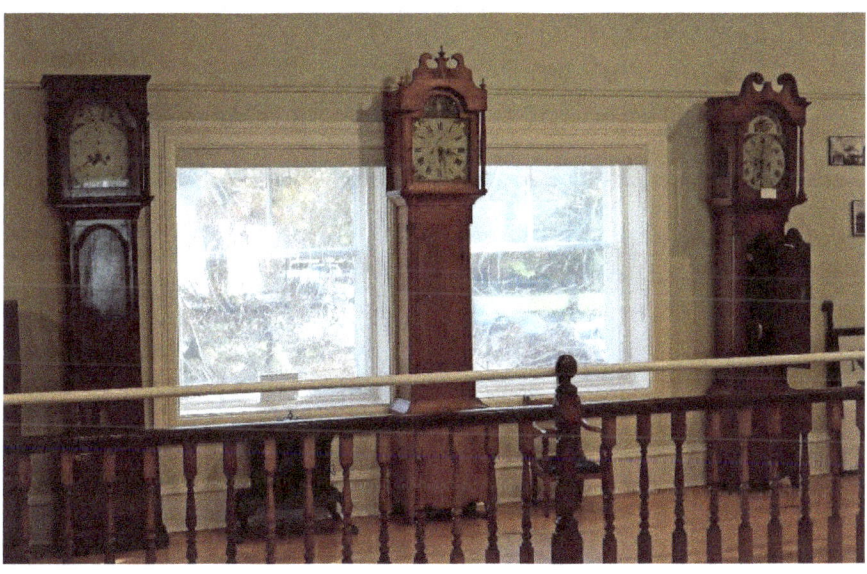

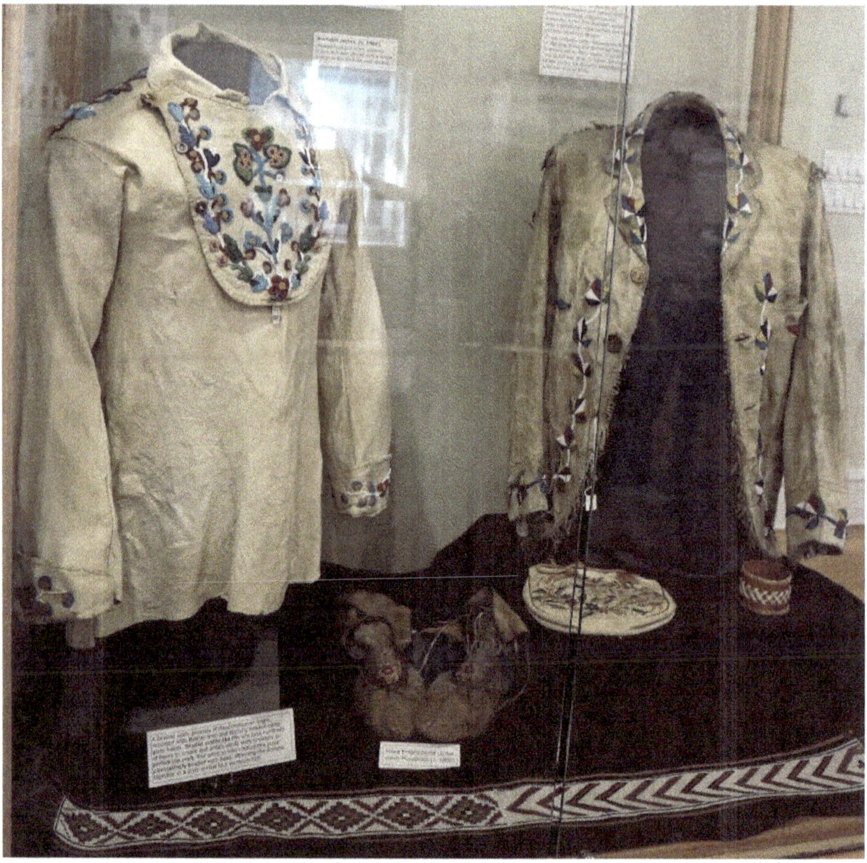

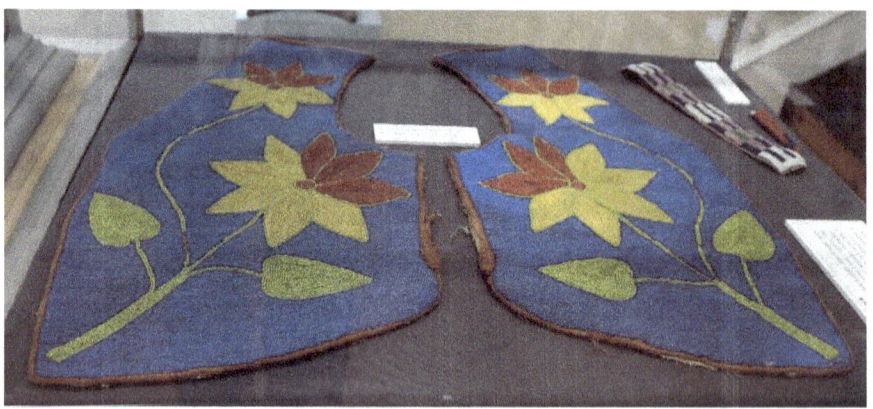

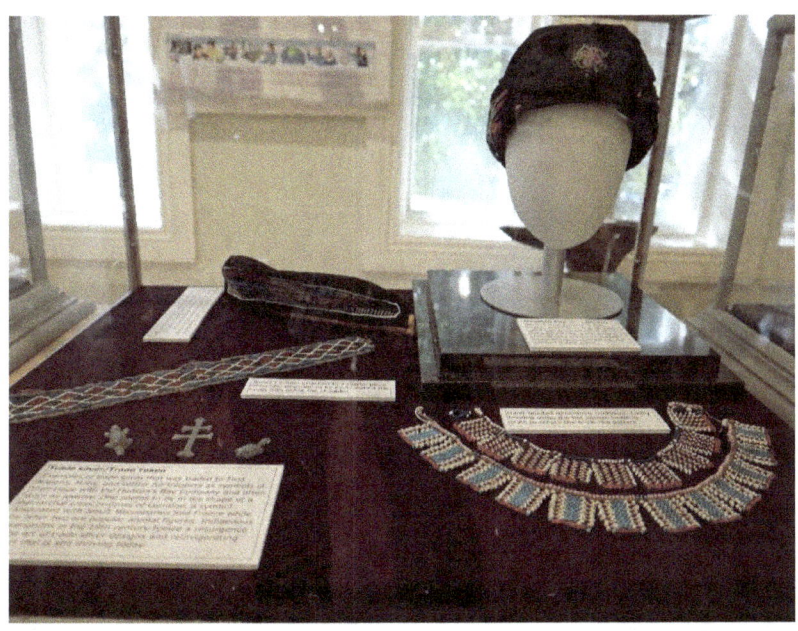

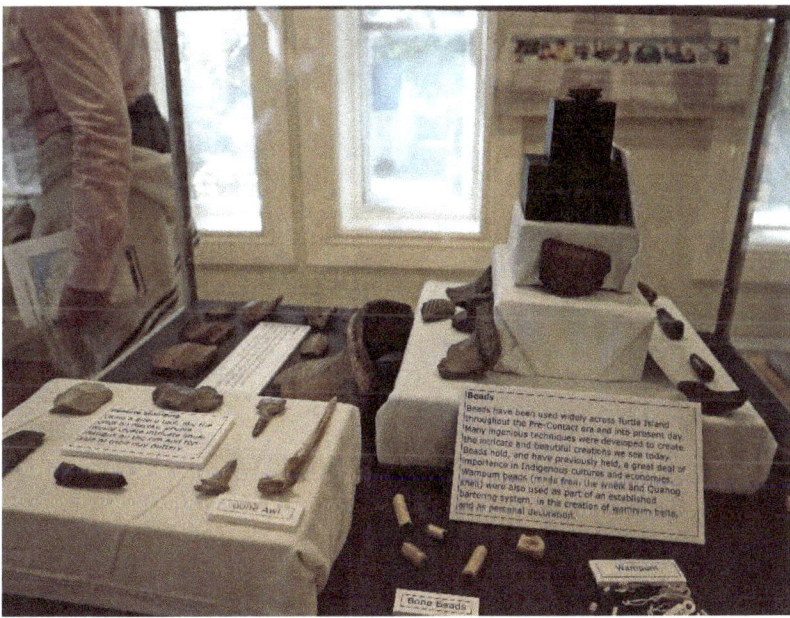

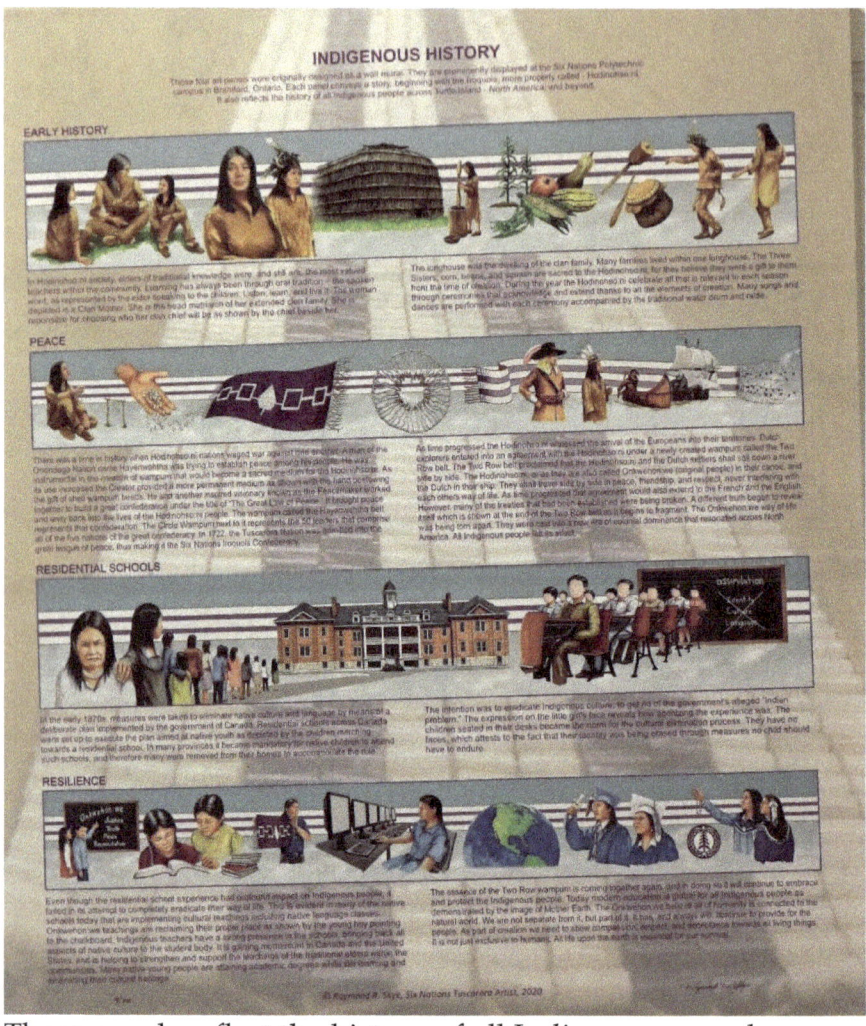

These panels reflect the history of all Indigenous peoples across Turtle Island (North America), and beyond.

In Iroquois society, more properly known as Hodinohso:ni, elders of traditional knowledge are the most valued teachers within the community. Learning is through oral tradition, represented by the elder speaking to the children. The woman depicted is a Clan Mother, head matriarch of her extended clan family; she chooses the chief, represented by the one standing beside her. The longhouse was the dwelling place of the clan family; many families lived in one longhouse. The Three Sisters, corn, beans and squash, are sacred to them as they believe they were a gift to them from the time of creation. The people celebrate throughout the year in ceremonies that extend thanks using the water drum and rattle.

There was a time when the Hodinohso:ni nations waged war against one another. A man of the Onondaga nation named Hayenwahtha, tried to bring peace by establishing wampum as a sacred medium for the Hodinohso:ni. As its use increased, the creator provided a more permanent medium as shown by the hand bestowing the gift of shell wampum beads. He and another inspired visionary known as the Peacemaker worked together to build a great confederation under the title of 'The Great Law of Peace' which brought peace and unity back into the lives of the Hodinohso:ni. The wampum called the Hayenwahtha belt represents that confederation. The circle wampum next to it represents the fifty leaders that comprise the five nations of the great confederacy. In 1722, the Tuscarora nation was admitted into the great league of peace, thus making it the Six Nations Iroquois Confederacy.

As time progressed, the Hodinohso:ni saw the arrival of the Europeans into their territories. Dutch explorers entered into an agreement with the Hodinohso:ni under a newly created wampum called the Two Row belt which proclaimed that the Hodinohso:ni and the Dutch would sail down a river side by side, shown by the Hodinohso:ni in their canoe and the Dutch in their ship, traveling side by side in peace, friendship and respect, never interfering with each other's way of life. Later this agreement extended to the French and English. Many of the treaties were broken. A different truth began to reveal itself which is shown at the end of the Two Row belt as it begins to fragment. The Onkwehon:we (original people) way of life was being torn apart. The new era was of colonial dominance that resonated across North America. All indigenous people felt its affect.

In the early 1870s, measures were taken to eliminate native culture and language. Residential schools were set up across Canada to execute the plan, as shown by the children marching towards a residential school. In many provinces it was mandatory for native children to attend such schools; many were removed from their homes to accommodate this rule. The intention was to eradicate Indigenous culture, to get rid of the government's alleged 'Indian problem.' The children at the desks have no faces indicating that their identity was being erased.

Even though the residential schools had a profound impact on Indigenous people, it failed to completely eradicate their way of life. Many native schools today are implementing cultural teachings, and native language classes.

The essence of the Two Row wampum is coming together again. Global education for all Indigenous people – represented by the globe of Mother Earth. As part of creation, we need to show compassion, respect and acceptance towards all living things. All life upon the earth is essential for our survival.

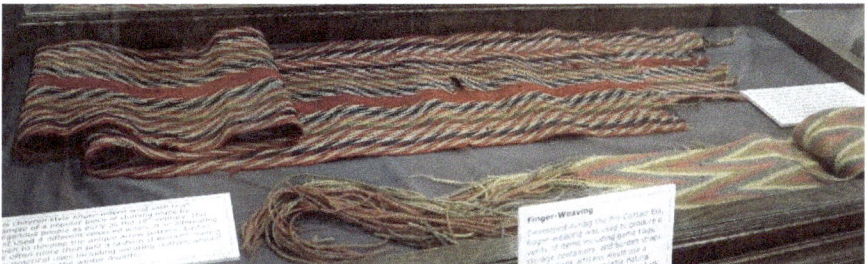

Finger weaving was used to produce a variety of items including game bags, storage containers and burden straps. First Nations artisans used readily available natural fibers including sinew, basswood bark, milkweed, cattail rushes, and buffalo hair. Following contact with Europeans, colored wool was introduced into the process. Glass beads could be added to further decorate the styled sashes. Sashes had practical uses such as securing clothing around the waist during the winter months.

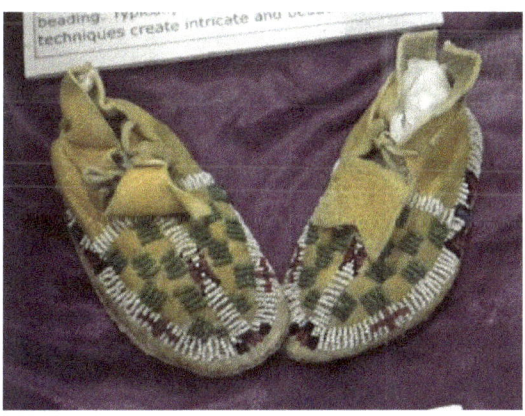
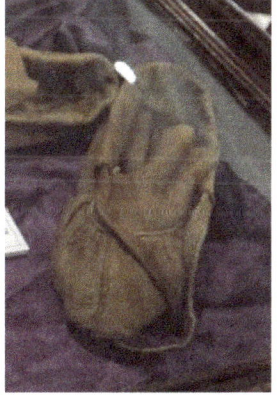

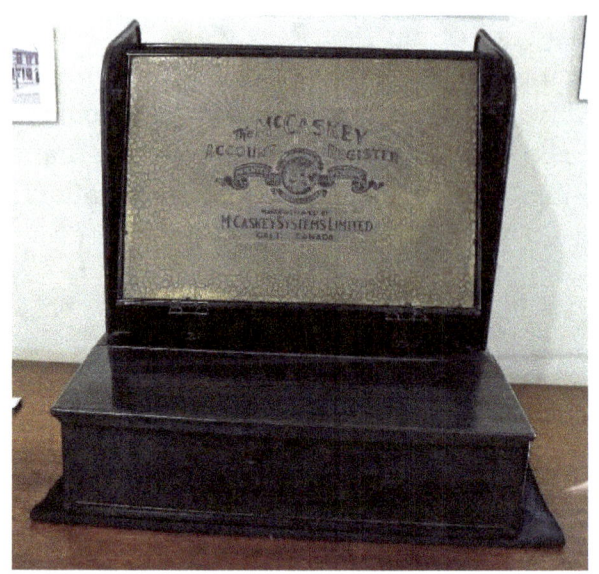

Account Register

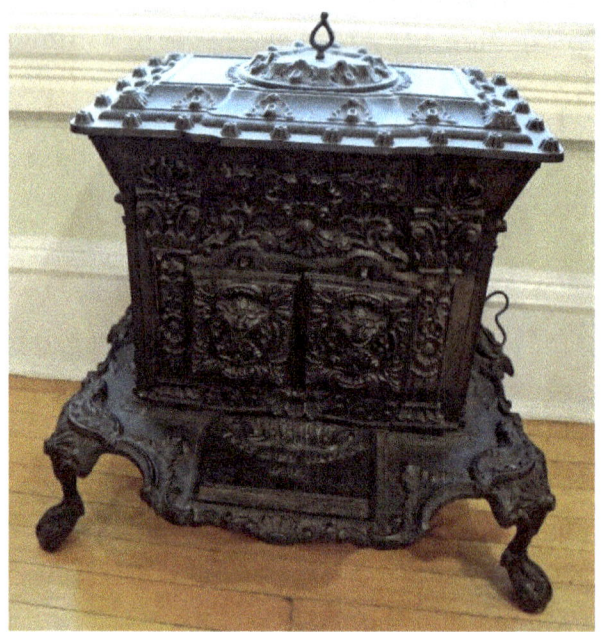

Parlor Stove c. 1850-1860

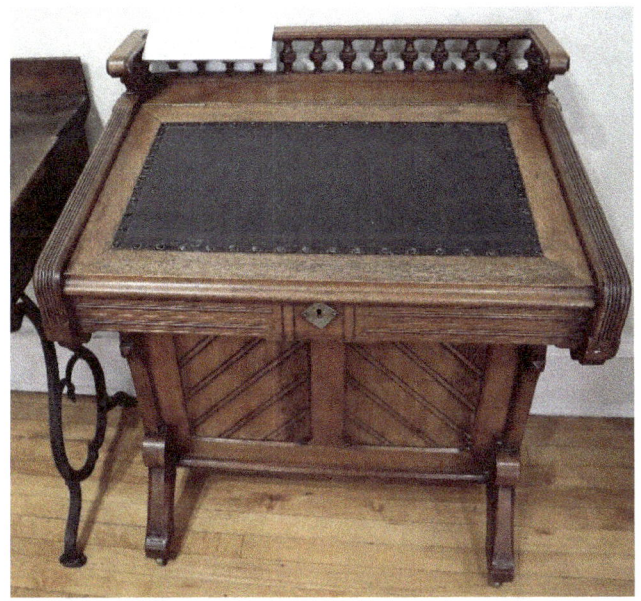

This desk belonged to Miss Maria Rye. She brought about 4,200 children, mostly girls, to Canada. Miss Rye used this desk at 'Our Western Home,' her receiving home in Niagara-on-the-Lake.

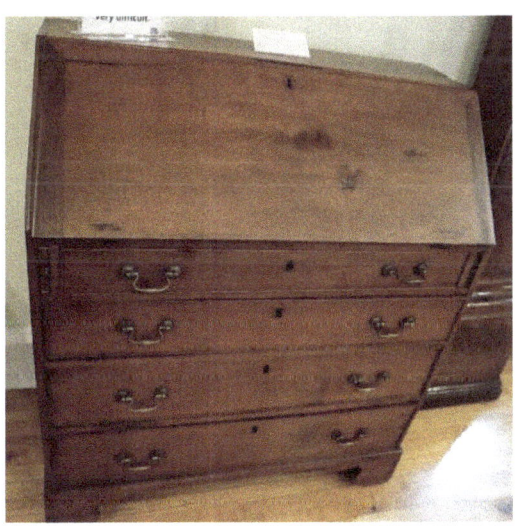

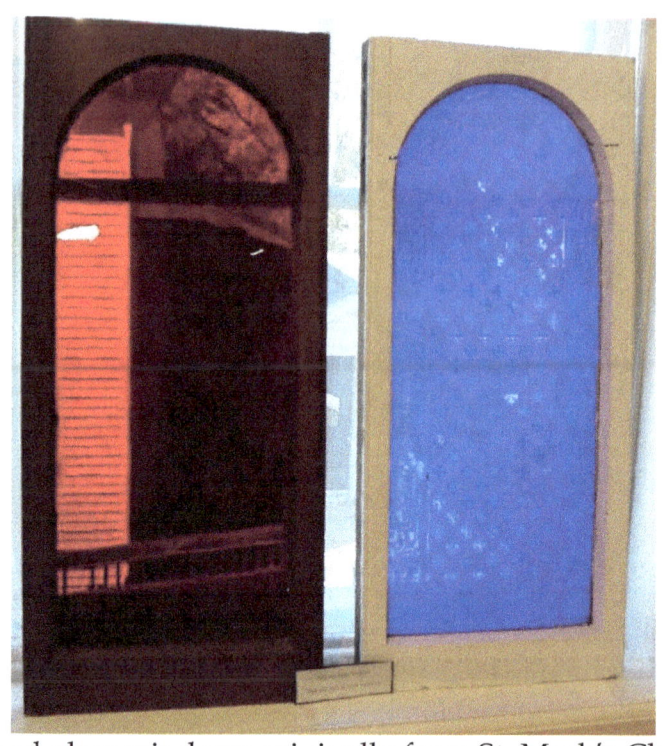

Stained glass windows originally from St. Mark's Church

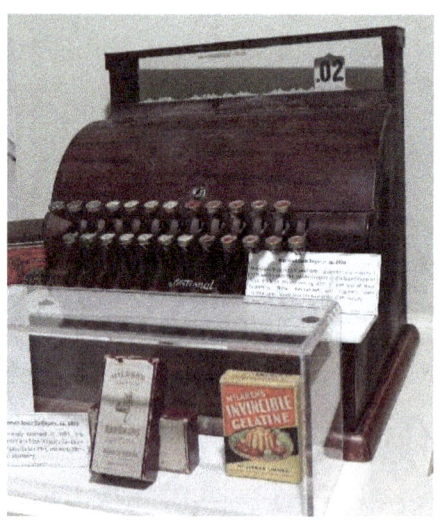

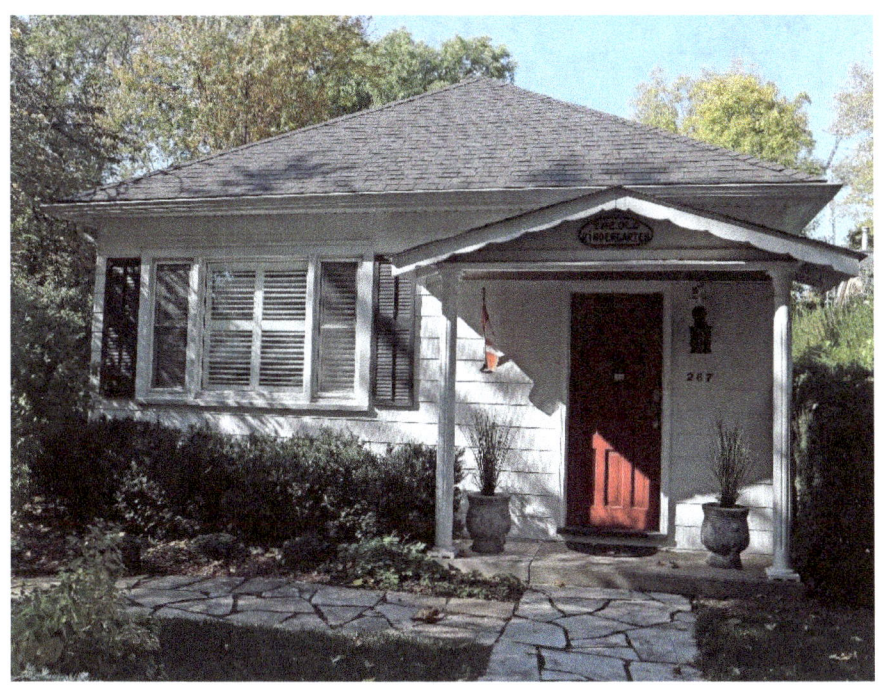

The Old Kindergarten

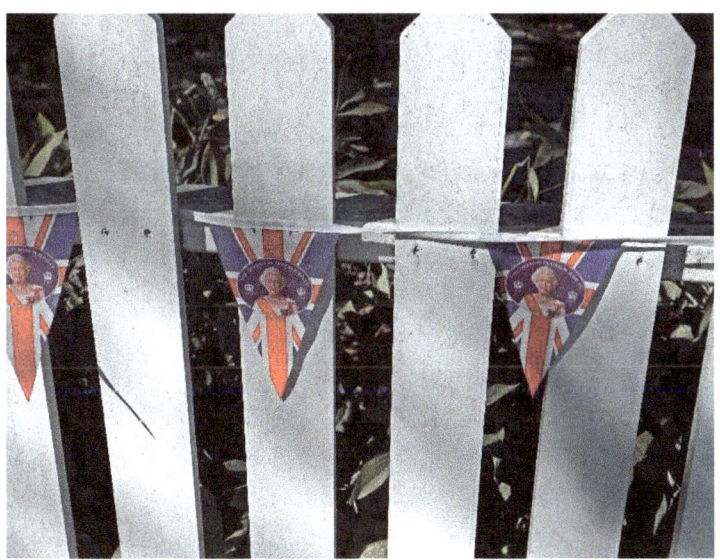

In honor of the passing of Queen Elizabeth II, flags decorate the picket fence.

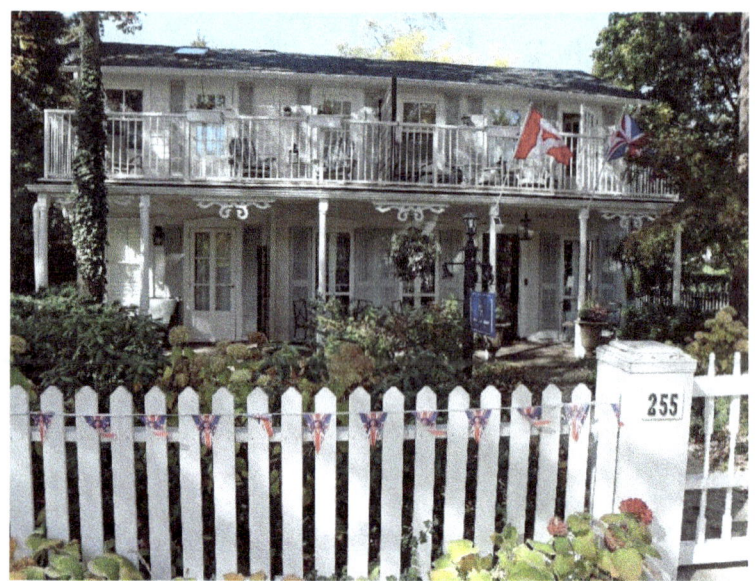

255 King Street – former Burns Bed & Breakfast – c. 1818 – now Harrogate House Inn. It is a warm and welcoming bed and breakfast with the privacy, charm and personalized service that a boutique hotel offers. It is centrally located in the heart of the historic downtown core and close to restaurants, theatres, boutique shopping, wineries and North America's oldest golf course.

The Niagara Agricultural Society (1792-1805) was devoted to the improvement of agriculture. Its members were mostly merchants, politicians, clergymen, and gentlemen farmers who met regularly for dinner and discussion. They introduced new varieties of fruit trees to the Niagara peninsula in 1794 and sponsored the province's first agricultural fair in Queenston in 1799. Although the society was short-lived, its scientific approach to farming anticipated the work of regional agricultural societies run by farmers after 1820.

Shaw Festival Theatre
10 Queen's Parade

At 856 seats, the Festival Theatre is the Shaw's largest venue. Built in the modernist style, it was designed to provide a spacious yet intimate audience experience. It was built in 1973. (Plans changed and the theatre was only open until 1:00 instead of the advertised 4:00.)

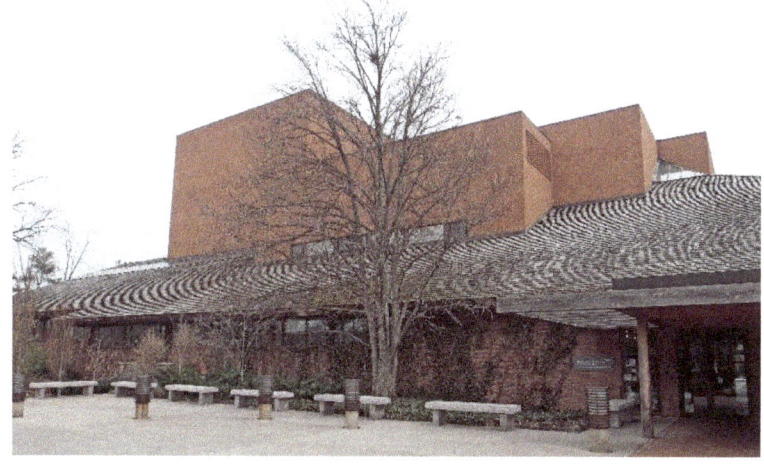

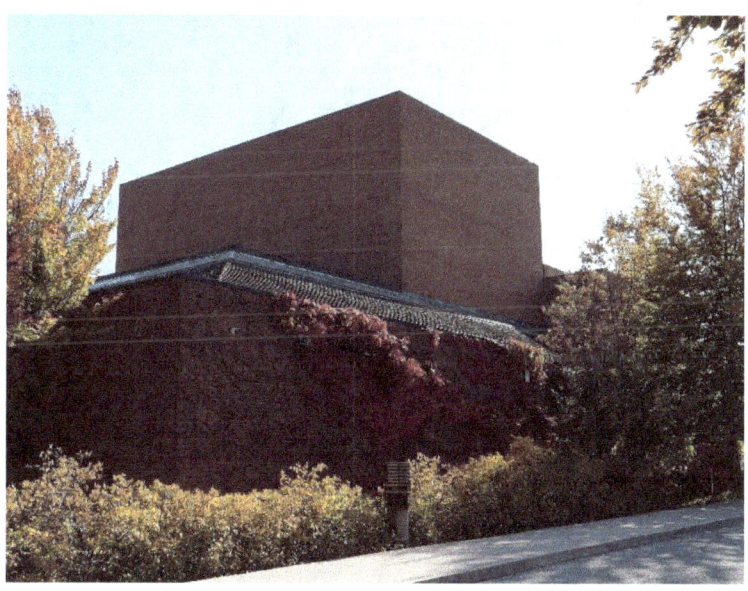

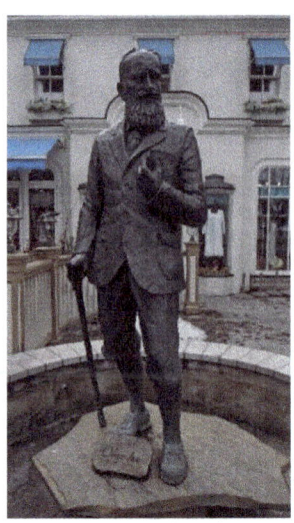

George Bernard Shaw (1856-1950) – born in Dublin, Ireland; spokesperson and playwright – awarded the Nobel Prize for Literature in 1925. Elizabeth Bradford Holbrook, sculptor 1996

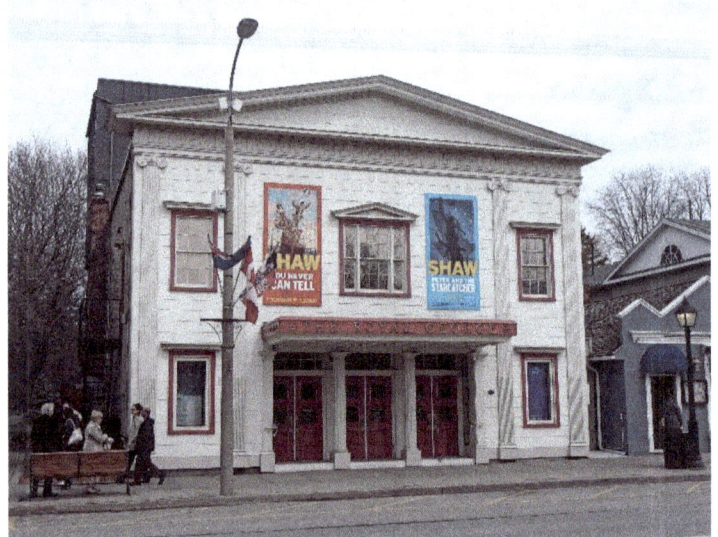

85 Queen Street – The Royal George Theatre - Built as a vaudeville house, this 328-seat theatre was used to entertain the troops during World War I. Now the red and gilt auditorium is home to mysteries and comedies.

RiverBrink Art Museum
116 Queenston Street. Queenston, Ontario

The former country home of lawyer Samuel E. Weir (1898-1981), RiverBrink opened to the public in 1983 as a fine art museum with exhibitions of historical and contemporary art. Construction on the Georgian-style building began in the 1960s and was completed in 1970. It has a mansard roof and gabled windows. Samuel Weir was an avid collector of fine and decorative arts, rare books, and historical documents. The collection includes art works by many well-known Canadian, U.S. American, and European artists.

The building has exhibition galleries on three levels, a library, and gift shop. In Fall 2022, Specimen will be on display (sculptures by Susan Low-Beer, curated by Sheila McMath), along with works by members of the Group of Seven in The Spirit Within the Form, an exhibition of stone-cut prints by Stanley Lewis.

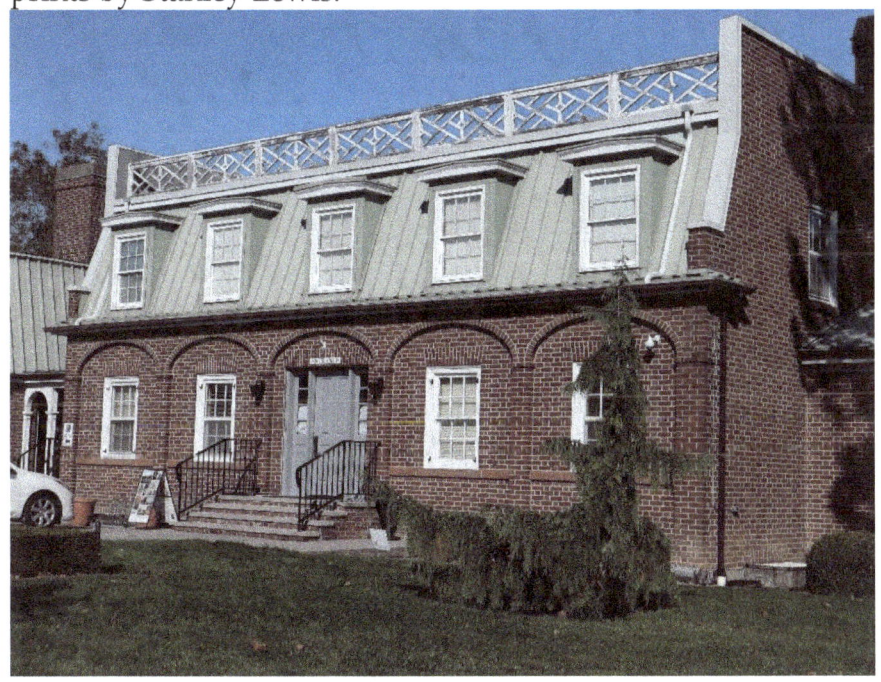

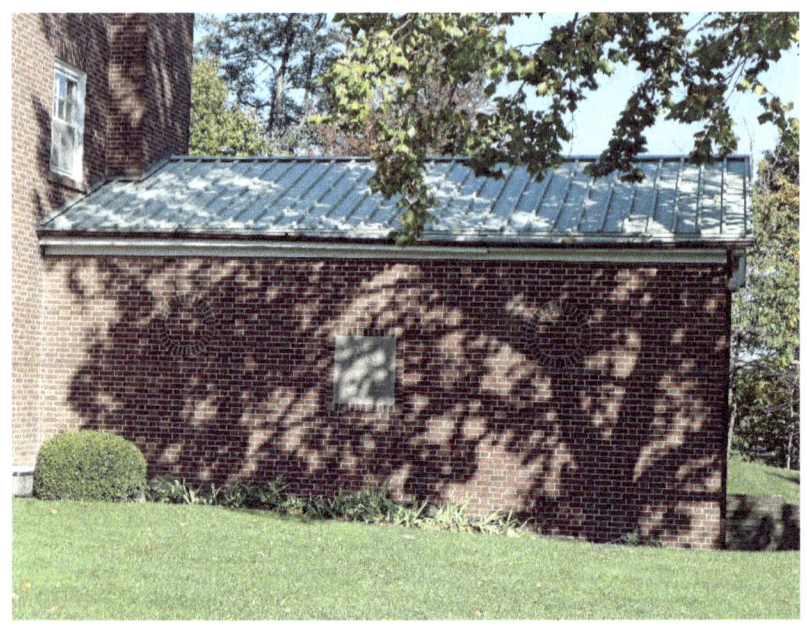

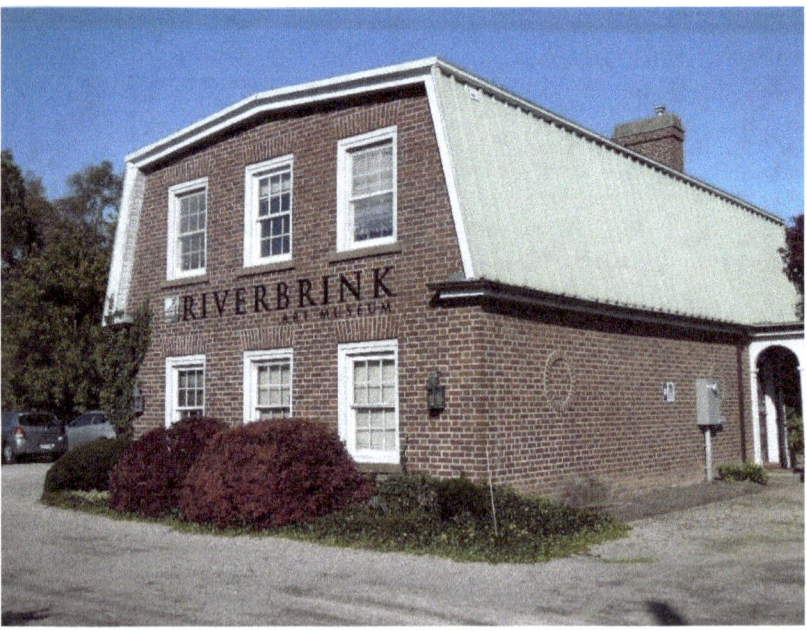

There is a self-contained apartment over the coach house.

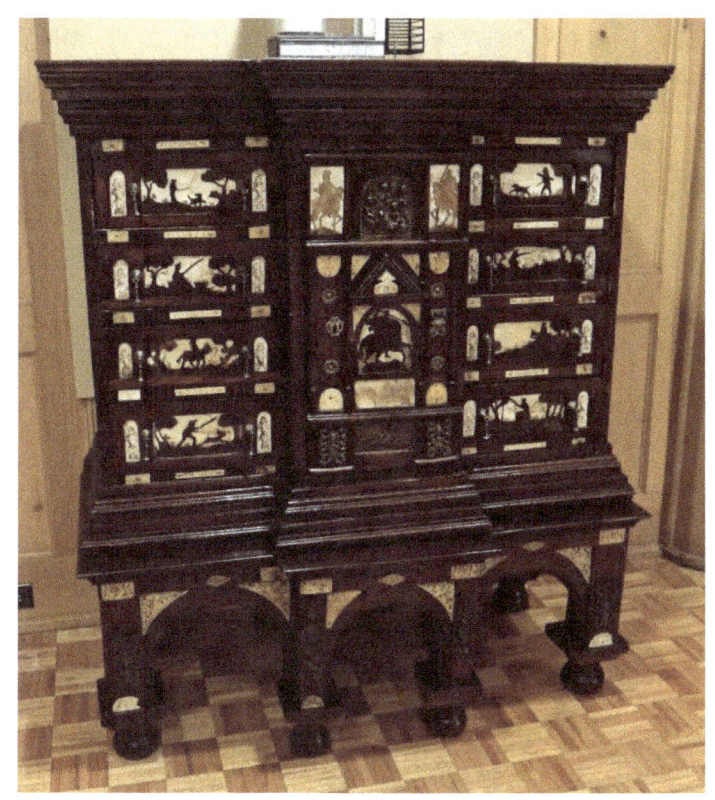

Hunting and fishing scenes on each panel

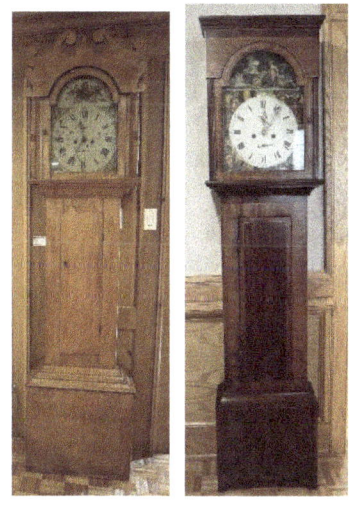

Susan Low-Beer's latest series *Specimen* – ceramic sculptures using fabric and wire – abstract organs of the body

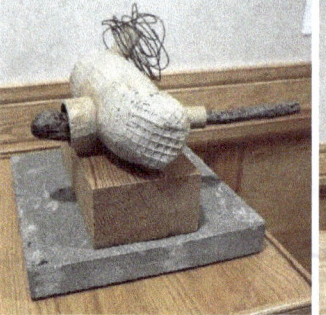
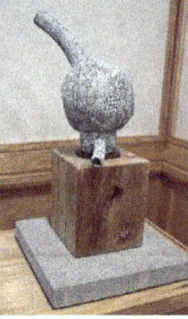

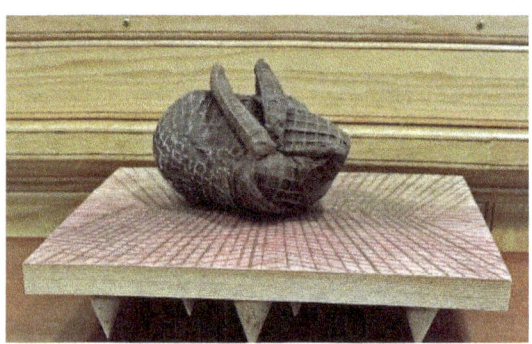

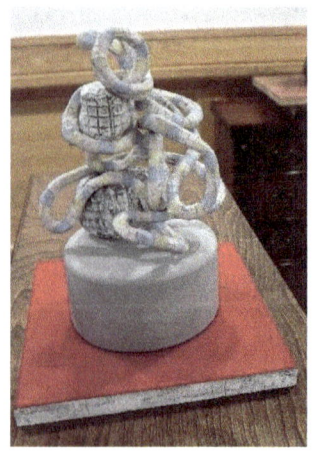
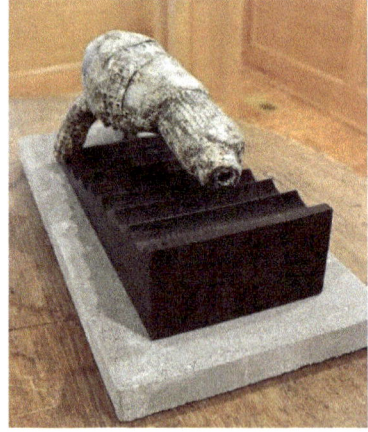

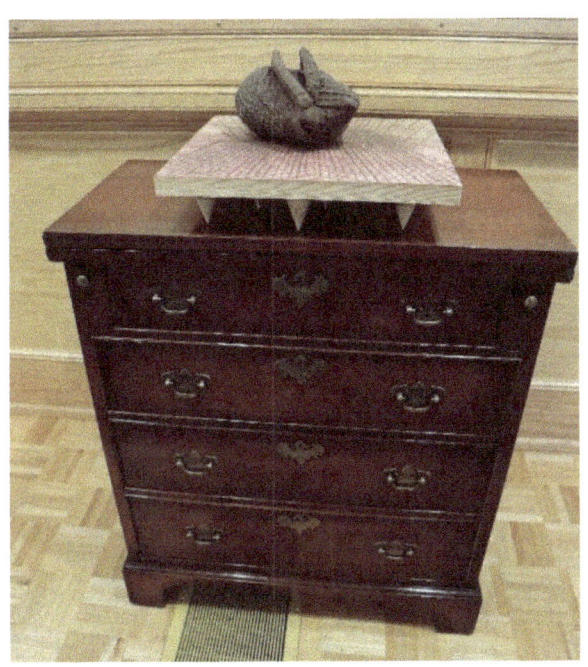

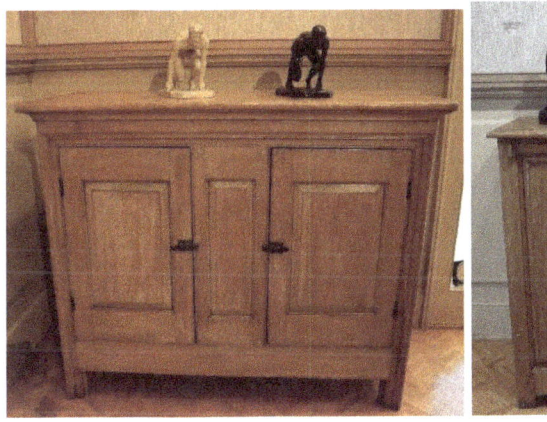

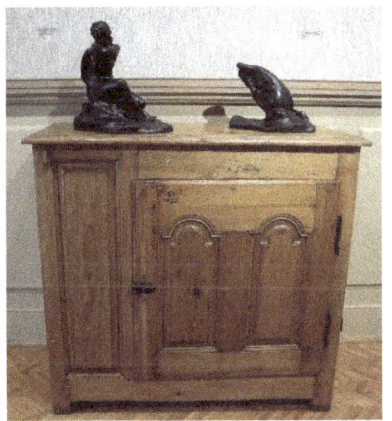

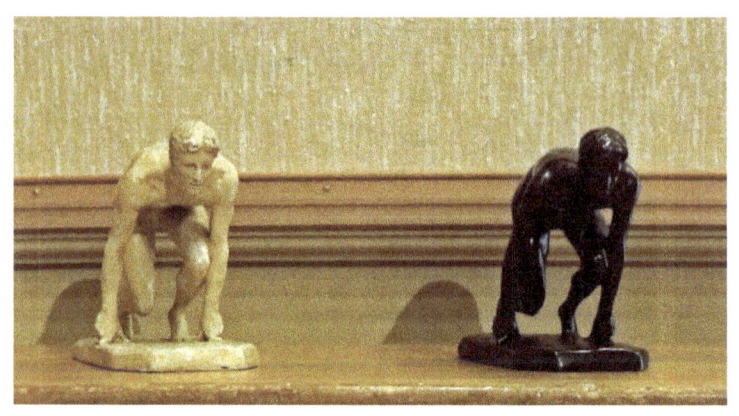

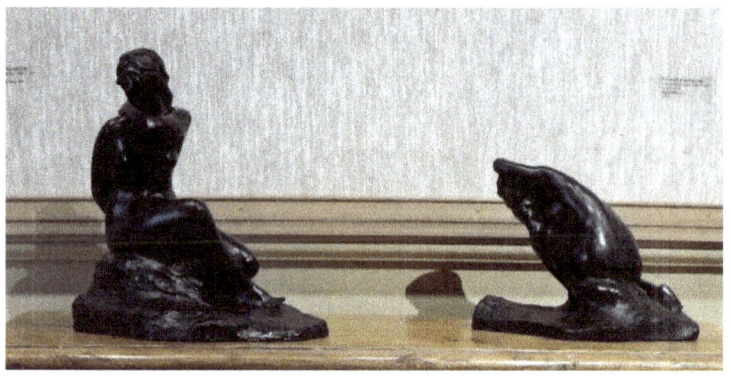

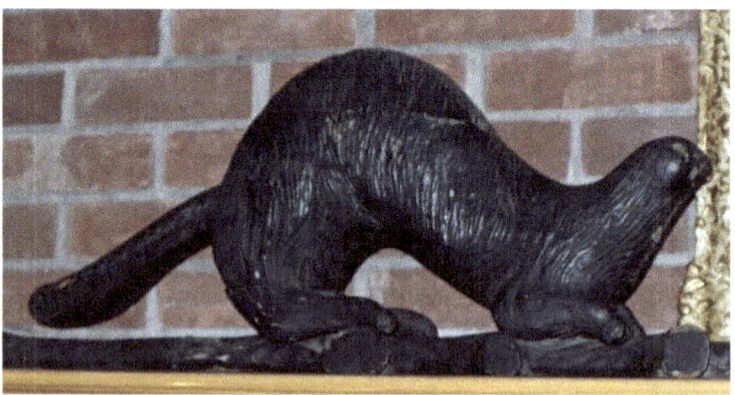

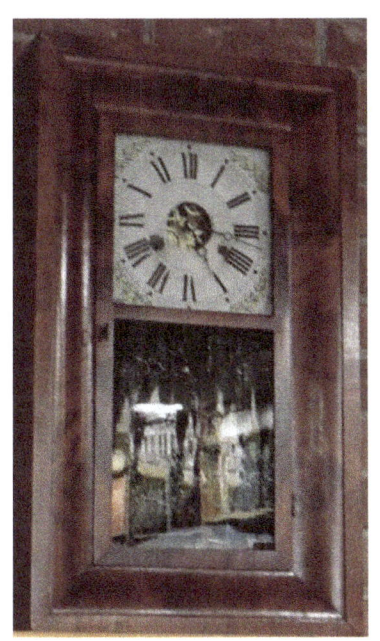

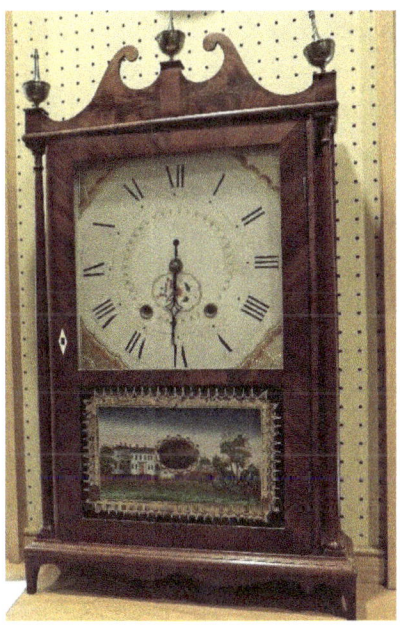

Pillar and Scroll Clock c. 1820

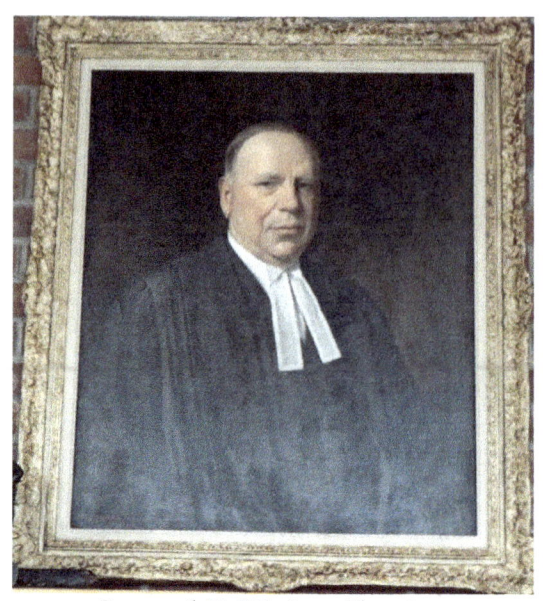

Samuel E. Weir collection

Marc-Aurèle de Foy Suzor-Coté (1869-1937) was a French-Canadian painter and sculptor. His works were directly influenced by French Impressionism and Post-Impressionism. He was born in Arthabaska, Quebec; his father was an artist. Suzor-Coté was a baritone and he studied music at the Conservatory of Music in Paris in 1890. Later he studied painting and sculpture at the École des Beaux-Arts with Léon Bonnat. At the school, he learned of the work of Swedish sculptor Carl Miles whose sculptures of indigenous people influenced him. After his return to Quebec in 1908, he established a studio in Montreal creating paintings with classic interpretations of Canadian landscapes. He produced many paintings of the Quebec landscape, as well as portraits, nudes, historical paintings and sculptures. He produced forty or fifty small bronze Impressionist figures and groups.

Bronze sculptures by Marc-Aurele de Foy Suzor-Coté

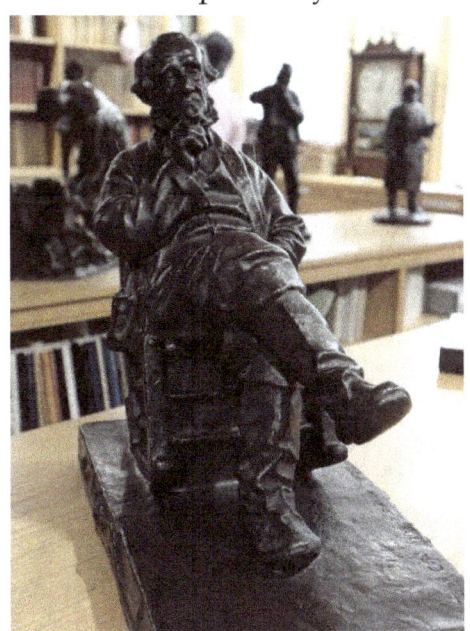 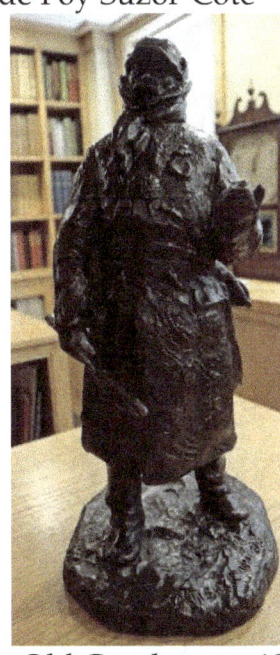

The Old Coachman - 1916

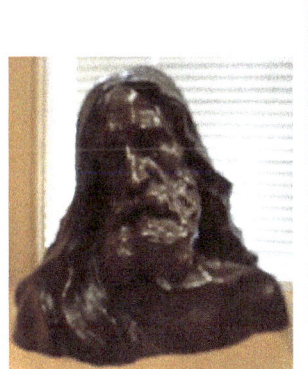 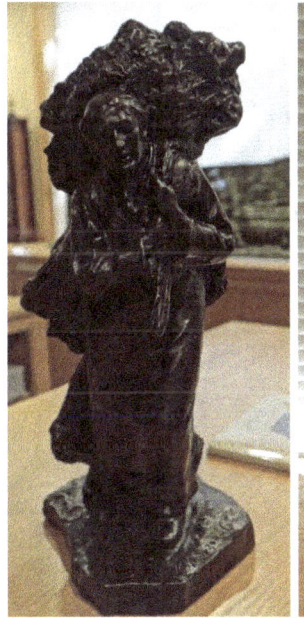 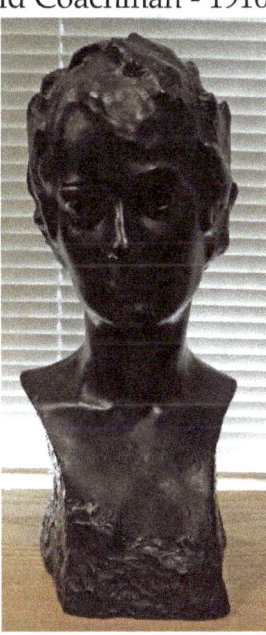

Je Me Souviens – 1924

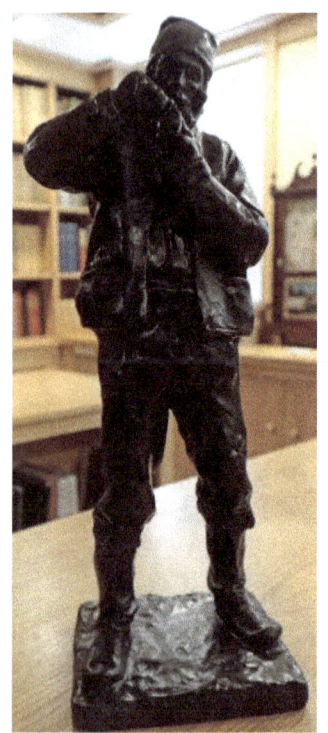
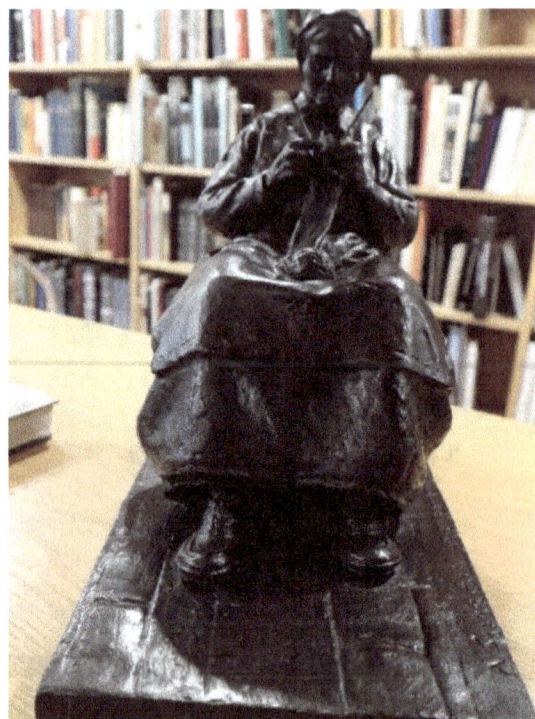

The Old Smoker

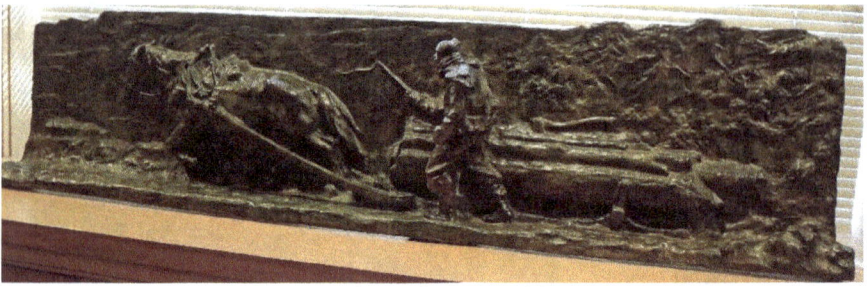

Hauling logs – 1924

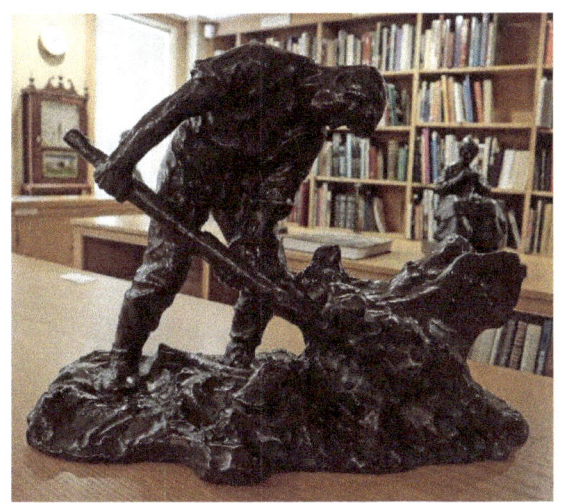

Root Digger - 1912

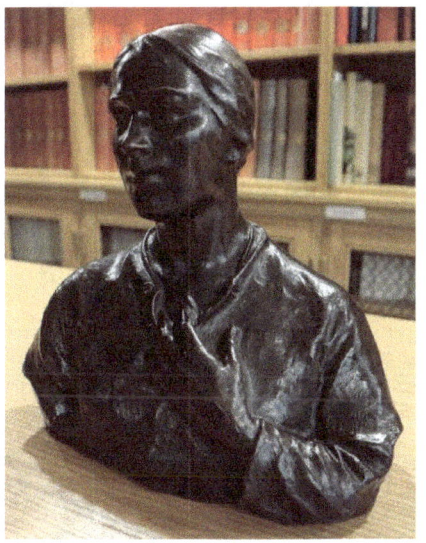

Maria Chapdelaine - 1925

Maria Chapdelaine is a romance novel written in 1913 by the Breton writer Louis Hémon. Aimed at young French and Quebecois people, the book was included in school curricula, translated, and has been extensively analyzed and adapted.

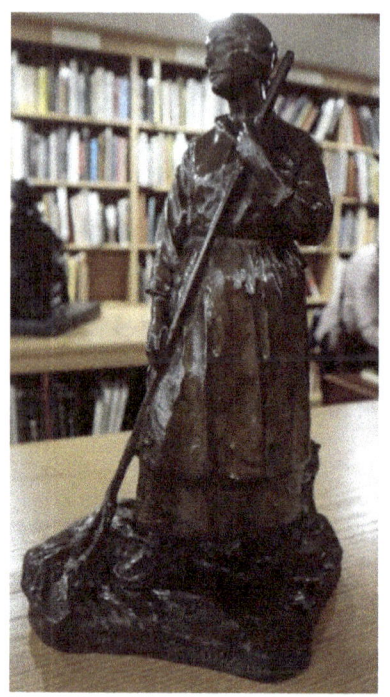 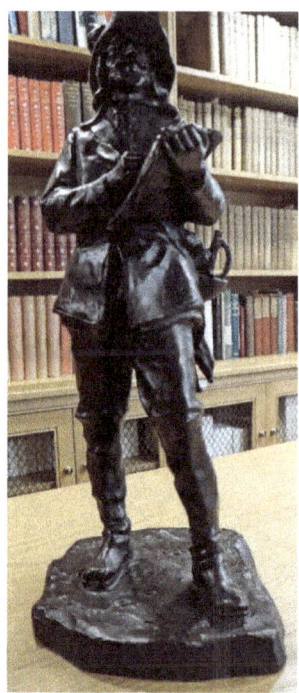

Maria Chapdelaine – 1925 The Surveyor - 1925

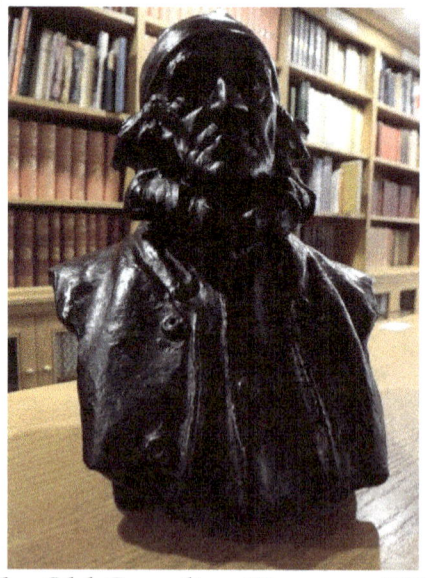

The Old Canadian Pioneer – 1912

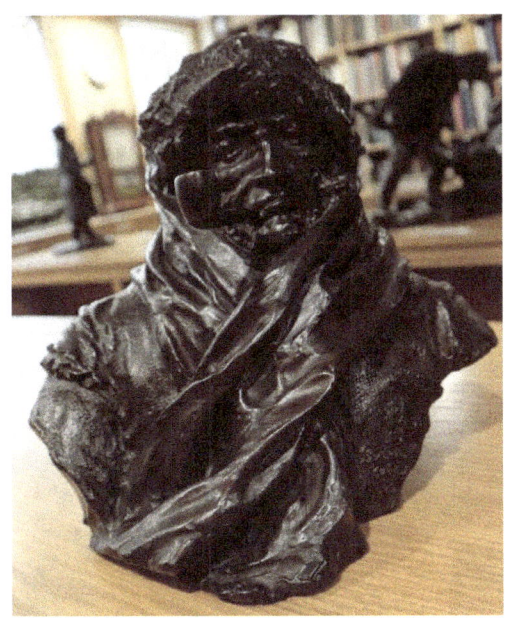

Pere Fleury – 1908

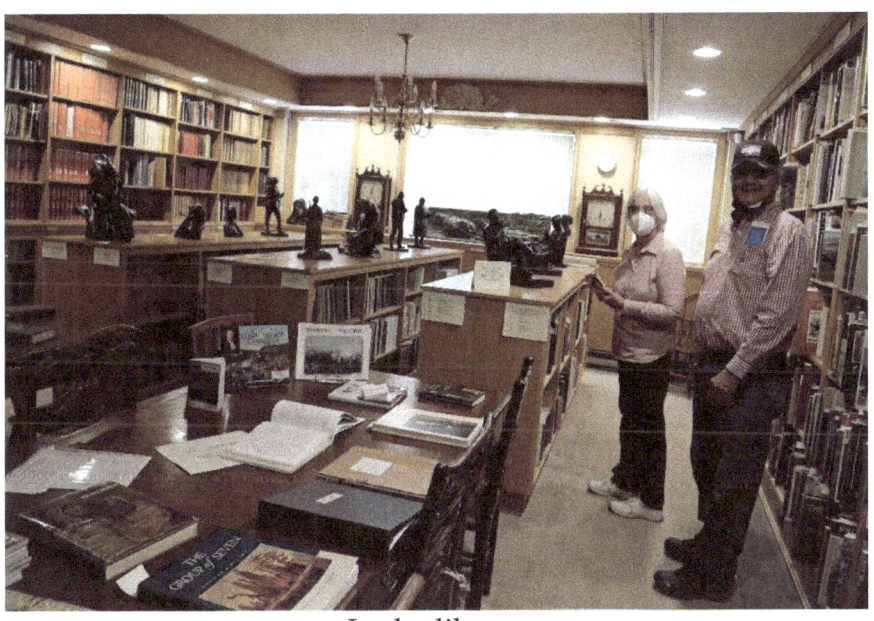

In the library

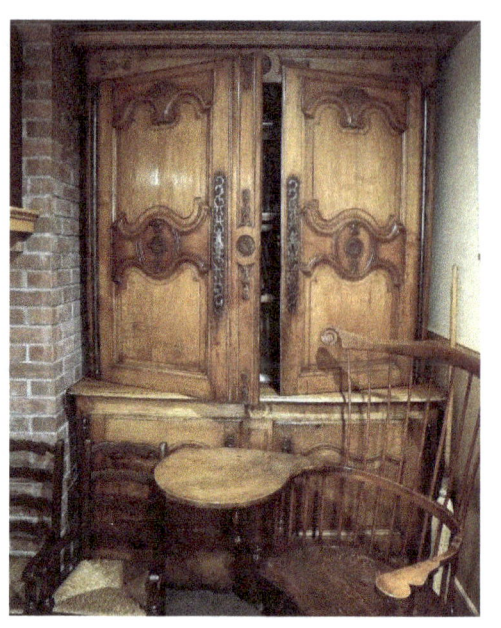

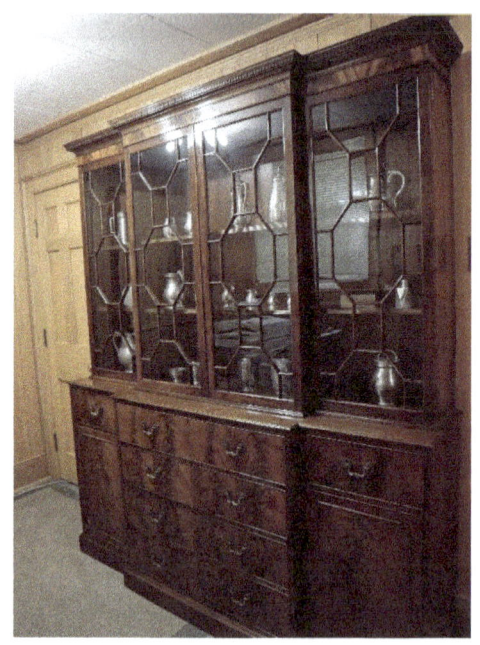

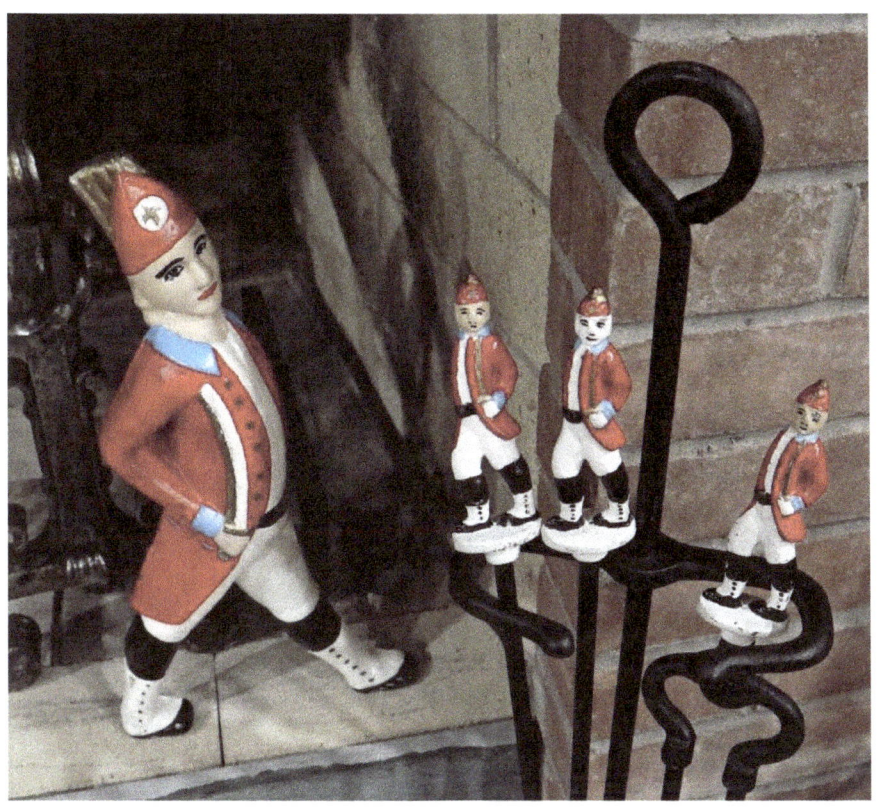

The Group of Seven have become synonymous with an untouched, seemingly uninhabited, Canadian wilderness. These artists also sketched and painted urban locations, with clear evidence of civilization and industry. These are a selection of artwork in the Samuel E. Weir collection showing the complex relationship between the urban center and rural periphery in paintings by members of the Group.

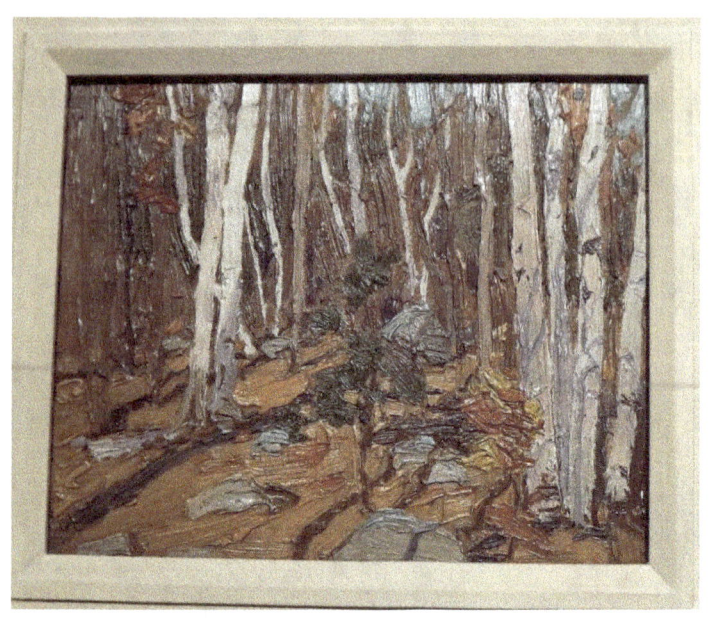

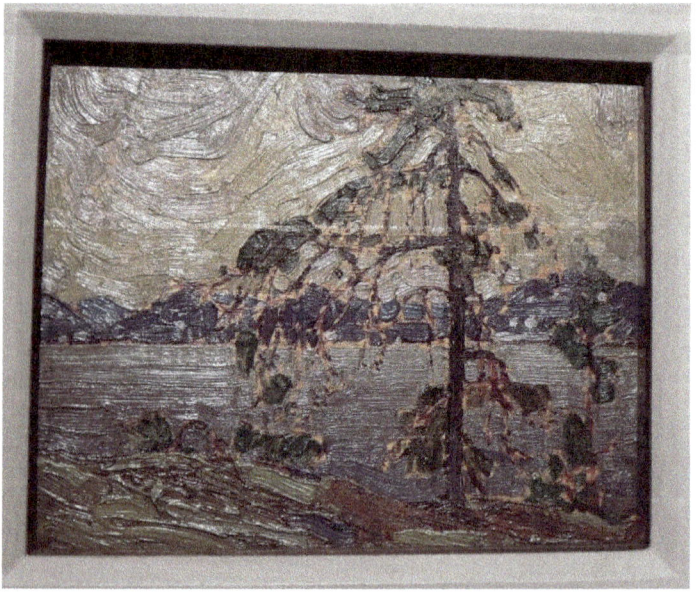

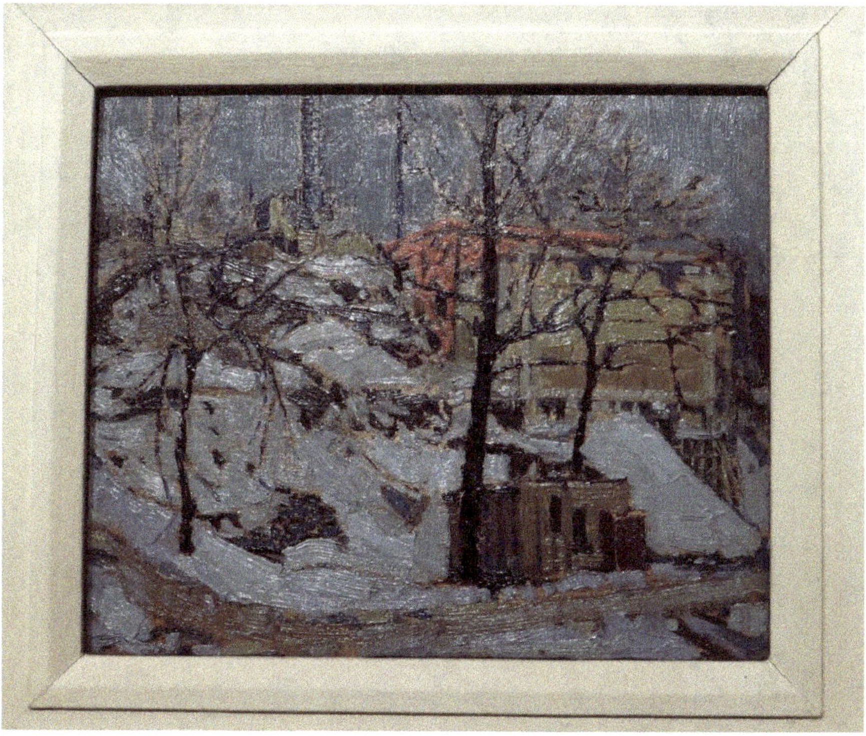

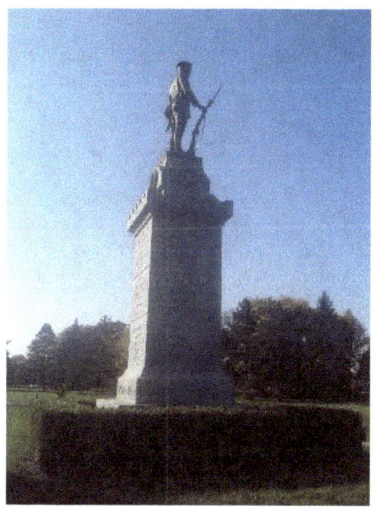

Military monument (located across from RiverBrink Art Museum, Queenston) – soldiers lost in World War I, World War II and Korea

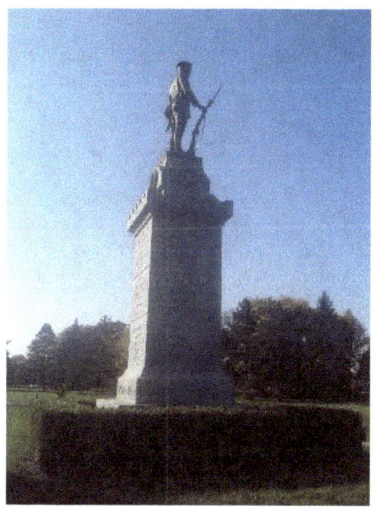

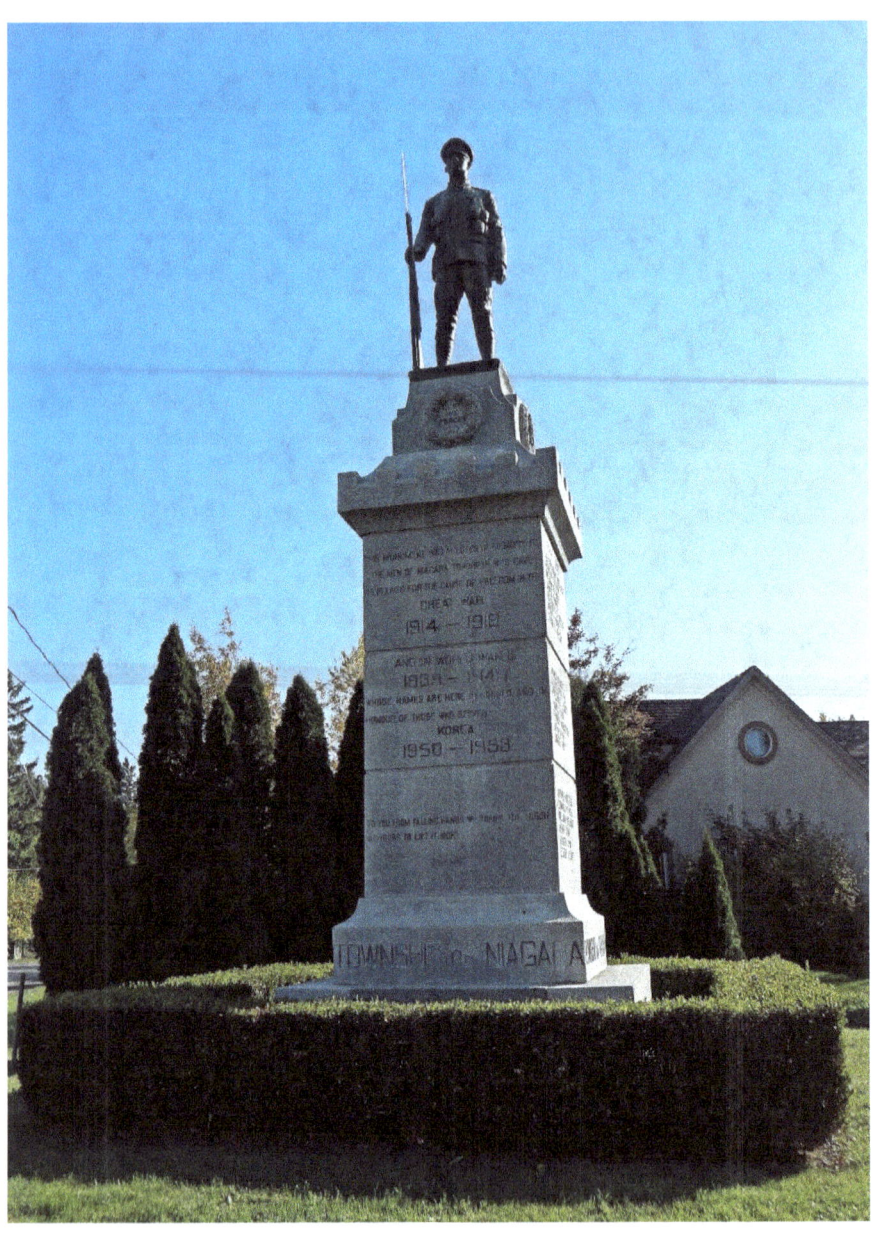

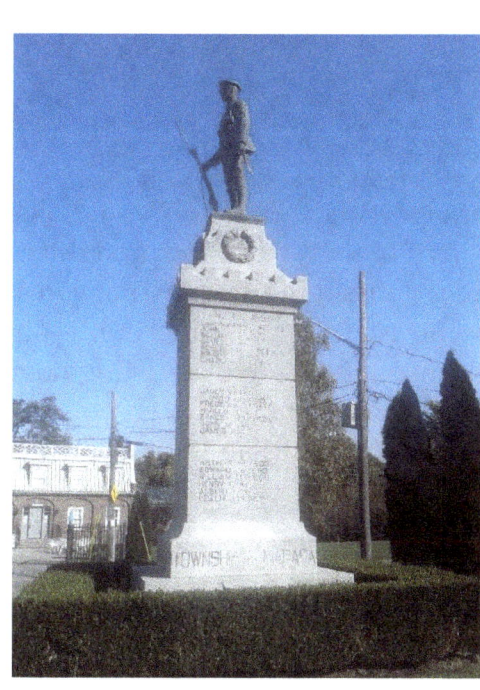

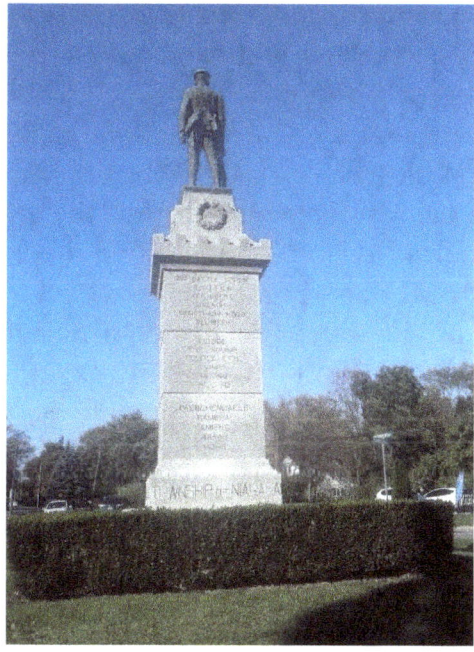

Willowbank
14487 Niagara Parkway, Queenston, Ontario

Willowbank is in the village of Queenston, halfway between Niagara Falls and Niagara-on-the-Lake. The natural and cultural history of this area is rich and interwoven. First Nations peoples identified the Queenston waterfront and the Willowbank ravine as an important terminus on the river. The mouth of the ravine was the logical starting point for a portage route to bypass the falls, known now as Portage Road.

In 1785, Scottish-Canadian trader Robert Hamilton established Hamilton Wharf on the Niagara River and created a rail system pulled by horses which runs up the ravine past Willowbank. In 1834, Robert's son, Alexander Hamilton and wife Hannah Jarvis commissioned master builder John Latshaw to build a Greek Revival stone mansion which they named Willowbank after the magnificent willow trees that once graced its grounds. Willowbank is an elegant example of the great rural estates of early nineteenth century Upper Canada. In 1934, John Bright and his wife Dorothy, bought and reoriented the estate toward the new Niagara Parkway.

In 2003, Willowbank was saved from the wrecking ball by a group of local residents who formed the group Friends of Willowbank. Laura Dodson founded the School of Restoration Arts as a not-for-profit corporation; the school opened in 2006 as a registered private career college offering a three-year diploma program. Its multi-disciplinary, experiential curriculum educates a new generation of leaders in the field of heritage conservation. In 2014, His Royal Highness The Prince of Wales became Royal Patron to Willowbank.

Willowbank Estate House & Grounds are available for rentals, ranging from as little as ten people, up to three hundred guests for a tented outdoor event. There is something for every size and cause to celebrate in this unique, elegant and historical setting.

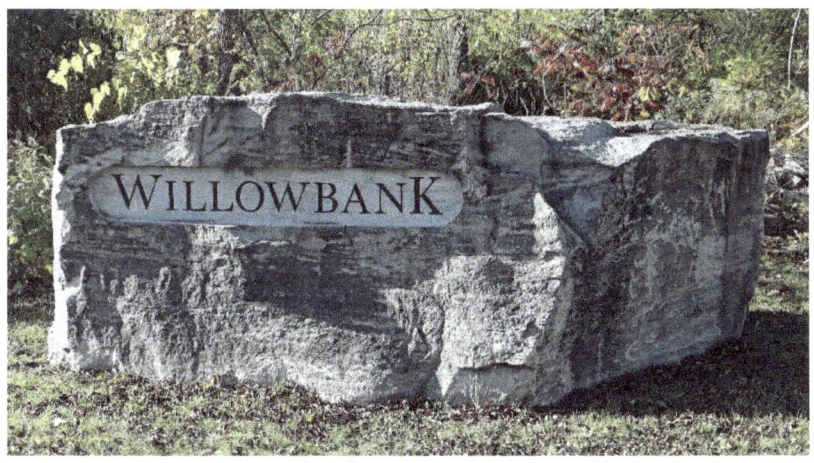

Erected 2012 – from Queenston Quarry

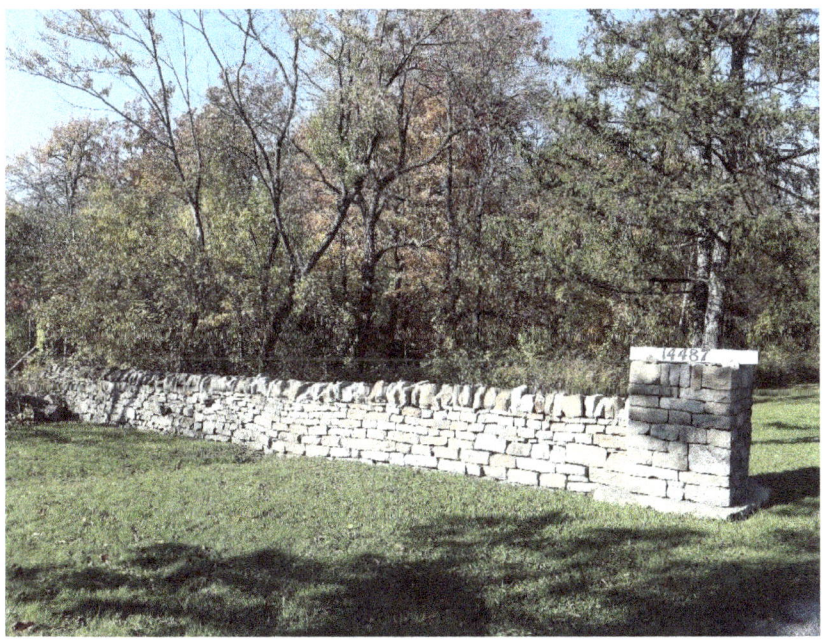

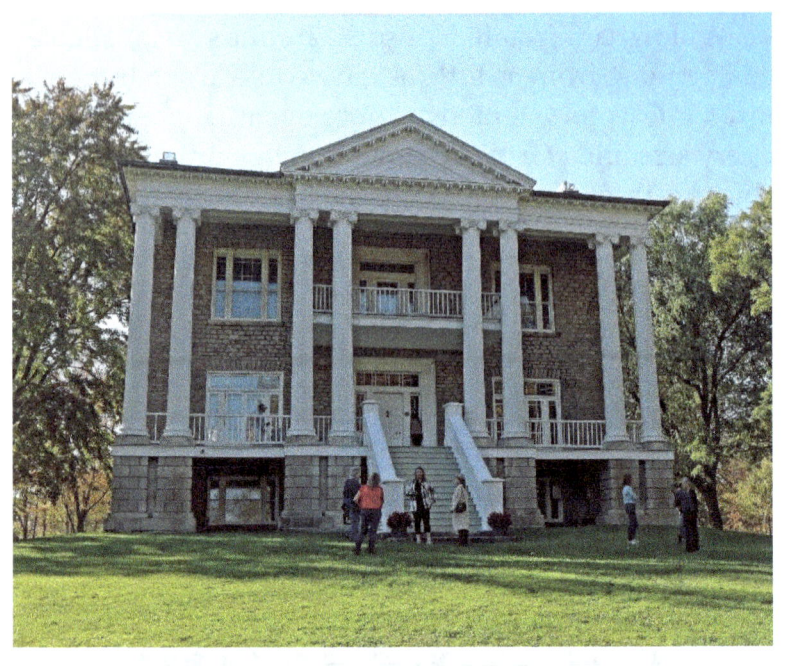

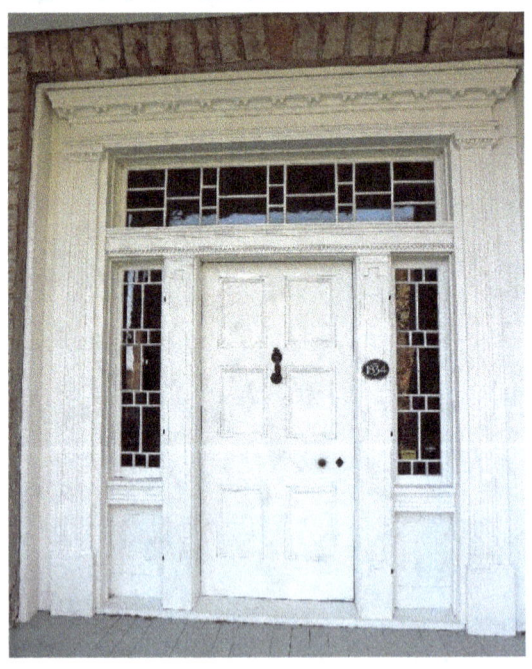

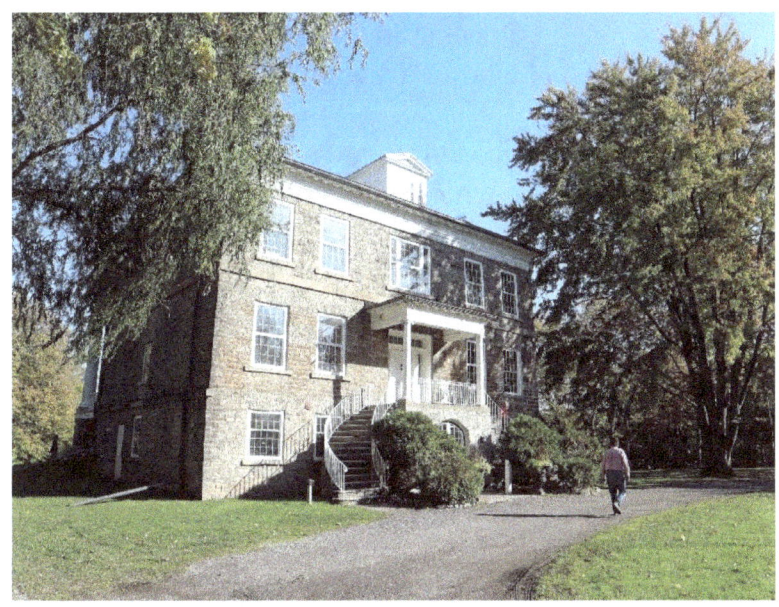

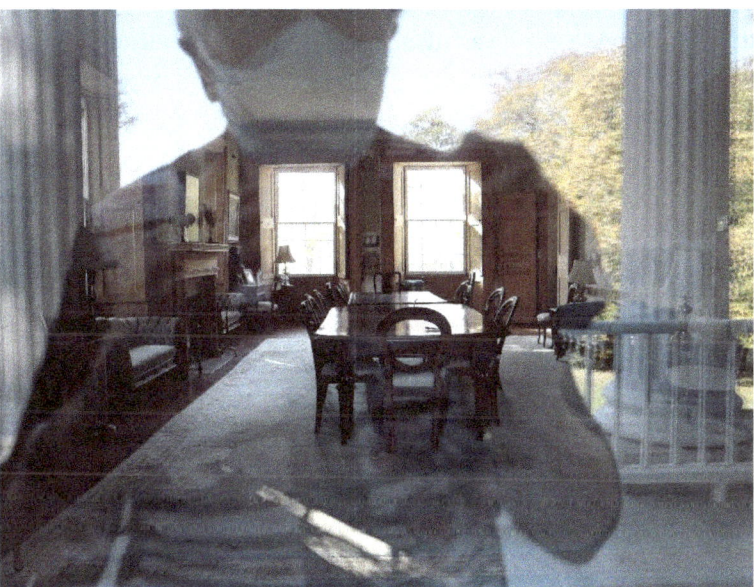

Inside as seen through the window – it closed early before we arrived

Queenston Heights
14184 Niagara Parkway, Queenston

Isaac Brock was born into a wealthy family in Guernsey, a British Isle which allowed him to become a career military officer. He was given charge of the 49th Regiment who came to Upper and Lower Canada in 1802. The Regiment went from Montreal to York (Toronto), and then on to Fort George in Newark (now Niagara-on-the-Lake). Appointed commander of military forces in 1810, Brock organized the militia, and prepared the colony for possible war with the United States. Following the outbreak of war, and the forging of a crucial alliance with Shawnee Chief Tecumseh, Brock led the daring capture of Detroit, securing the western frontier and boosting the morale of Upper Canadians.

On October 13, 1812, an American army, under the command of Major-General Stephen van Rensellaer, crossed the Niagara River and took possession of Queenston Heights. Major-General Isaac Brock hurried from Fort George to lead a small force against the invaders to try to regain the heights. He was killed at the age of 42 years. Mohawk Chiefs, John Norton and John Brant and a group of eighty allied Indigenous warriors played a critical role. After Brock was killed, the Indigenous warriors climbed the escarpment out of sight of the American forces. They pinned down the Americans until reinforcements arrived under the leadership of Major-General Roger Hale Sheaffe. Upper Canada's all-Black Regiment, known as the "Colored Corps," were under Sheaffe's command. Together they helped win the Battle of Queenston Heights.

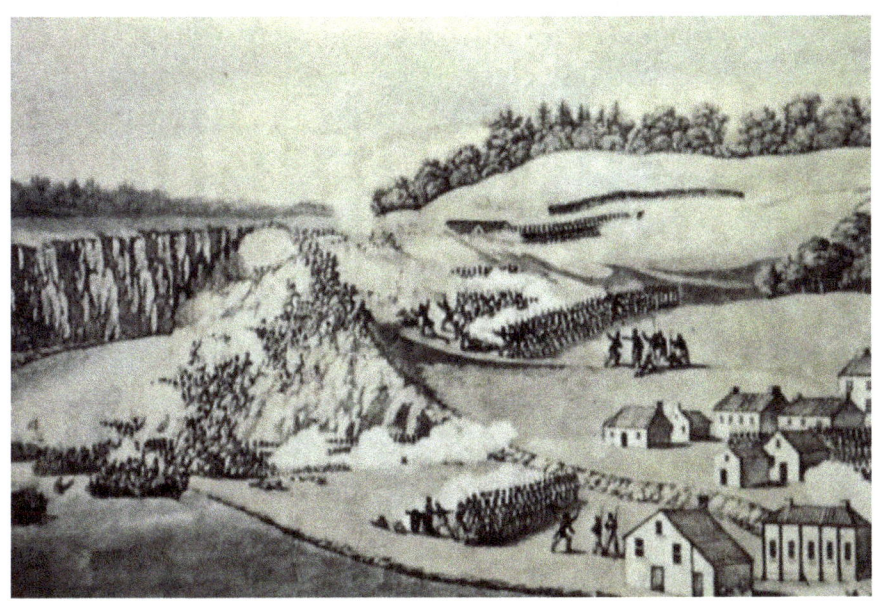

Even though Brock died in the battle, he became known as the "Hero of Upper Canada." He was remembered as being benevolent, brave, and patriotic. The first Brock monument, a 135-foot Tuscan-style monument at Queenston was completed in 1824. Major General Sir Isaac Brock's body was removed from the bastion at Fort George and interred under Brock's Monument in a solemn event. Over 8,000 spectators gathered to watch the procession along the route from Fort George to Queenston. By 1827, the tower was completed and measured forty meters in height.

On April 17, 1840, Brock's Monument was severely damaged by a bomb set off at the base of the stairs by Benjamin Lett, an American sympathizer who was part of the Upper Canada Rebellion. Rather than try to repair it, many felt that a new tower should be erected to highlight their respect for Brock.

The second monument, designed by William Thomas, was built entirely out of Queenston limestone, measures fifty-six meters (185 feet) in height, and was opened to the public in 1859.

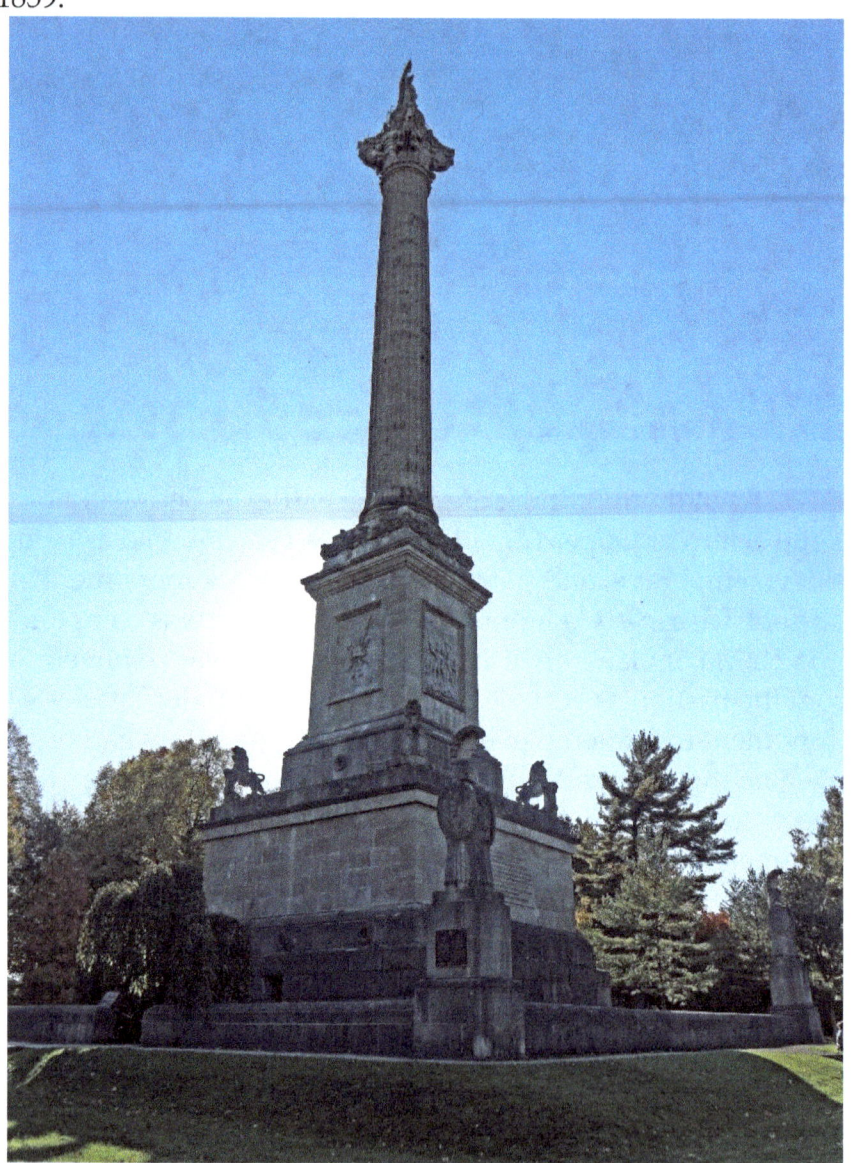

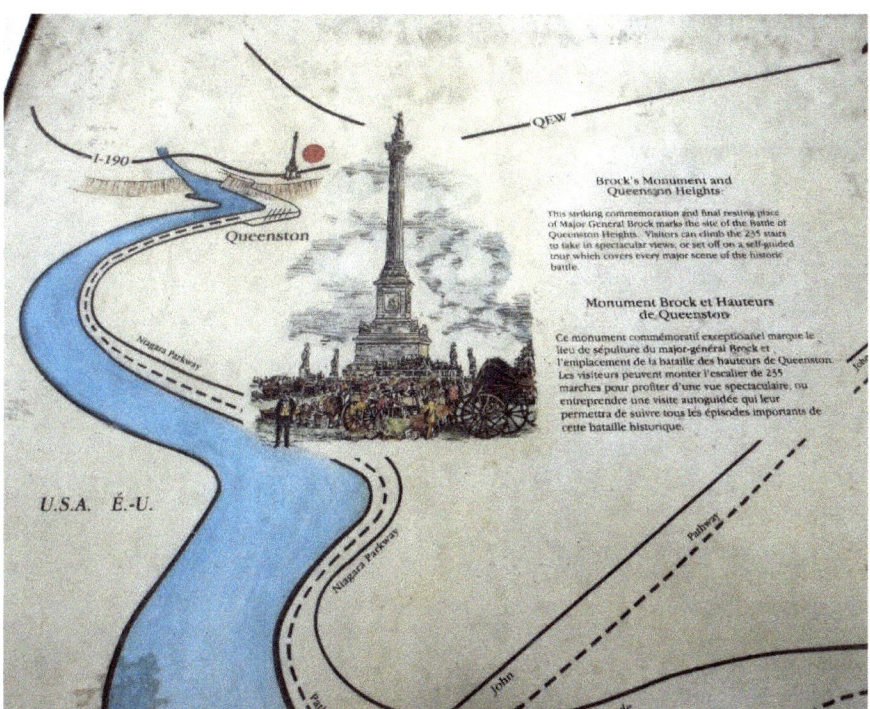

This striking commemoration and final resting place of Major General Sir Isaac Brock marks the site of the Battle of Queenston Heights.

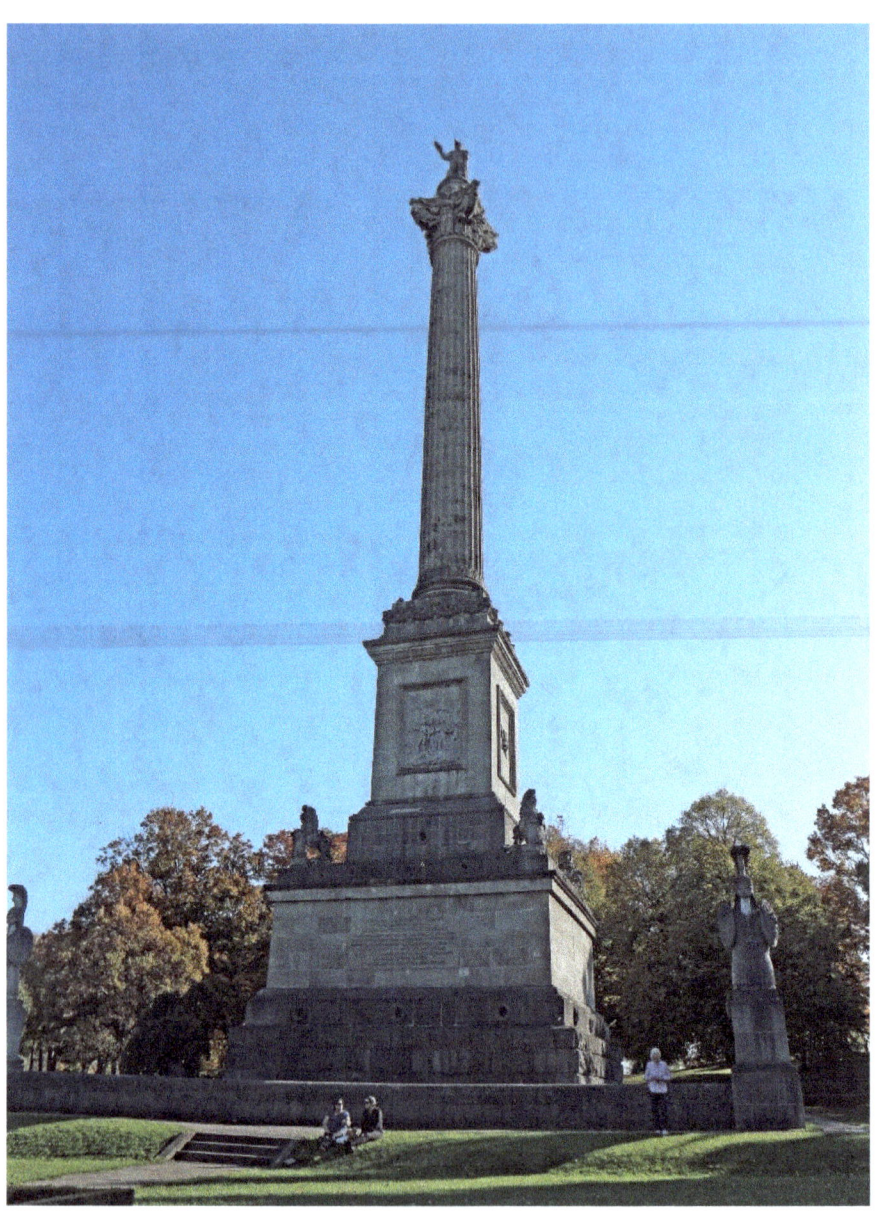

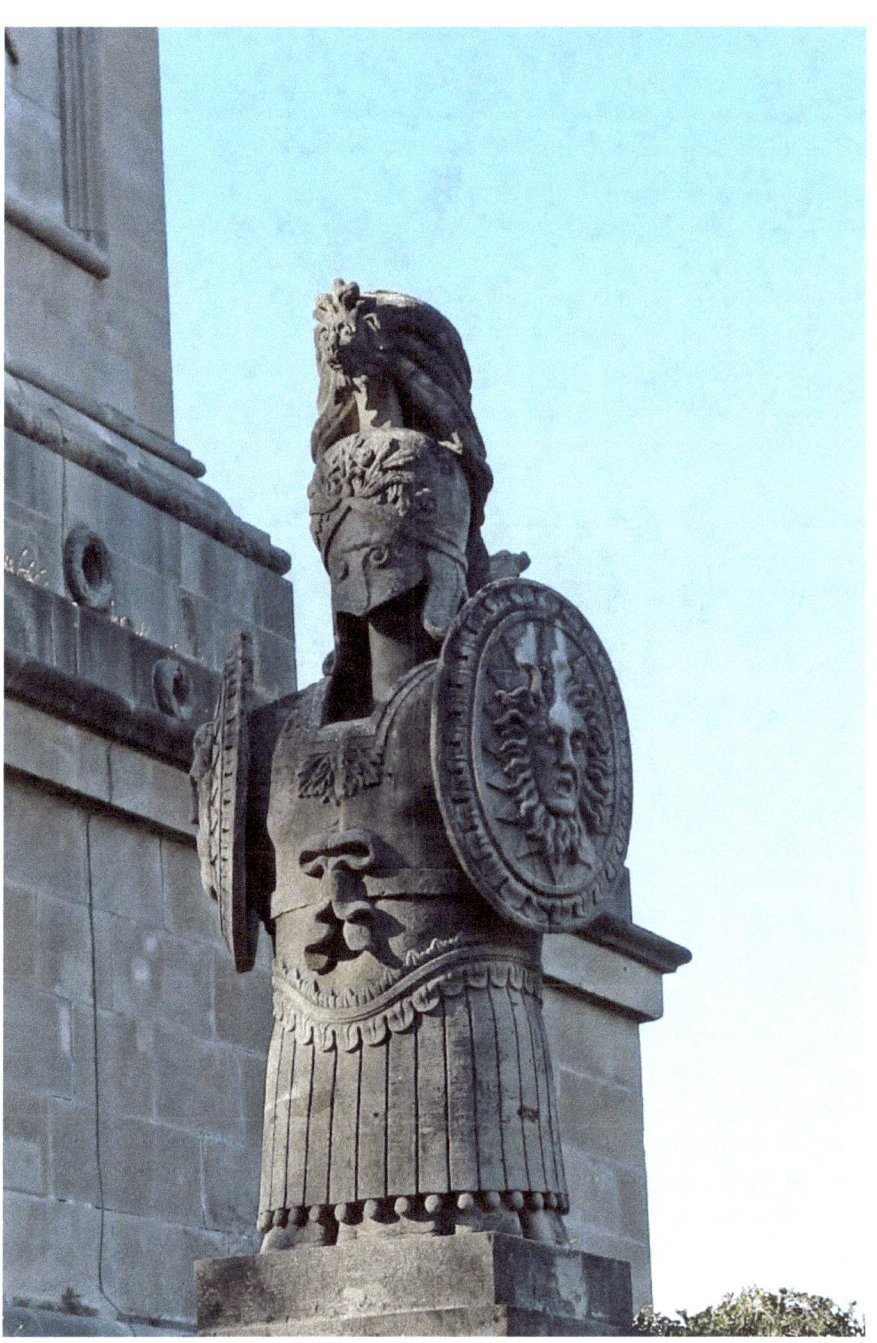

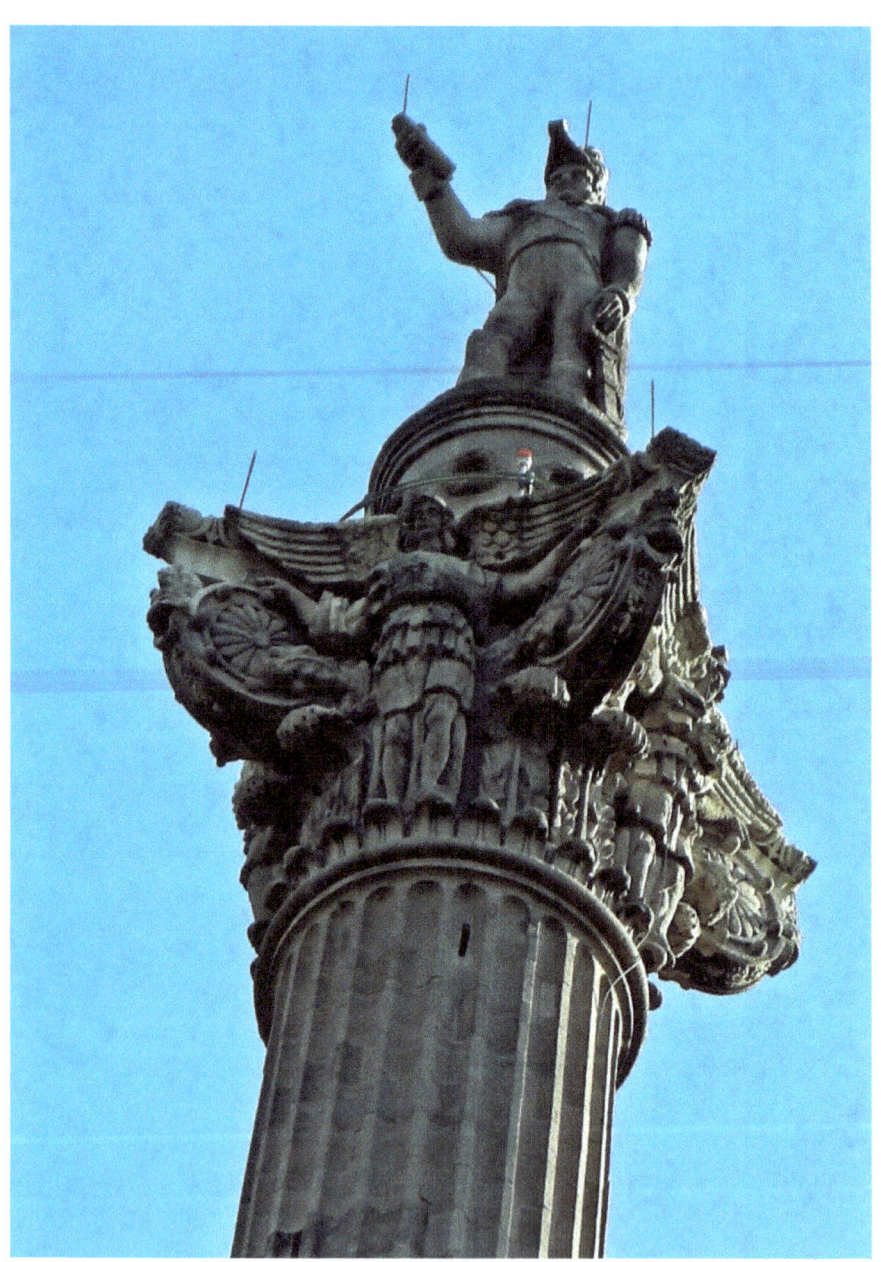

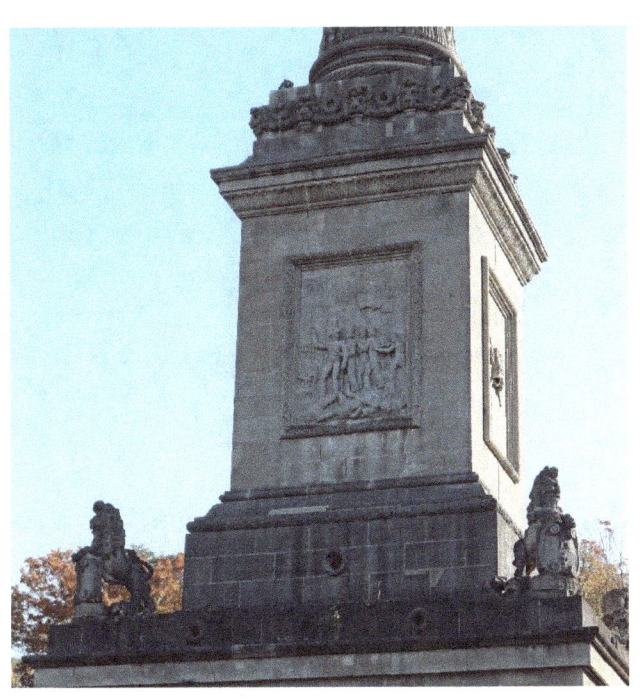

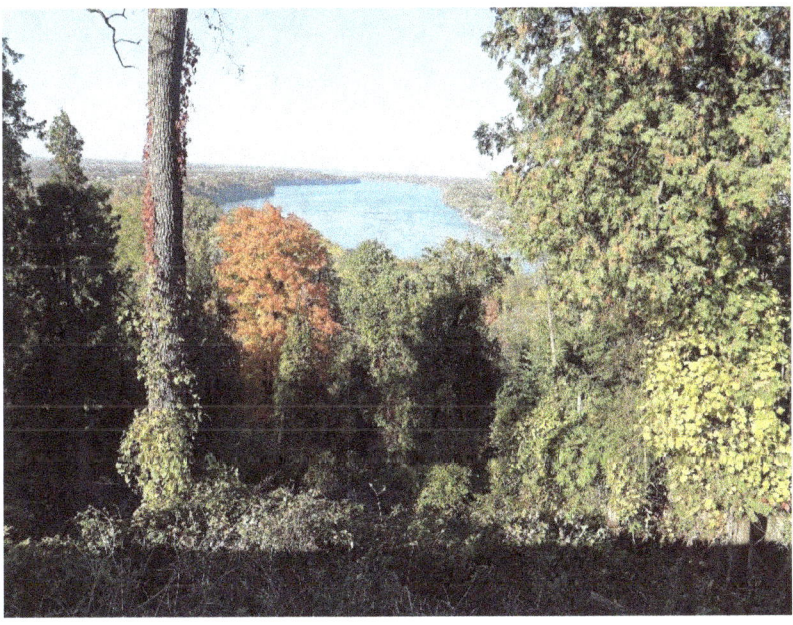

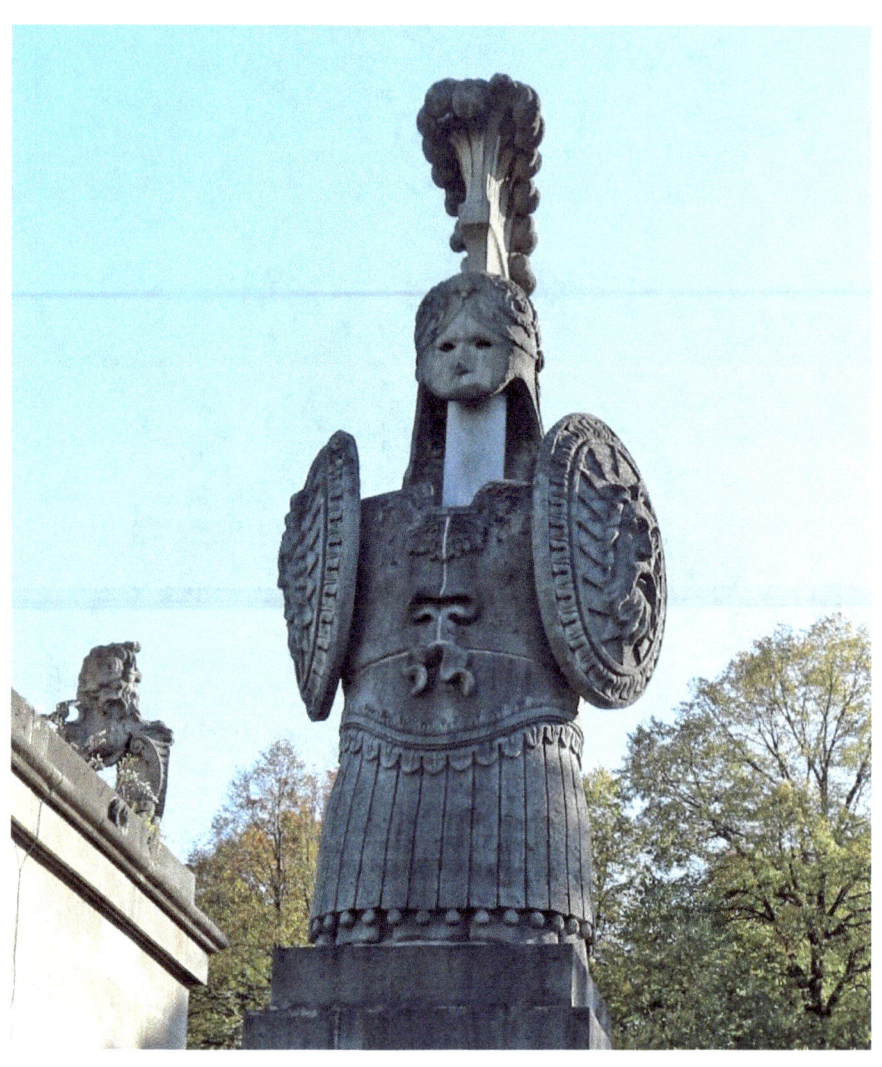

Landscape of Nations
14184 Niagara Parkway, Niagara-on-the-Lake

The Landscape of Nations is a living memorial dedicated to the contributions and sacrifices made by Six Nations and Native Allies on Queenston Heights and equally important, throughout the War of 1812. The memorial also recognizes the historic ceremony of peace and reconciliation held in Niagara on August 31 and September 1, 1815 that restored peace among the Native nations who fought on opposing sides.

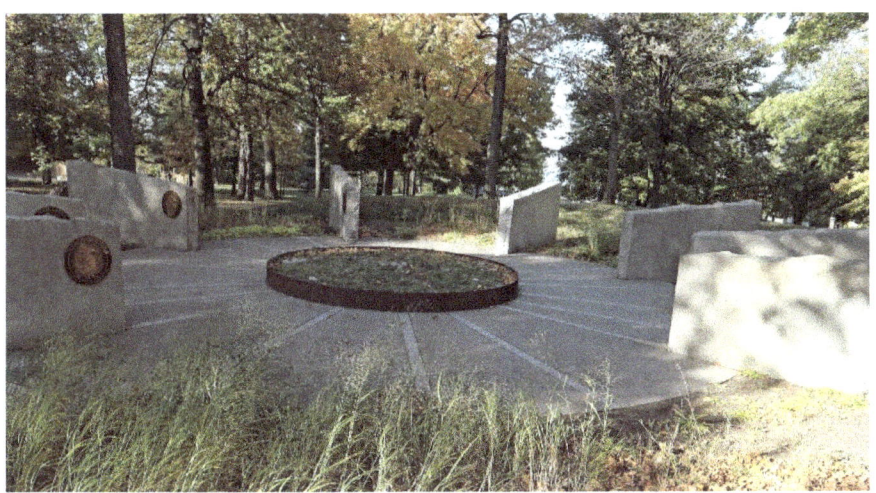

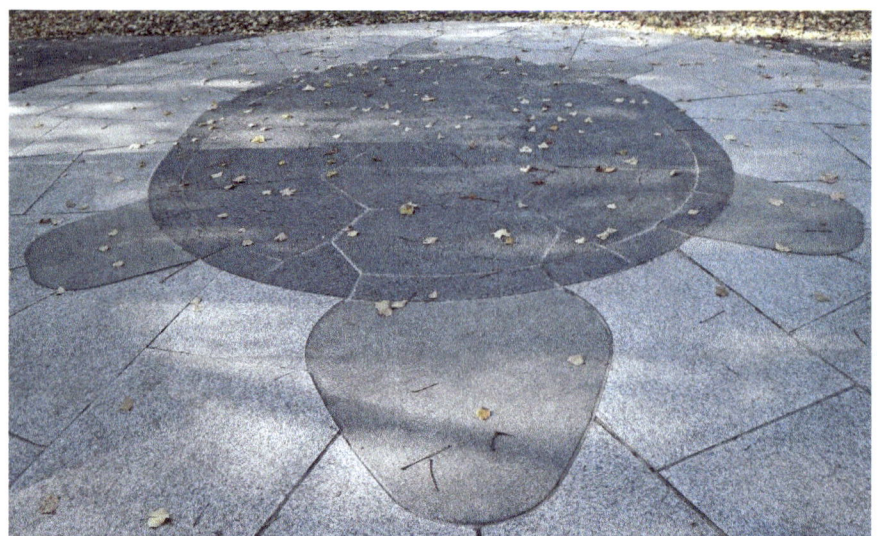

In the Six Nations creation story, the earth was created on the back of a giant turtle when Skywoman fell from the sky. She fell with the help of geese and ducks that gently set her on the back of a turtle. Dirt was pulled from the ocean floor by the muskrat that was given to Skywoman to spread on the turtle's back which is the ground we walk upon. Skywoman brought plants with her that are used as medicine and food within the Haudenosaunee culture.

Major John Norton (Teyoninhokarawen) was adopted into the Mohawk Nation by Joseph Brant. He led fighters from Six Nations of the Grand River into battles at Queenston Heights, Stoney Creek and Chippawa.

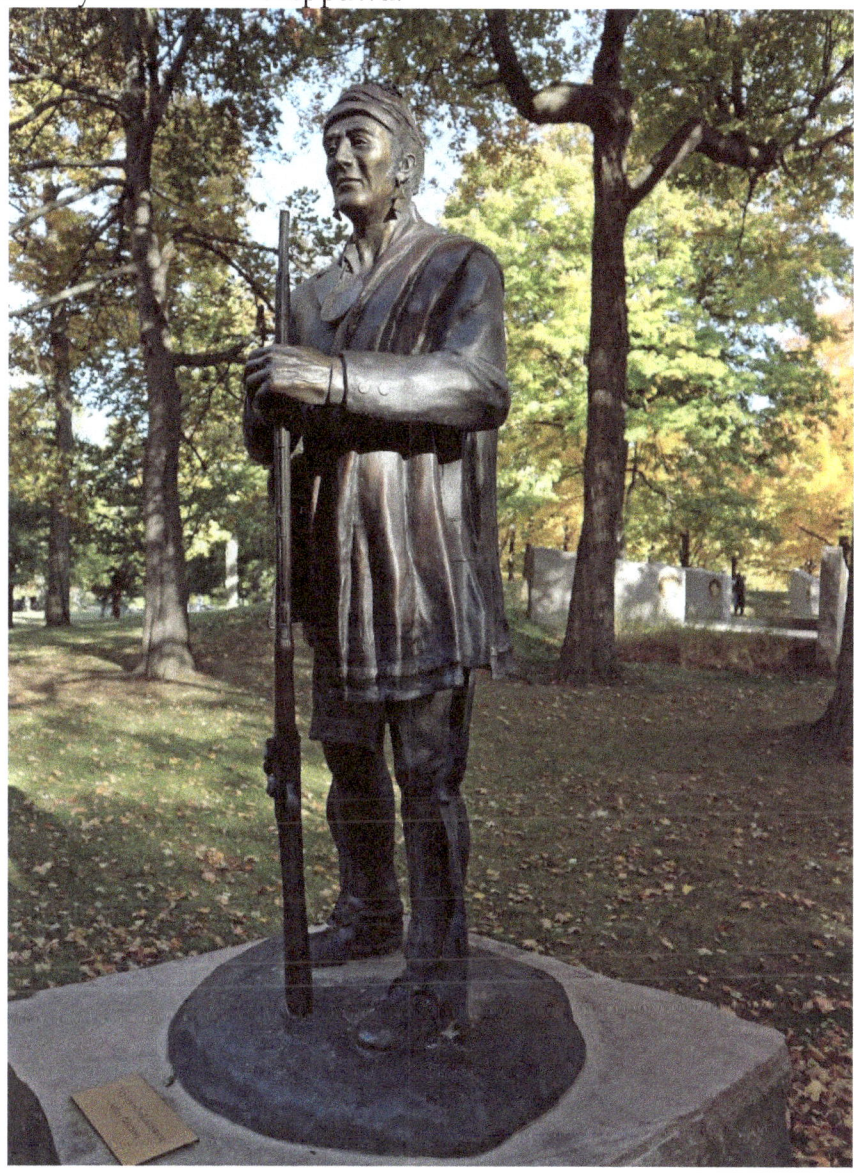

John Brant (Ahyouwa'ehs) was the son of Joseph Brant. Along with John Norton, he led warriors at the Battle of Queenston Heights along with other engagements. He was a strong advocate for building schools. He was elected to the Legislative Assembly of Upper Canada for Haldimand.

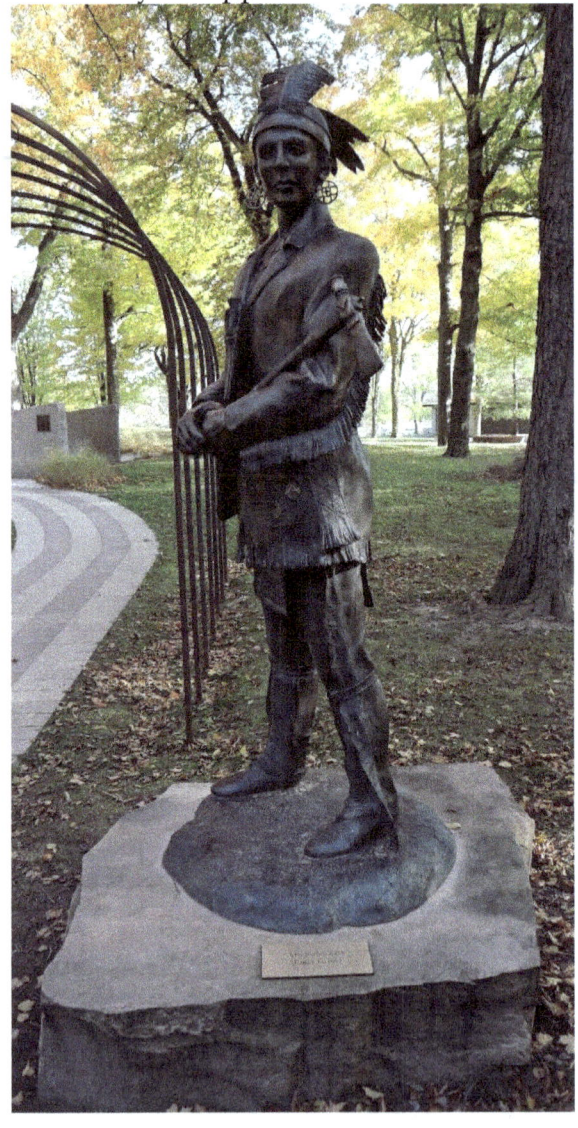

The Six Nations refer to themselves as Haudenosaunee, or "People of the Longhouse. The longhouse is a traditional architectural structure and a symbol of the member nations living under one Great Law of Peace.

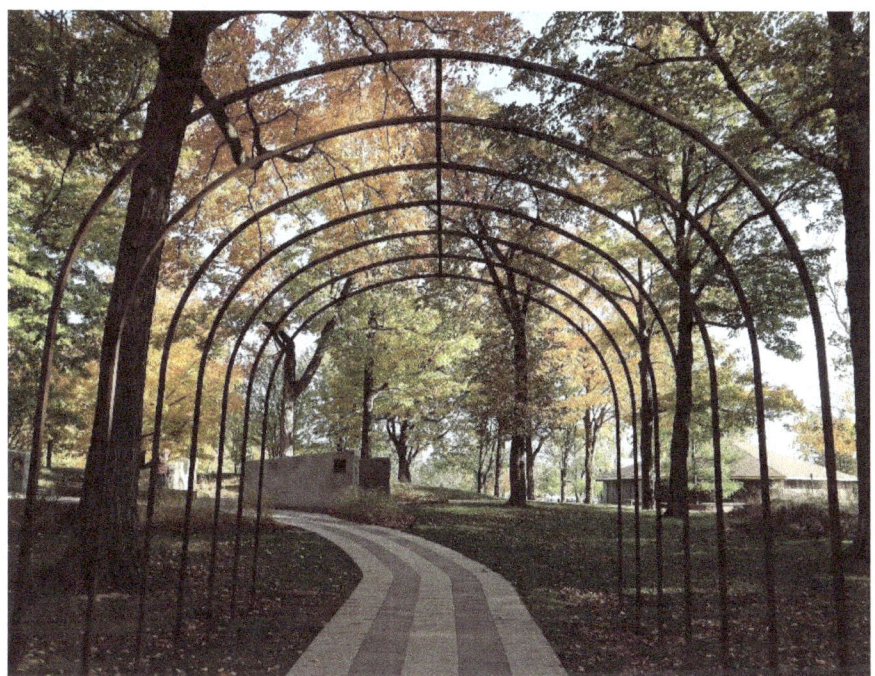

The walkway represents the Two-Row Wampum Belt, the first treaty between the Haudenosaunee and Europeans, representing their agreement to co-exist on parallel paths. Wampum are tubular white or purple beads made from the quahog shell that were found on the eastern shore of North America.

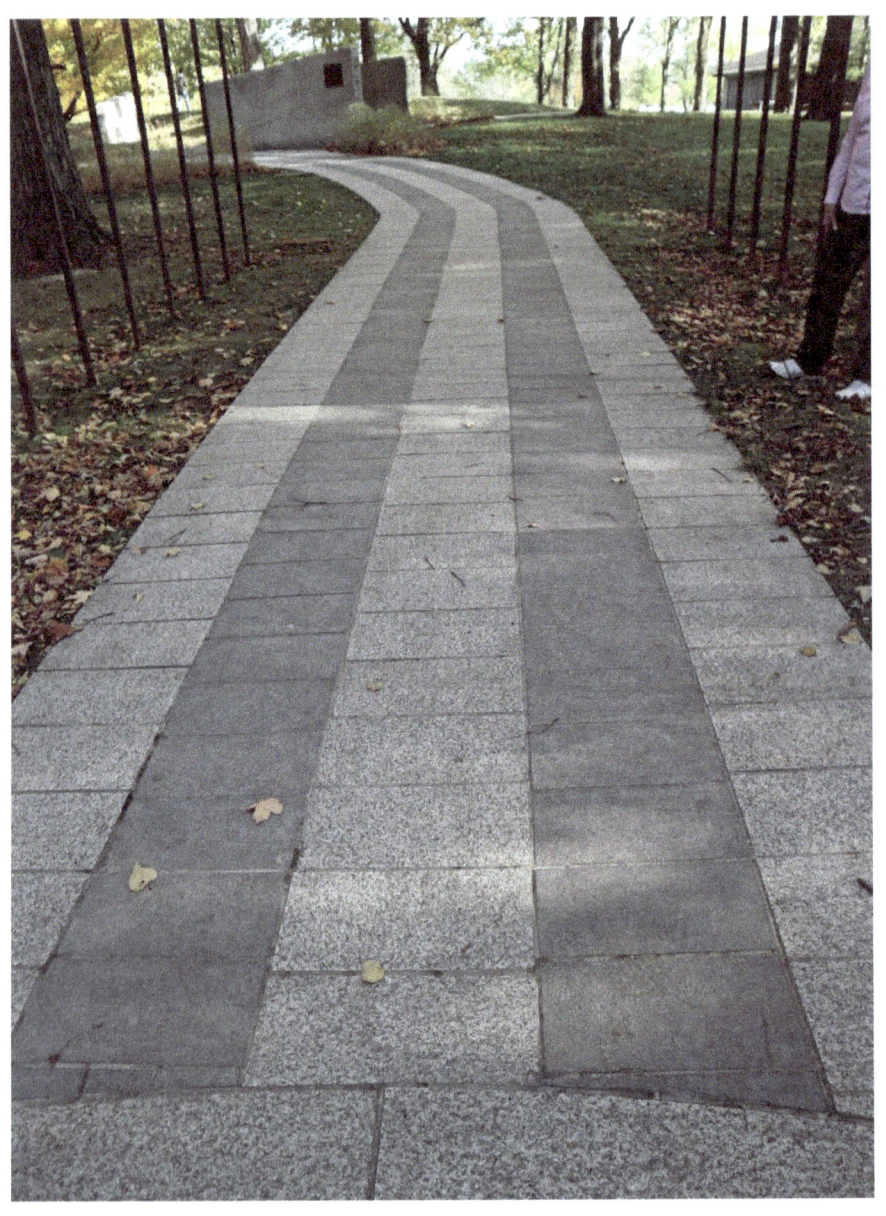

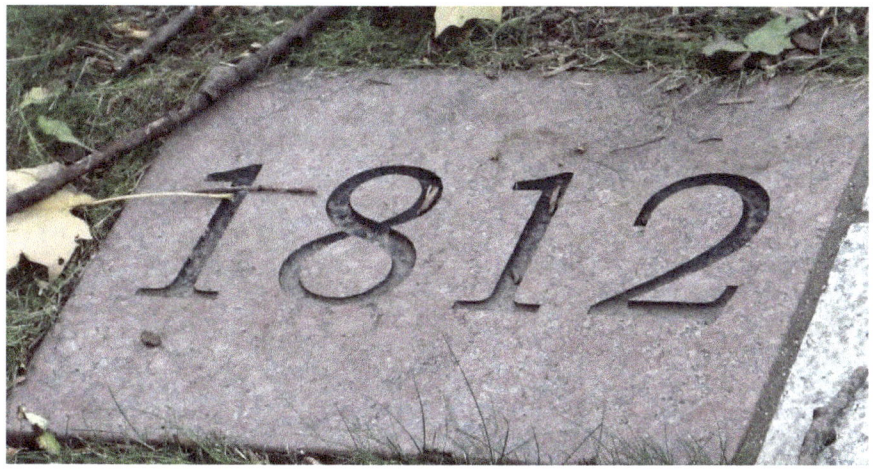

Time marker – the start of the War of 1812

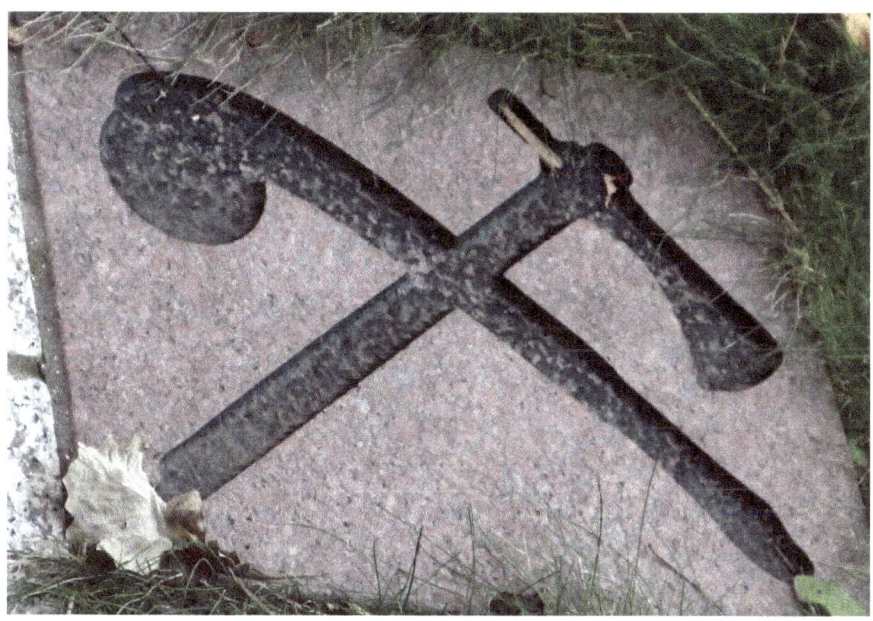

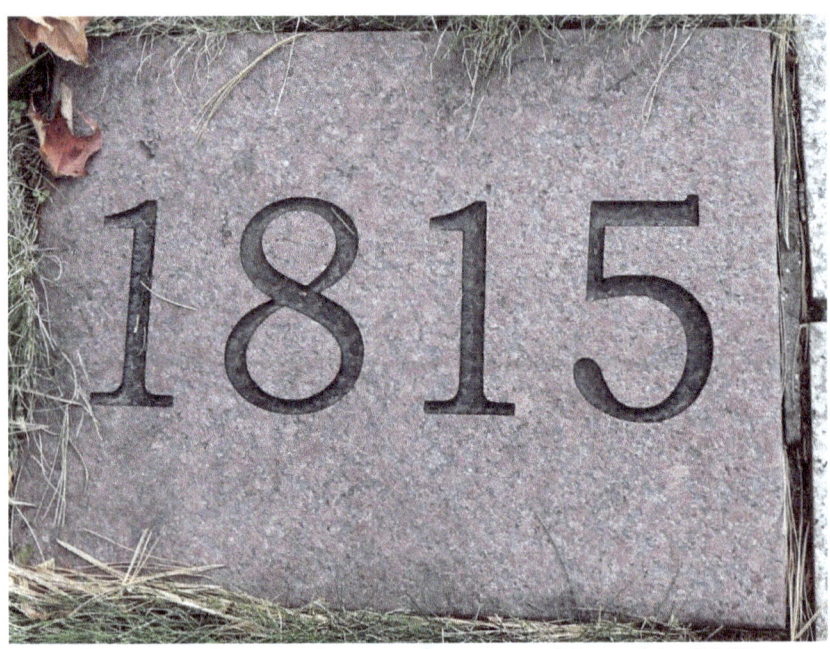

Time marker – when peace was achieved in 1815

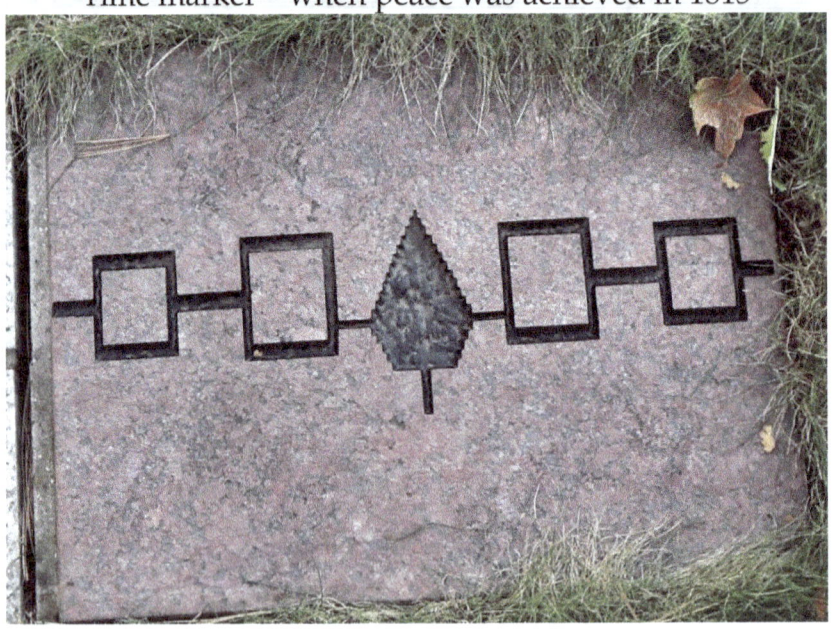

The red and blue squares inside Fort Riall serve as symbols for all who fought. Fort Riall was an artillery battery built during the War of 1812 named after Major-General Phineas Riall.

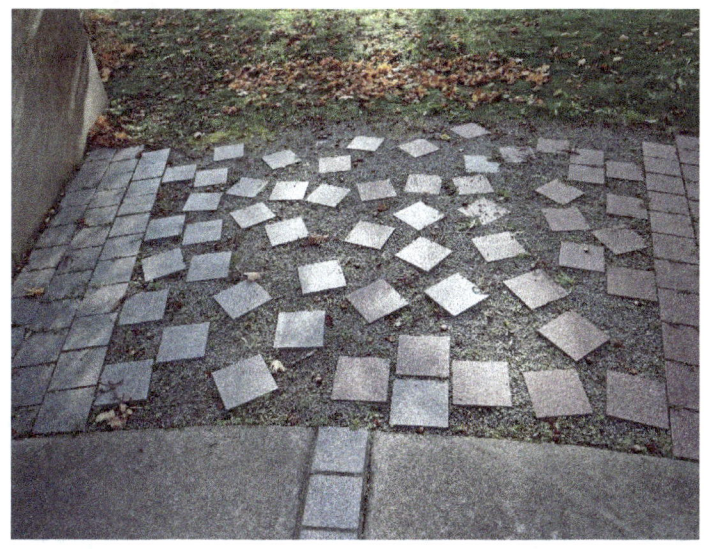

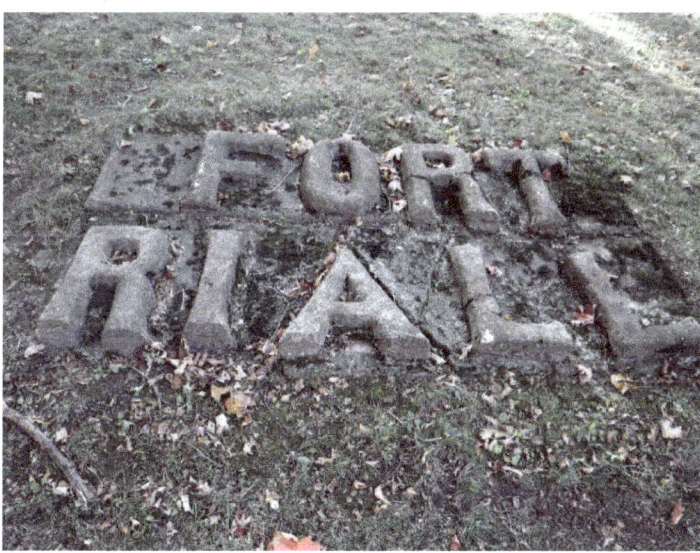

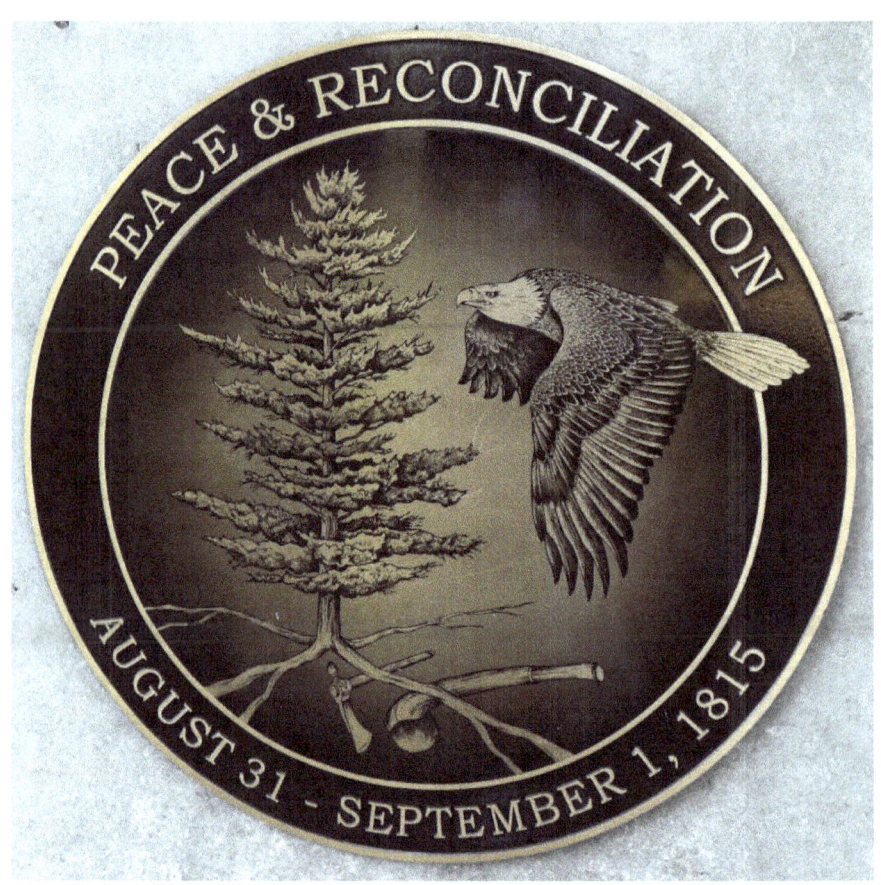

Here we remember the contributions of Six Nations and Native Allies who participated in the War of 1812. The historic ceremony of Peace and Reconciliation held at Niagara on August 31 and September 1, 1815 is commemorated here.

Eight limestone walls, sourced from the Queenston Quarry, emanate from the Memory Circle like a sunburst. Inside the circle, sweetgrass is grown; it is a sacred medicine among the Haudenosaunee and other Indigenous Nations across North America.

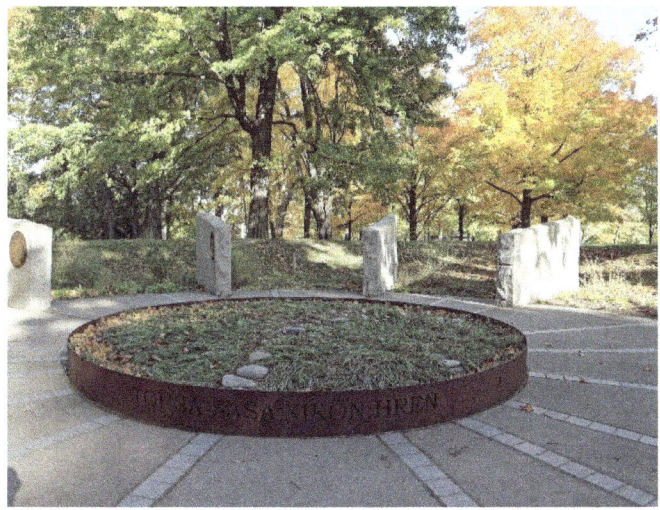

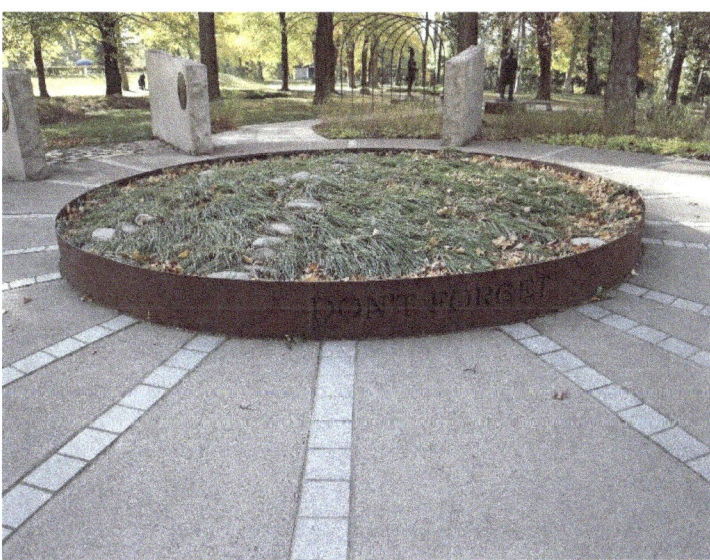

Don't Forget

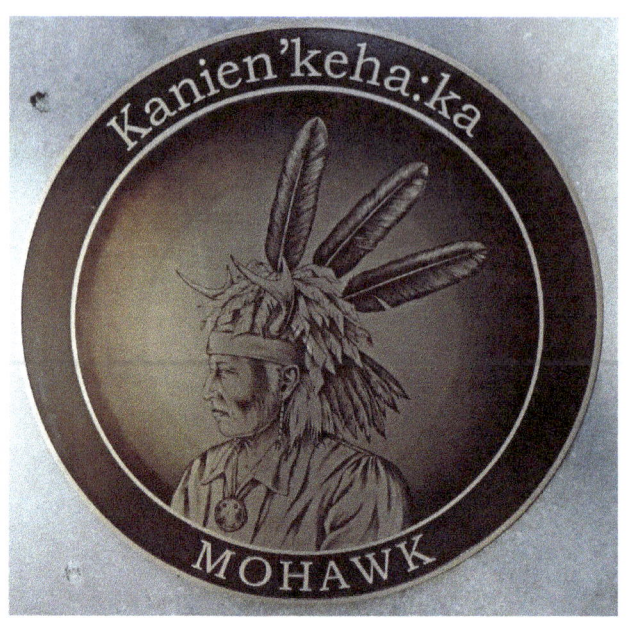

People of the Flint

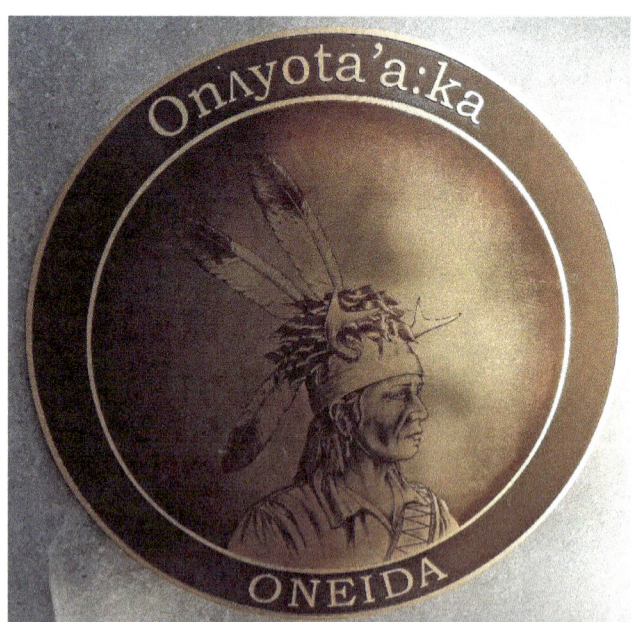

People of the Standing Stone

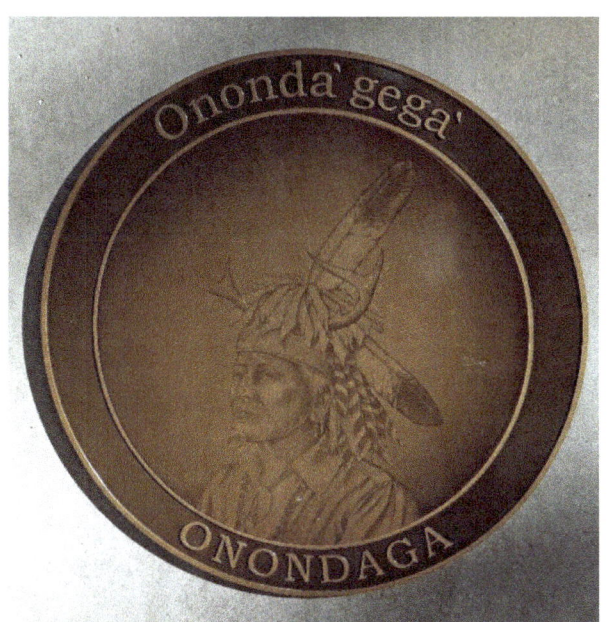

People of the Hills

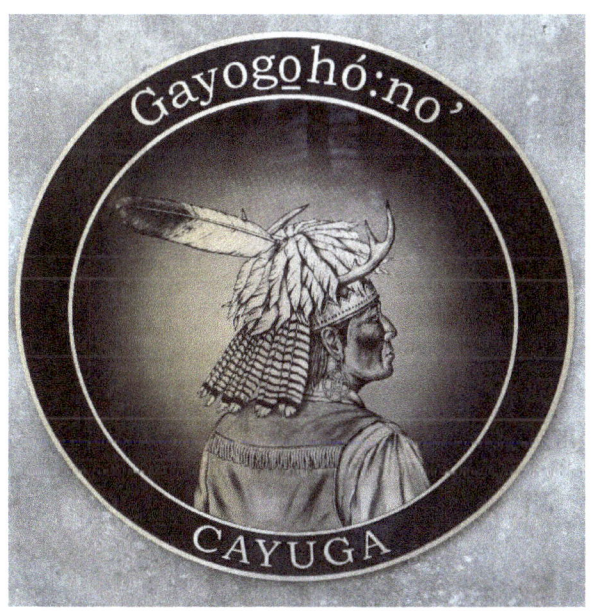

People of the Great Swamp

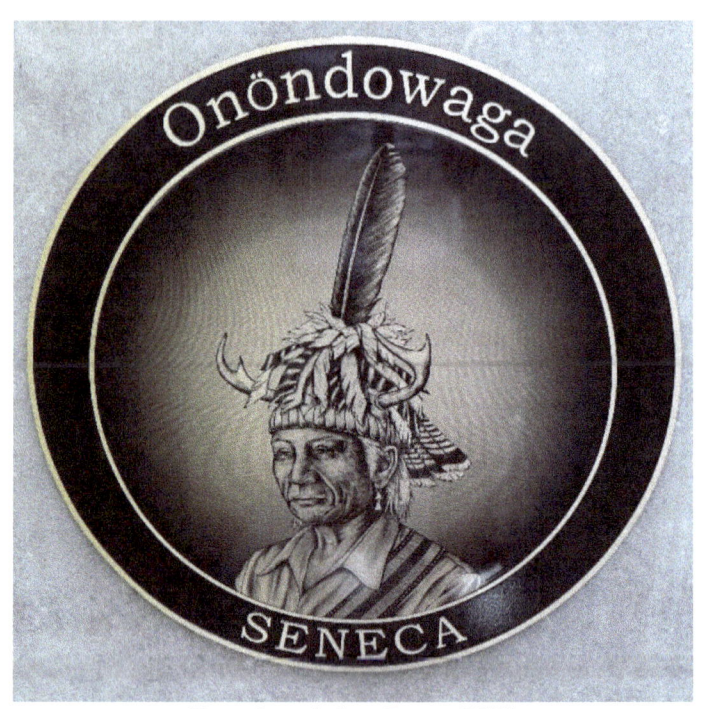

People of the Great Hill

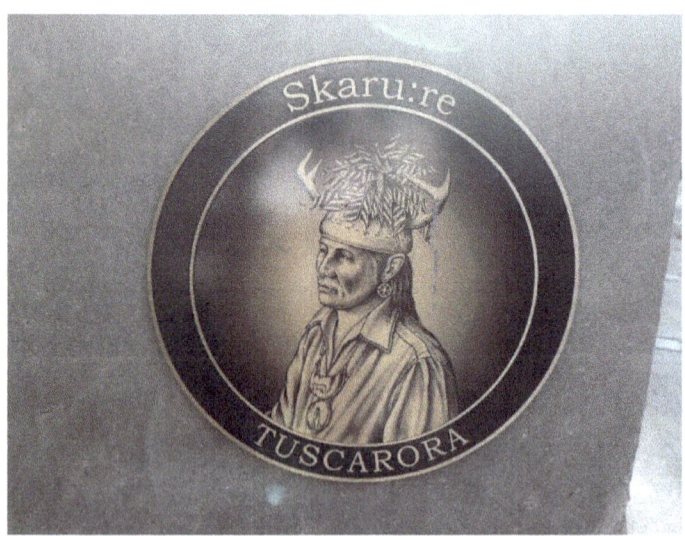

People of the Long Shirt

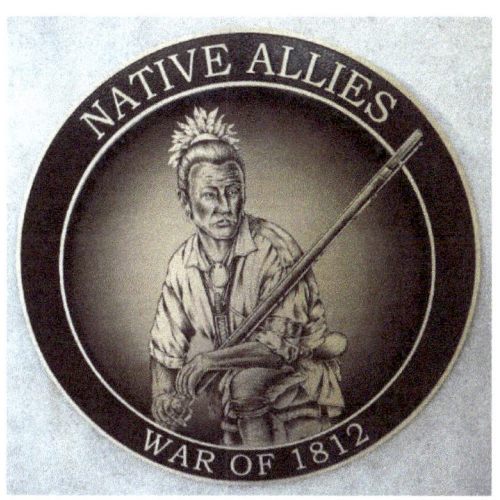

NATIVE ALLIES

In addition to the Six Nations named on the limestone walls, the members of these Native Nations also took part in the War of 1812:

ALLIES AUTOCHTONES

En plus des Six Nations nommées sur les murs de calcaire, les membres de ces nations autochtones ont également participé à la guerre de 1812:

Abenaki of Three Rivers and St. Francis	Métis
	Miami
Algonquin	Mississauga
Anishnaabeg	Mohican
Akwesasne Mohawk	Moravian
Cherokee	Muncey
Dakotah (Sioux)	Nanticoke
Delaware	Odawa
Fox	Ojibwe
Huron of Lorette	Potowatomi
Kahnawake Mohawk	Sauk
Kanesatake Mohawk	Shawnee
Kickapoo	Tyendinaga Mohawk
Menominee	Winnebago (Ho Chunk)
Mesquakie	Wyandot

An eastern white pine stands as a symbol of the Haudenosaunee constitution known as the Great Law of Peace. It stands as a living memorial dedicated to the contributions and sacrifices made by Six Nations and Native Allies on Queenston Heights and throughout the War of 1812.

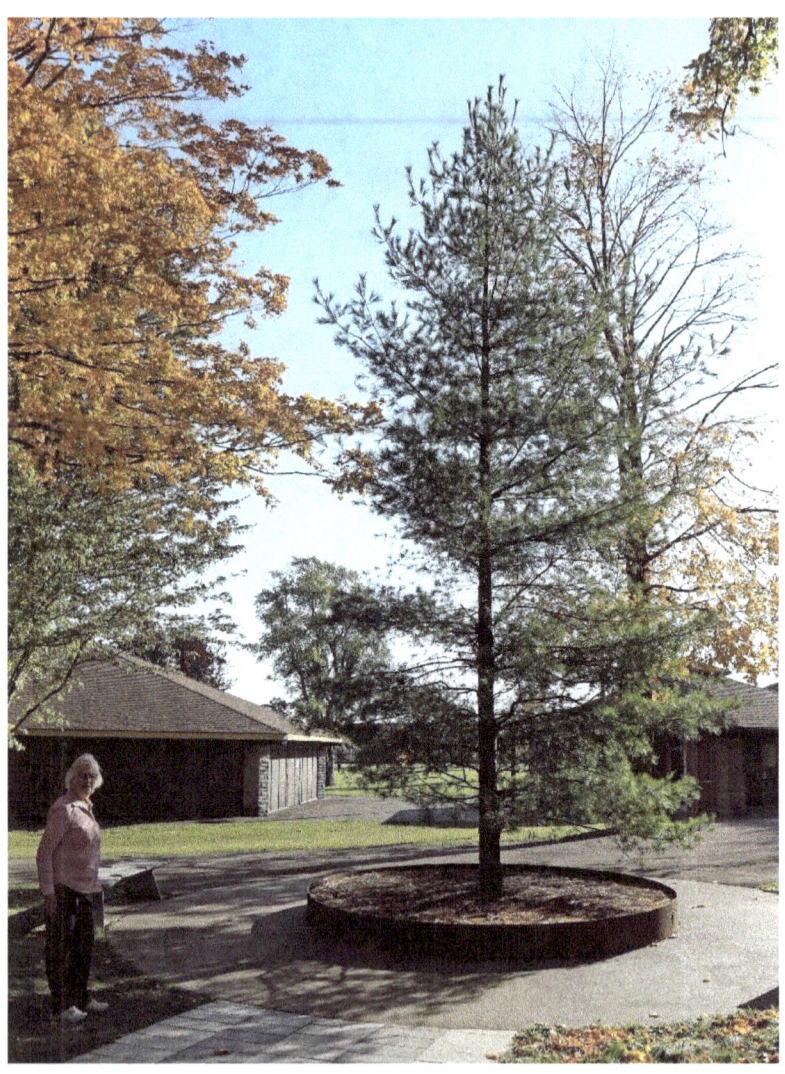

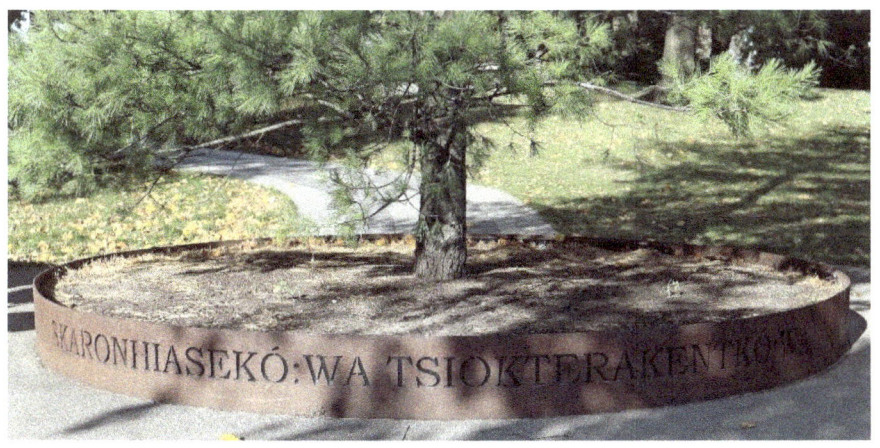

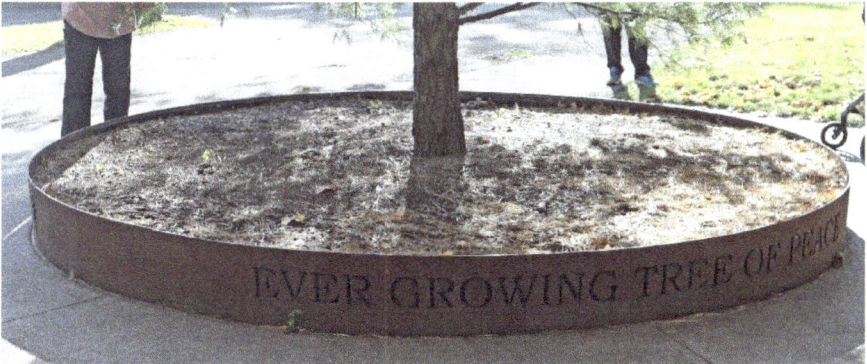

This symbol is represented on the Haudenosaunee 'flag' as the middle symbol out of the five symbols. Originally, it was a wampum belt that was modernized into a flag to symbolize the Haudenosaunee.

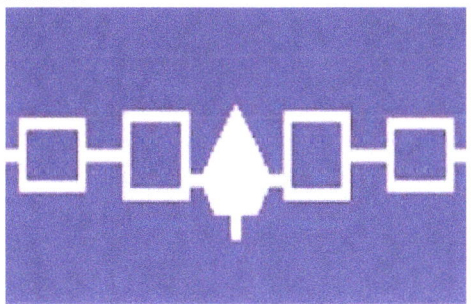

Other Books by Barbara Raue

Coins of Gold
Arrows, Indians and Love
The Life and Times of Barbara
The Cromwell Family Book
Laura Secord Discovered
Daddy Where Are You?

Montana Series
Book 1: Montana Dream
Book 2: Life on the Montana Frontier
Book 3: Montana to Boston and Back
Book 4: Montana Sons Go to War
Book 5: Montana Sons Return from War

Donaldson Series
Book 1: Rite of Passage
Book 2: Rite of Marriage

Our Tour of Doors Open 2019 (Hamilton, Grimsby,
Burlington, St. Thomas)

Our Tour of Doors Open 2022 Hamilton
Our Tour of Doors Open 2022 Niagara-on-the-Lake

Barbara is The Authority on Saving Our History One Photo at a Time. She is pursuing her interest in photography and architecture by preserving a record through photos of old buildings from the 1800s and 1900s with their unique architecture. Enjoy the beautiful architecture in the comfort of your living room. Dream about what it was like in those by-gone days. Dream about what it was like to live in a mansion like one of those in this book.

Barbara Raue, a wife, mother and grandmother, is an avid reader and writer. She has researched and compiled several family histories. In 2010, Barbara published her book "Coins of Gold," which celebrates the courageous life of her mother, May Todd. Barbara's second book is a historical fiction "Arrows, Indians and Love" which takes place in Boonesborough, Kentucky during the time of Daniel Boone. In 2013, Barbara published *The Cromwell Family Book* in which she traces her ancestry generations back into Great Britain. Her second novel is called *Laura Secord Discovered,* in which the story of Laura Secord's service during the War of 1812 is shared. Barbara's memoir is titled *Daddy Where Are You?* It tells of her life growing up without a father. Five novels in the Montana Series have been published, *Montana Dream, Life on the Montana Frontier, Montana to Boston and Back, Montana Sons Go to War*, and *Montana Sons Return from War*. The Donaldson series of two novels is available: *Rite of Passage* and *Rite of Marriage.*

This is a link to Barbara's website to view all her books
http://barbararaue.ca

www.ingramcontent.com/pod-product-compliance
Lightning Source LLC
Chambersburg PA
CBHW070336220526
45467CB00001B/145